Two week loan

Please return on or before the last
date stamped below.
Charges are made for late return.

OXFORD SERIES ON EUROPEAN COMMUNITY LAW

General Editor: Professor F.G. Jacobs QC
Professor of European Law, King's College London

LEGAL ASPECTS OF AGRICULTURE IN
THE EUROPEAN COMMUNITY

OXFORD SERIES ON EUROPEAN COMMUNITY LAW

The aim of this new series is to publish important and original studies of the various branches of European Community Law. Each work will provide a clear, concise, and critical exposition of the law in its social, economic, and political context, at a level which will interest the advanced student, the practitioner, the academic, and government and Community officials.

Legal Aspects of Agriculture in the European Community

J. A. USHER

CLARENDON PRESS · OXFORD
1988

Oxford University Press, Walton Street, Oxford OX2 6DP
Oxford New York Toronto
Delhi Bombay Calcutta Madras Karachi
Petaling Jaya Singapore Hong Kong Tokyo
Nairobi Dar es Salaam Cape Town
Melbourne Auckland
and associated companies in
Berlin Ibadan

Oxford is a trade mark of Oxford University Press

Published in the United States
by Oxford University Press, New York

British Library Cataloguing in Publication Data
Usher, J.A. (John Anthony), 1945–
Legal aspects of agriculture in the
European Community.
1. European Community countries.
Agricultural industries. Policies of European
Economic Community. Common Agricultural Policy.
Legal Aspects.
I. Title II. Series
341.7'5471
ISBN 0–19–825565–9

Library of Congress Cataloging in Publication Data
Usher, J. A. (John A.)
Legal aspects of agriculture in the European Community / J.A. Usher.
(Oxford series on European Community law)
Includes index.
1. Agricultural laws and legislation—European Economic Community
countries. I. Title II. Series.
KJE6605.U84 1988   343.4'076—dc19 [344.0376] 88–12107
ISBN 0–19–825565–9

Text translation by Hope Services (Abingdon) Limited
Printed and bound in Great Britain by
Biddles Limited, Guildford and King's Lynn

General Editor's Foreword

The Common Agricultural Policy is in many respects the most significant structure in the entire edifice of the European Community, as well as in some quarters the most notorious. Its notoriety is attributable, of course, to its vast cost, consuming as it does a large proportion of the entire Community budget, and to the chronic surpluses which have been engendered by the attempt to ensure self-sufficiency in production and to protect the living standards of the agricultural populace. It has to be remembered, however, that all European countries, and indeed all developed economies, have found it necessary to protect the agricultural sector from market forces. Once the premiss is accepted that the common market should extend to agriculture, a high degree of intervention was probably inevitable, as was the centralized management and centralized financing of the various markets, together with the vast corpus of directly applicable legislation which is the subject of this book.

Remarkably, Professor Usher's work is the first extended book on the subject in the English language. That fact alone might be regarded as sufficient to justify its appearance in the Oxford European Community Law Series, and indeed to demonstrate the need for a series of monographs on the main branches of Community law. This book is thus able to deal in a systematic way, yet within a manageable compass, with the different regimes adopted for the whole range of agricultural products; with the financial mechanisms which provide the synchromesh between common prices and fluctuating national currencies; and with the attempts to introduce the necessary long-term re-structuring of European agriculture.

Apart from the intrinsic importance of the subject, expounded concisely and with a clarity that belies its complexity, the book has a wider significance since it covers the network of constitutional and administrative issues underlying the relationship between directly applicable Community legislation and its detailed implementation in the Member States. As by far the most developed of Community policies, agriculture illustrates better than any other the contribution of the law to the resolution of those issues: in particular the scope and limits of the power of the Community institutions, on the one hand, and of the authorities of the Member States—their government departments and their intervention agencies—on the other. Agriculture has been a fertile field for litigation, and has required the European Court to develop fundamental principles of judicial review. Drawing on the fragmentary indications in the EEC Treaty, and on the legal traditions of the Member States, the Court has developed an impressive body of case-law, constructing 'general principles of law' which have been erected into quasi-constitutional principles to control the Community legislature and to ensure so far as possible a fair and even-handed application of the law.

This book thus does more than provide a detailed but succinct analysis of an elaborate system of legislation; it also performs a wider function in illustrating the techniques by which the Community's legal order has evolved to provide a means of subjecting the legislative and administrative apparatus to the rule of law.

Preface

While the Common Agricultural Policy may be well known for the political and financial problems to which it gives rise, the legal issues underlying it have not been so widely discussed. Yet the Common Agricultural Policy lies behind many of the institutional developments in the Community, and is all too closely intertwined with the system of Community finance. Agricultural markets formed the first 'single markets' within the EEC, and agricultural legislation forms the background to much of the European Court's case-law on the relationship between Community law and national law. It is also in the context of agricultural disputes that the European Court has developed many of the general principles of Community law.

My own interest in the subject developed while I was a Legal Secretary at the European Court in Luxembourg from 1974 to 1978, when it became very clear that agriculture was the largest single cause of litigation before that Court. However, the genesis of this book was a request by Professor Sir Thomas Smith, while I was teaching at Edinburgh University, to write a section on the Common Agricultural Policy in the chapter on Agriculture in the *Stair Memorial Encyclopedia of the Laws of Scotland*, under a contract which expressly permitted the material to be used in a monograph. The present book is therefore essentially a much-expanded and updated version of that text, taking account in particular of the experience gained while using it as the basis for an LL M course at University College London.

A particular feature of the Common Agricultural Policy is the frequency and bulk of the legislation to which it has given rise. Indeed, while writing on milk quotas for the *Stair Memorial Encyclopedia* I was driven to suggest to the editors that the experience resembled that of chasing a moving target through a thick fog. In recent years there have even been changes in those fundamental characteristics of common organizations which appeared to be pillars of relative stability, so that, for example, intervention in the cereals market is no longer at the intervention price. On the other hand, the agreement reached in the European Council in February 1988 on 'stabilizers' and 'set-aside' may, if it fulfils its authors' wishes, usher in a new era of relative stability. In general, the law is stated as at 30 April 1988.

Finally, I should like to express my thanks to Peter Oliver and Grant Lawrence of the Legal Service of the Commission, and Nick Green, barrister, for having taken the time to read through the manuscript and for the valuable and constructive comments which they made. I am of course responsible for all remaining errors and omissions. My particular thanks go to Monique Bertoni, who turned my illegible handwriting into a clear typescript, and, last but not least, to my family for their patience and encouragement.

John A. Usher
May 1988

Contents

Table of Cases
(In Alphabetical Order)

Cases before the French Courts

Cases before United Kingdom Courts

Table of Cases
(*In Numerical Order*)

Table of Legislation
Table of Community Treaties

Treaty Provisions

EEC Treaty

Art. 5	96, 146–7
Art. 9	14
Art. 10	14
Art. 13	30
Art. 16	30
Art. 30	11, 28, 165, 166
Art. 33	13
Art. 34	11, 13, 23, 28
Art. 36	25, 27–34, 47
Art. 37	21
Art. 38	3, 6, 9, 21, 91
Art. 39	23, 35, 39, 41, 53, 133, 141
Art. 40	12, 20, 41–4, 45, 53, 107, 133
Art. 42	15, 21
Art. 43	1, 12, 26, 108, 137, 144, 145
Art. 44	41
Art. 45	12
Art. 46	12, 15, 19–20
Art. 85	15, 17, 150, 165
Art. 86	17, 150, 165, 166
Art. 90	15
Art. 92	18, 150
Art. 93	18, 150
Art. 94	18, 150
Art. 100	26, 137, 145
Art. 100A	26–7, 145
Art. 103	108, 144
Art. 105	114
Art. 130d	143
Art. 155	146–7
Art. 169	13, 20, 150, 152–3
Art. 173	149, 164
Art. 227	93, 94, 162
Art. 232	3
Art. 234	102
Art. 235	137
Annex II	3, 17

1972 Act of Accession

Art. 9	13
Art. 26	93
Art. 44	21
Art. 55	122
Art. 60	13
Art. 100	92
Art. 101	92, 94
Art. 102	24, 95, 96
Art. 103	93
Art. 104	25
Art. 105	25

Declaration on Liquid Milk	81
Protocol No. 2	93
Protocol No. 3	93, 94
Protocol No. 17	88
Protocol No. 18	82

Greek Act of Accession

Art. 61	122
Art. 65	14
Arts. 99–101	86
Art. 112	25

Spanish and Portuguese Act of Accession

Table of Community Legislation

Table of Community Legislation

Other Acts

Table of U.K. Legislation

Table of U.K. Statutory Instruments

1

Introduction

'It is inconceivable that any common market should be established in Europe which did not include agriculture':[1] this book is concerned with the legal consequences of that approach to European integration. The agricultural policy of the European Community is probably the area of Community activity of which the general public in the United Kingdom is most aware, if only because of the critical comment to which it has given rise. However, it is also in the sphere of agriculture that many of the fundamental institutional, financial and legal developments in the history of the Community have occurred.

Thus, it was in anticipation of the introduction of qualified majority voting in the Council of Ministers with regard to agricultural legislation under art. 43(2) and (3) of the EEC Treaty, at the end of the second stage of the original transitional period (i.e. 1 January 1966) that the French government pursued its 'empty chair' policy in the second half of 1965, resulting in the so-called Luxembourg Accords of January 1966; yet it was also in the context of agricultural legislation that the system of delegating discretionary powers to the Commission subject to consultation with a management committee representing the Member States was evolved. Financially, it has been argued that it is only 'the accident of history which led to the establishment of the CAP in a particular form' which resulted in the adoption of the 'own resources' system of financing Community expenditure with the core principle of 'financial solidarity' or common financing.[2] Be that as it may, agricultural expenditure consumes the greater part of the Community budget, even if in percentage terms the proportion diminished from 80.6 per cent at the time of United Kingdom Accession to 72.9 per cent in 1985.[3]

Legally, the introduction in the late 1960s of common organizations of agricultural markets based on a single Community market was one of the factors which enabled the Common Customs Tariff to be introduced eighteen months early in July 1968,[4] and the regulations creating those

[1] Spaak Report 1956 p. 44 as translated by E. Neville-Rolfe in *The Politics of Agriculture in the European Community* (Policy Studies Institute, London, 1984) p. 185.

[2] H. Wallace, 'A European Budget Made in Strasbourg and Unmade in Luxembourg', *Yearbook of European Law 1986* p. 263.

[3] EC Commission, European File 17/86 pp. 2, 5.

[4] An account of the interrelationship is contained in Neville-Rolfe, *The Politics of Agriculture* pp. 239–242.

common organizations expressly reproduced the provisions of the EEC Treaty relating to the free movement of goods and applied them to trade in the relevant agricultural products at a time when the basic Treaty rules had not become fully effective. Moreover, it is in the context of such common organizations that the European Court's theories on the relationship between national law (and the powers of national legislatures) and Community law have largely been developed.[5] Finally, it may be observed that agricultural disputes have been the most frequent source of litigation before the European Court[6] and hence, hardly surprisingly, the source of many of the general principles of Community law.[7] The aim of this book is, essentially, to examine the legal issues to which the Common Agricultural Policy gives rise, rather than to discuss aspects of that policy itself, although this is an area where it is not always possible to separate the law from the policy to which it gives effect.

[5] See ch. 6 *infra*.
[6] According to the running totals recorded in the annual *Synopsis of the Work of the Court of Justice*. (Official Publications Office of the EC, Luxembourg).
[7] See *infra*. pp. 40–48.

2

Agriculture in the EEC Treaty

(a) Definition of agricultural goods

The characteristic distinction between the ECSC and Euratom Treaties, on the one hand, and the EEC Treaty, on the other, is that the former only apply to the goods, activities, and persons expressly listed therein, whereas the EEC Treaty is limited only by reference to the scope of the other two Treaties.[1] However, the agricultural provisions of the EEC Treaty are an exception to this generalisation, at least with regard to the definition of agricultural goods. Art. 38(1) of the EEC Treaty provides that the common market should extend to agriculture and trade in agricultural products, and defines agricultural products as products of the soil, of stock farming and of fisheries, and products of first-stage processing directly related to these products. By virtue of Art. 38(3), a specific list of the products subject to the agricultural rules of the Treaty is contained in Annex II, but the Council was empowered to decide what products should be added to this list within two years of the entry into force of the Treaty. This power was exercised in Council Regulation 7a which, however, is not without controversy. The two year period expired on 31 December 1959, and although the Regulation is dated 18 December 1959, it was not published in the Official Journal of the European Communities until 30 January 1961.[2] Under art. 191 of the EEC Treaty, publication is an essential requirement for the entry into force of a Regulation, and in Case 185/73, *HZA Bielefeld* v. *König*,[3] it was, therefore, argued that Regulation 7a was invalid. This argument was rejected by the European Court on the ground that the late publication of the Regulation had no significance save as to the date from which it could be applied and take effect.

Perhaps of greater importance, however, is the fact that the Court in this judgment gave a purposive interpretation to the phrase 'products of first-stage processing directly related' to basic agricultural products, holding that what was relevant was the economic relationship between the basic product and the processed product, rather than the number of processing operations involved. It was held that there should be a clear economic interdependence between the basic products and processed products, but that where processed products have undergone a productive process the

---

[1] EEC Treaty, art. 232.   [2] JO 1961 p. 71.   [3] [1974] ECR 607.

cost of which is such that the price of the basic agricultural raw materials becomes a completely marginal cost, they do not fall within the definition. Applying this economic criterion, the Court held that the fact that ethyl alcohol of less than 80° strength would be diluted with water (not an agricultural product!) after distillation did not prevent its being included in the list in Regulation 7a.

Whilst the definition in *König* sets the overall limits on what may or may not be included in the lists of agricultural products, the lists themselves are highly specific, using the same nomenclature as the Common Customs Tariff. There are two major legal consequences of this system. The first is that products falling within the definition in *König* will not be treated as agricultural products unless they are specifically listed in Annex II or Regulation 7a, and the second is that in interpreting these lists regard may be had to the other headings of the Common Customs Tariff (CCT) and to the accepted aids to the interpretation of that tariff.[4] Hence, in Case 77/83, *CILFIT* v. *Italian Ministry of Health*,[5] it was held that whilst wool was undisputably grown on sheep, it did not fall within the concept of 'animal products not elsewhere specified or included' under CCT heading 05.15b, which was included in Annex II, since a note to chapter 5 of the CCT specifically stated that it did not cover animal textile materials, and wool was the subject of a separate Chapter 53 of the CCT which was not included in Annex II.

Indeed, in so far as the CCT was based on the 1950 Customs Co-operation Council Convention on Nomenclature for the Classification of Goods in Customs Tariffs,[6] reference may be made in interpreting Annex II to the Explanatory Notes to that Convention, as in Case 61/80, *Cooperatieve Stremsel-en Kleurselfabriek* v. *Commission*.[7] There, in the absence, as the Court pointed out, of any Community provisions explaining the concepts contained in Annex II, those Explanatory Notes were followed in so far as they indicated that animal rennet should be classified under heading 35.07 as an enzyme or prepared enzyme rather than under headings 05.04 or 05.15, which are included in Annex II, as a gut, bladder, or stomach of an animal, or as other animal produce, even though the rennet there at issue was extracted from calves' fourth stomachs. Annex II has not been altered to take account of the International Convention on the Harmonized Commodity Description and Coding System,[8] on which the Common Customs Tariff has been based

---

[4] See Usher, 'Uniform External Protection: EEC Customs Legislation before the European Court of Justice' (1982) *CML Rev*. 389.
[5] [1984] ECR 1257.   [6] See n. 4 *supra*.
[7] [1981] ECR 851, 869.
[8] OJ 1987 L198/1. The new text of the Common Customs Tariff is contained in Council Reg. 2658/87 (OJ 1987 L256/1).

since 1 January 1988, since this would require a Treaty amendment and could conceivably lead to changes of substance.

With regard to the overall scope of the concept of agricultural products, particular attention may be drawn to the products of fisheries. After the Accession of the United Kingdom in 1973, the view was put forward that art. 102 of the 1972 Act of Accession, which laid down a time limit for the adoption of fishery-conservation measures, conferred a new competence on the Community.[9] However, the European Court affirmed in Case 61/77, *Commission* v. *Ireland*,[10] and in Case 141/78, *France* v. *United Kingdom*,[11] that sea fisheries had always fallen within the scope of the Common Agricultural Policy, and that art. 102 of the 1972 Act of Accession merely confirmed that conservation measures were included in the Community's powers. Indeed, it may be observed that 'fish, crustaceans and molluscs' are expressly included in the list in Annex II.

Readers of Annex II might, however, be surprised to see that the last item on the list is cannabis (in the form of 'true hemp'). Of the items not included in the list, on the other hand, particular attention may be drawn to cotton, with regard to which the Accession of Greece, followed by that of Spain and Portugal, has resulted in the adoption of special measures. Although Annex II itself was not amended to include cotton, specific provisions were introduced under Protocol No. 4 to the Greek Act of Accession, on the grounds of the great importance that cotton production represented for the Greek economy and 'recognising the specifically agricultural character of this production'. To avoid discrimination, these provisions apply throughout the territory of the Community, and the aims are to support the production of cotton in regions where it is important for the agricultural economy, to permit producers to earn a fair income, and to stabilise the market—aims remarkably similar to those of the Common Agricultural Policy itself.[12] The basic system of support is a production aid, paid through cotton ginning undertakings to cover the difference between a guide price and the world market price (concepts familiar in common organizations of agricultural markets), subject to quantitative restrictions (also now familiar in common organizations). The link with agricultural organizations is further confirmed by Council Regulation 2169/81,[13] the basic implementing regulation, which used as the management committee[14] in the cotton sector the already-existing management committee for flax and hemp created by Regulation 1308/70[15]—hence the link with the first sentence of this paragraph.

[9] See e.g. Hiester, 'The Legal Position of the European Community with Regard to the Conservation of the Living Resources of the Sea' (1976) *Legal Issues of European Integration* 55.

[10] [1978] ECR 417.   [11] [1979] ECR 2923.

[12] As set out in art. 39 of the EEC Treaty.

[13] OJ 1981 L211/2.   [14] See *infra.* pp. 147–9.   [15] JO 1970 L146/1.

There is a double reason for the importance of the definition of agricultural products in the EEC Treaty: certain of the general rules of that Treaty do not apply to agricultural products, even if the basic principle laid down in art. 38 is that they do, and, conversely, certain special rules apply only to agricultural products, much of this Chapter being devoted to their consideration. However, in practical terms it has not always been possible to operate a clear distinction between agricultural goods, and non-agricultural goods which, nevertheless, incorporate an agricultural element. Hence, a series of Regulations may be found, currently exemplified in Council Regulation 3033/80,[16] laying down the trade arrangements applicable to certain goods resulting from the processing of agricultural products. The effect of these Regulations is that certain provisions of the special agricultural legislation, particularly trading rules relating to levies and refunds, may be applied to processed products not defined in Annex II, in order to take account of the basic agricultural products considered to be comprised in those processed products.

(b) Definition of agricultural producers and agricultural holdings

Whilst the Treaty defines agricultural products, it mentions 'persons engaged in agriculture'[17] and 'producers'[18] without defining those terms, and does not even mention 'agricultural holdings'; nevertheless, these terms have been widely used in the secondary legislation. A simplistic definition would be to say that an agricultural producer is a person producing agricultural products as defined in the Treaty, and that an agricultural holding is land used to produce such products, but this is not really sufficiently specific when it becomes necessary to categorize farmers who also carry out processing operations or have other part-time employment, or to categorize land which is also used for processing operations or part of which is used for non-agricultural purposes.

The argument that an agricultural producer is simply a producer of an agricultural product defined in the Treaty was put to the European Court in Case 139/77, *Denkavit v. FZA Warendorf*,[19] in the context of a Regulation which, following the revaluation of the German mark in 1969, allowed Germany to grant compensation 'in the form of direct aid to agricultural producers', to make up for the fact that such producers would receive fewer DM when Community prices expressed in units of account were converted at the new parity.[20] The plaintiff company produced

---

[16] OJ 1980 L323/1.   [17] Art. 39(1)b.
[18] e.g. arts. 40(3) and 43(3).   [19] [1978] ECR 1317.
[20] This may be contrasted with what happened in 1971, when the German and Dutch currencies floated upwards, leading to the introduction of monetary compensatory amounts. See *infra*, pp. 108–13.

feeding stuffs and fattened calves on substitute milk-based fodder which it produced itself, but under the German implementing legislation the breeding and keeping of livestock was deemed to be agricultural only if a defined quantity of livestock was kept in a defined area of land, whereas the plaintiff company, having bought its calves, entered into contracts with other farmers to have them fattened, thus, not using any agricultural land of its own. In response to the plaintiff's argument that it should, nevertheless, in Community law be regarded as an agricultural producer, the Court emphasized that the concept of agriculture (as opposed to that of agricultural products) was not precisely defined in the Treaty, and concluded that 'for the purposes of the agricultural rules derived from the Treaty, it is for the competent authorities where necessary to define the scope of such rules in relation to persons and in relation to subject-matter'. On the particular legislation at issue, the Court took the view that although the expression 'agricultural producer' was broad enough to include the production of agricultural products by any method whatever, the Regulation conferred a power rather than a duty on the German authorities, and the distinction which the German authorities had chosen to make could be objectively justified and was therefore not a discriminatory exercise of their discretion.

A more specific Community definition may be found in the context of structural (i.e. guidance) policy. Here, Council Regulation 797/85,[21] reproducing the terminology of the 1972 Directives which it replaced,[22] provides in art. 2(1) for aid to be granted to agricultural holdings when the 'farmer' practises farming as his main occupation, and, whilst the Member States are left to define this concept further, art. 2(2) provides that the definition must require such a farmer to earn more than 50 per cent of his income from farming and to devote less than half his total working time to work unconnected with the holding. However, farmers not falling within this definition may still be eligible for national aids within certain limits, and this appears to have been the background to Case 152/79, *Lee* v. *Minister for Agriculture*,[23] where the plaintiff was an office clerk as well as being a part-time farmer. Furthermore, in the context of the 1972 Directives, it was clearly held in Case 312/85, *Villa Banfi* v. *Region of Tuscany*,[24] that the concept of a 'farmer' is not limited to human beings and that a legal person carrying on a farming activity is not excluded if it complies with the other criteria—indeed it would be a breach of the prohibition on discrimination between producers laid down by art. 40(3) of the Treaty to exclude a producer who was a legal person from the scope of the structural legislation.

---

[21] OJ 1985 L93/1. [22] See ch. 7 *infra*.
[23] [1980] ECR 1495. See the Opinion of A.-G. Warner at p. 1514.
[24] 18 Dec. 1986.

The dividing line between producer and processor was at issue in Case 107/80, *Adorno* v. *Commission*,[25] where the applicant sought the annulment of a Commission decision refusing to grant aid for an investment project under Council Regulation 355/77, on common measures to improve the conditions under which agricultural products are processed and marketed.[26] The applicant ran a farm comprising two holdings traditionally devoted to wine-growing and capable of producing high-quality wine, and his investment project involved the creation of a new wine-making centre at the farm to improve the processing of his grapes into wine. The Commission rejected his claim on the basis that it fell within the scope of one of the 1972 structural Directives benefiting farmers, Directive 72/159 on the modernization of farms,[27] and that it, therefore, could not fall within the scope of the Regulation benefiting processors; however, the applicant fell outside the income criteria laid down by that Directive. In its judgment, the Court effectively rejected the contention that a person who was also a producer was necessarily excluded from the processing Regulation, holding that 'projects for improving the processing and marketing of agricultural products from the same farm as that in which the investment is to be made are in no way excluded from the scope of the Regulation if they are capable of making an effective contribution towards standardizing processing and marketing structures'.[28] On the other hand, in the Court's view, even though the applicant was a producer his project was not concerned with improving production conditions for basic agricultural products but with improving the processing and marketing of those products, so that it did not, in any event, fall within the scope of the 1972 Directive.

Similar problems of definition have also arisen in the context of an 'agricultural holding', a term used in a range of Community legislation, being the basic entity qualifying for assistance under Council Regulation 797/85 on structural policy,[29] but also being mentioned in, for example, Commission Regulation 3254/86,[30] which exempted the crushing of maize ears for ensilage on an agricultural holding from the co-responsibility levy on cereals.[31] The basic question was put in Case 85/77, *Santa Anna* v. *INPS*,[32] in relation to an Italian undertaking marketing eggs, day-old chicks and fattened poultry, produced on a holding of some three hectares. The dispute before the national court related to the question whether the undertaking should have to pay social security contributions covering its employees as an agricultural undertaking (apparently liable to pay at lower rates) or as an industrial undertaking. In its reference for a preliminary

[25] [1981] ECR 1469.   [26] OJ 1977 L51/1. See *infra*, p. 140.
[27] JO 1972 L96/1.   [28] [1981] ECR at p. 1485.
[29] OJ 1985 L93/1.   [30] OJ 1986 L302/2.
[31] See *infra*, p. 56.   [32] [1978] ECR 527.

ruling, the Italian court asked if there was a Community concept of an 'agricultural holding' and whether the Member States were obliged to follow this concept. The Court again noted that the Treaty contained no precise definition of agriculture, and still less of an agricultural holding, so that it was for the Community institutions to work out such a definition where appropriate. After observing that the phrase was widely used in secondary legislation, the Court stated that 'the definition of these words is far from being uniform throughout these rules . . . but on the contrary varies according to the specific objectives pursued by the Community rules in question';[33] it therefore concluded that it was impossible to find in the provisions of the Treaty or in the rules of secondary Community law any general, uniform Community definition of 'agricultural holding' universally applicable in all the provisions relating to agricultural production.

Whilst, therefore, the meaning of the phrase 'agricultural holding' may depend on its context, it would appear that the fact that part of the land is used for non-agricultural purposes does not necessarily take it outside the scope of Community agricultural legislation. In Case 152/79, *Lee* v. *Minister of Agriculture*,[34] the plaintiff had bored for water on his land and installed a pump and an underground pipe to a drinking trough for cattle, but he had also inserted a T-junction in the pipe, leading to a tank acting as a reservoir for a water-supply in houses built on his land for sale. The basic issue was whether this fell within the scope of the former Directive 72/159 on the modernization of farms,[35] and the European Court held that that depended on whether the provision of a water supply was carried out principally in order to service dwelling-houses or whether a *part* (emphasis added) of that work related to the modernization of a farm; a question which it was for the national court to decide.

(c) *Application of general rules of the EEC Treaty*

(i) **The basic principle in common organizations**

The basic principle laid down in art. 38 of the EEC Treaty is that the rules laid down for the establishment of the common market shall apply to agricultural products 'save as otherwise provided in articles 39 to 46'. These exceptional cases will be considered below,[36] but it is a distinctive feature of the European Economic Community that the 'common market' it creates extends not only to industrial products but also to agricultural products, whereas the European Free Trade Association, for example, expressly excluded agricultural products from the system of free trade which it created.[37] Indeed, Council Regulations establishing common

---

[33] Ibid. at p. 540.   [34] [1980] ECR 1495.   [35] JO 1972 L96/1.
[36] See *infra*, pp. 14–20.   [37] EFTA Treaty art. 21.

organizations of the market before the end of the transitional period (1st January 1970) reproduced the basic Treaty provisions concerned with the free movement of goods, expressly prohibiting charges equivalent to customs duties and measures equivalent to quantitative restrictions in trade between Member States, and it has long been held by the European Court that these concepts have exactly the same meaning when used in secondary agricultural legislation as they have when used in the Treaty itself.[38]

To some extent, the agricultural Regulations went beyond the express Treaty provisions, as where they prohibited Member States from imposing charges equivalent to customs duties not only in trade between Member States but also at the external frontiers of the Community with regard to goods imported from third countries.[39] The Treaty itself does not expressly prohibit such charges on direct imports from third countries, and for goods not covered by agricultural common organizations of the market, such a prohibition was developed by the European Court as case law, notably in its judgment in Cases 37 and 38/73, *Sociaal Fonds voor de Diamentarbeiders* v. *Indiamex*,[40] where it was held that it was incompatible with the concepts of a Common Customs Tariff and a Common Commercial Policy for Member States unilaterally to alter the level of external protection through such charges. Indeed, in that case, specific reference was made to the fact that instruments of the Common Agricultural Policy expressly prohibited such charges.

After the end of the transitional period, the reproduction of the Treaty provisions in agricultural Regulations has become otiose, as was pointed out by A.-G. Warner in relation to a 1970 Regulation on the common organization of the market in wine,[41] since these provisions have been held to be of direct effect, that is, they give rise to rights enforceable by individuals before national courts, since that date. Hence, the modern versions[42] of the basic agricultural Regulations do not reproduce the basic Treaty provisions. The status of a modern Regulation codifying the provisions governing a common organization of the market, without expressly repeating the Treaty provisions relating to the abolition of customs duties and quantitative restrictions was considered by the Court in Case 83/78, *Pigs Marketing Board* v. *Redmond*,[43] in relation to Regulation No. 2759/75[44] on the common organisation of the market in pigmeat, and it

---

[38] See, for example, Case 34/73, *Variola* v. *Italian Finance Administration* [1973] ECR 981.

[39] See, for example, Case 84/71, *Marimex* v. *Italian Finance Administration* [1972] ECR 89, with regard to the regulations establishing the common organization of the market in beef and veal.

[40] [1973] ECR 1609.

[41] In his Opinion in Cases 80 and 81/77, *Ramel* v. *Receveur des Douanes* [1978] ECR 927.

[42] In practice, those adopted after the judgment of the Court in Case 48/74, *Charmasson* [1974] ECR 1783 (see *infra*, p. 12).

[43] [1978] ECR 2347.   [44] OJ 1975 L282/1.

was there said that the provisions of the Treaty relating to the abolition of tariff and commercial barriers to intra-Community trade, and in particular arts. 30 and 34 on the abolition of quantitative restrictions and of measures having equivalent effect on imports and exports 'are to be regarded as an integral part of the common organisation of the market'. In so far as Regulations are still in force which reproduce, for example, arts. 30 and 34 of the EEC Treaty, the view was expressed in Case 118/86, *Nertsvoederfabriek*,[45] that account should simply be taken of the Treaty provisions.

On the other hand, it is clear that the Council and Commission cannot prevent the application of the basic Treaty rules to agricultural products except to the extent that arts. 39 to 46 so provide. This is illustrated in Cases 80 and 81/77, *Ramel* v. *Receveur des Douanes*,[46] where France imposed levies on imports of Italian wine, claiming to be so authorized under Council Regulation 816/70[47] on additional provisions for the common organization of the market in wine. Whilst art. 31(1) of that Regulation repeated the basic prohibition on the levying of charges equivalent to customs duties, art. 31(2) contained a derogation to the effect that 'so long as all the administrative mechanisms necessary for the management of the market in wine are not in application producer Member States shall be authorised in order to avoid disturbances on their markets to take measures that may limit imports from another Member State'. The French view was that the relevant 'administrative mechanisms' were not in application in Italy, and the fundamental question referred to the European Court was whether this provision was compatible with the Treaty. In its judgment, the Court held that in order to justify the establishment of charges having equivalent effect to customs duties after the end of the transitional period, it must be shown that arts. 39–46 contain a provision which expressly or by necessary implication provides for or permits such charges. After considering those articles, the Court found that there was no such provision; indeed, it found that under art. 44, even during the transitional period, in so far as the abolition of customs duties and quantitative restrictions between Member States might have resulted in prices likely to jeopardize the attainment of the objectives of the Common Agricultural Policy, Member States could only, subject to certain conditions, introduce a non-discriminatory system of minimum prices, and that it would be manifestly contrary to the Treaty to allow greater restrictions after the end of the transitional period.

The Court concluded from this that, at all events after the end of the transitional period, the Community institutions' powers in agricultural matters should be used with the unity of the market in mind, to the exclusion of measures breaching the prohibition on customs duties and

---

[45] 6 Oct. 1987.   [46] [1978] ECR 927.   [47] JO 1970 L99/1.

quantitative restrictions and charges and measures having equivalent effect. It went on to hold that art. 31(2) of Regulation No. 816/70, in so far as it permitted Member States to levy charges having equivalent effect to customs duties in trade with other Member States on the products covered by the Regulation, was incompatible with arts. 13(2) and 38–46 of the EEC Treaty, and, hence, invalid.

It would appear to follow from this decision that the treatment of agricultural products under the EEC Treaty may not be as exceptional as is sometimes thought, and in particular that it may be difficult to give special treatment to a certain national interest simply by clothing it in Community legislation. Indeed, the Court has now held clearly, in Case 288/83, *Commission* v. *Ireland*,[48] that the Commission cannot, even by approving expressly or by implication a measure adopted unilaterally by a Member State, confer on that State the right to maintain provisions which are objectively contrary to Community law. The extent to which arts. 39–46 do allow exceptional treatment of agricultural products will be considered later in this Chapter.[49]

(ii) The basic principle in the absence of a common organization

Under art. 40(1) of the EEC Treaty, common organizations of the market should have been established by the end of the transitional period. For most products this was, in fact, done, notable exceptions being alcohol, potatoes, and sheepmeat (for which an organization was eventually created in 1980). It may, however, be suggested that at the end of the transitional period there was a widely held view that, by virtue of arts. 43, 45, and 46 of the EEC Treaty, national organizations of the market could be protected until they had been replaced by common organizations of the market. Art. 43(3)(a), in particular provides that a national market organization may be replaced by a common organization only if the latter offers Member States which are opposed to it and have a relevant national organization 'equivalent safeguards for the employment and standard of living of the producers concerned'.

This view was accepted both by the Commission and by A.-G. Warner in Case 48/74, *Charmasson* v. *Minister for Economic Affairs*,[50] but not by the Court. In that case, a trader was challenging a French quota system applying to the importation of bananas into France. There was not at the time, and, it might be added, is still not, any common organization relating to the market in bananas. Whilst it held that a simple quota system could not amount to a national organization of the market, the Court did state its view on the position of a national organization of the market after the end

---

[48] [1985] ECR 1761.   [49] See *infra*, pp. 14–20.   [50] [1974] ECR 1383.

of the transitional period. The view accepted by the Court was that since the common organizations of the market should have been introduced by the end of the transitional period then the protected position of national organizations could also only last until the end of the transitional period. Hence, national organizations of the market become subject to the general rules of the Treaty; notably, those on free movement of goods; in the Charmasson case, it was held that art. 33, on the elimination of quotas would be applicable. This doctrine was reaffirmed in Case 68/76, *Commission* v. *France*,[51] an action brought by the Commission against France for breach of a Treaty obligation in subjecting exports of potatoes, even within the EEC, to the requirement that an officially certified export declaration must be presented. Following earlier case-law, the Court held such a requirement, even if purely formal, to be a measure having equivalent effect to a quantitative restriction, on the basis that arts. 39–46 could not justify a unilateral derogation from art. 34 of the EEC Treaty, prohibiting measures having equivalent effect to quantitative restrictions on exports, even if no common organization had been introduced.[52]

A similar view has been taken with regard to the expiry of the transitional period under the 1972 Act of Accession. Art. 9 of the Act provided that 'subject to the dates, time-limits and special provisions provided for in this Act', the accession transitional period should expire at the end of 1977. Art. 60(2) of the Act, on the other hand, provided that, in respect of products not covered by a common organization of the market at the time of accession, the general provisions of the Act relating to the abolition of charges having equivalent effect to customs duties, and of quantitative restrictions and measures having equivalent effect thereto, should not apply to those products if they formed part of a national market organization on the date of accession, and further stated that it should apply 'until the common organisation of the market for these products is implemented'. In Case 231/78, *Commission* v. *UK*,[53] where the Commission brought an action against the United Kingdom under art. 169 of the EEC Treaty for breaching a Treaty obligation in continuing a ban on the import of main-crop potatoes after the end of 1977, under the aegis of what was admitted to be a national organization of the potato market, it was argued by the United Kingdom that art. 60(2) constituted a 'special provision', so that the general time-limit did not apply. The Court, however, held that the only special provisions which could alter the basic transitional period were those which were clearly delimited and determined in time, and not a

---

[51] [1977] ECR 515.

[52] It was following this judgment that the French Conseil d'Etat awarded damages against the French government, when it had prevented the performance of a contract to sell French potatoes to an Italian undertaking by refusing to grant an export licence in *Alivar* v. *Ministre du commerce extérieur* (23 Mar. 1984).

[53] [1979] ECR 1447.

provision like art. 60(2) which referred to an uncertain future event. Indeed, the Court went so far as to suggest that even during the accession transitional period, Art. 60(2) could only have been invoked by the new Member States. This tends to support the view that those who drafted it, working before the decision in *Charmasson*, must have thought that national organizations of the market continued to be protected after the ending of the transitional period until common organizations were adopted, since such unilateral generosity seems highly unlikely.[54] Having found that the ordinary transitional period applied to national market organizations, the Court then repeated what it had said in *Charmasson*, that after expiry of the transitional period the operation of a national market organization could no longer prevent full effect being given to the Treaty provisions on the elimination of quantitative restrictions and measures having equivalent effect. This view of the accession transitional period was repeated in Case 232/78, *Commission* v. *France*,[55] an action brought by the Commission against France in relation to French measures restricting the importation of mutton and lamb. In the light of the earlier judgments, it was not disputed that these measures were incompatible with the Treaty, and the French government largely invoked economic and social justifications for its actions. It is, no doubt, as a result of these judgments that the equivalent art. 65(2) of the Greek Act of Accession limited the protection of national organizations of the market to the specific date of 31 December 1985. Similarly, arts. 76 and 244 of the Spanish and Portuguese Act of Accession limit such protection to 31 December 1995.

The effect of this case law has been clearly reaffirmed in Case 288/83, *Commission* v. *Ireland*,[56] with regard to Irish measures restricting the import of potatoes in free circulation in other Member States (i.e. potatoes which have been imported from non-Member States on payment of the appropriate duties etc., and are, therefore, under arts. 9 and 10 of the EEC Treaty, entitled to internal free movement in the Community). It was there stated that 'agricultural products in respect of which a common organisation of the market has not been established are subject to the general rules of the Common Market with regard to importation, exportation and movement within the Community'.

(iii) Competition, state aids, and countervailing charges

Leaving aside certain transitional provisions, the only express derogations from specific Treaty rules in favour of agricultural products are to be found

---

[54] See, for example, Wyatt, 'British Import Controls on Main Crop Potatoes' (1979) 4 EL Rev. 359.
[55] [1979] ECR 2729.   [56] [1985] ECR 1761.

in arts. 42 and 46 of the EEC Treaty. Art. 42 provides that the rules on competition shall apply to agricultural products only to the extent determined by the Council within the framework of the Common Agricultural Policy, and specifically enables the Council to authorise the granting of certain forms of aid. It should be observed that the relevant chapter of the EEC Treaty relates not only to the practices of private (and public) undertakings but also to the payment of state aids, and in practice the role of art. 46 is to allow import charges to be imposed on agricultural products in so far as state aids may be paid by the exporting Member State.

The basic rules in the matter were laid down by Council Regulation 26/62,[57] which treats the practices of private and public undertakings differently from the payment of state aids. With regard to the anti-competitive practices of private and public undertakings, art. 1 of the Regulation provides in principle for the application of the general rules contained in arts. 85–90 of the EEC Treaty to the production of or trade in agricultural goods. There is, however, an exception to this laid down by art. 2(1), the first sentence of which provides that art. 85(1) of the Treaty, prohibiting certain agreements, decisions, and concerted practices of or between undertakings, shall not apply to agreements, decisions, and concerted practices which are either an integral part of a national market organization or are necessary for the attainment of the objectives of the Common Agricultural Policy. In particular, according to the second sentence of art. 2(1) of the Regulation, art. 85(1) does not apply to agreements, decisions, and practices of farmers, farmers' associations, or associations of such associations belonging to a single Member State which concern the production or sale of agricultural products or the use of joint facilities for the storage, treatment, or processing of agricultural products, and under which there is no obligation to charge identical prices, unless the Commission finds that competition is thereby excluded (rather than simply restricted) or that the objectives of the Common Agricultural Policy are jeopardized. The Commission is given exclusive power to determine which agreements etc. fall within this exception. With regard to the attainment of the objectives of the Common Agricultural Policy, this effectively means that arts. 85 to 90 of the EEC Treaty are read subject to the specific provisions of the legislation establishing common organizations of agricultural markets. This legislation will frequently have the effect of severely restricting price competition (being, as will be seen, based on 'common' prices with compensation for exchange-rate fluctuations) and may, to give a random example, require non-members to abide by the rules of producer organizations, as under art. 7 of Council Regulation 3796/81,[58] on the common organization of the market in fish products. It is not, however,

[57] JO 1962 p. 993.   [58] OJ 1981 L379/1.

permissible for undertakings further to restrict the degree of competition left open to them, as is evident from the cases involving alleged concerted practices in the sugar market,[59] although these cases do also show, in relation to the Italian market for sugar at the relevant period, that a combination of Community and national rules may leave so little room for manoeuvre that the conduct of undertakings is incapable of appreciably impeding competition.[60] With regard to the other markets at issue in these cases, however, the applicants were not able to show that their practices were 'necessary' for the attainment of the objectives of the common agricultural policy.[61] Similarly, in Case 71/74, *Frubo* v. *Commission*,[62] which concerned an agreement relating to the import of fruit into the Netherlands from outside the Community, the Court took the view that such an agreement could not be necessary to achieve the first two objectives of the Common Agricultural Policy, that is, to increase agricultural productivity and to ensure a fair standard of living for the agricultural community. This statement is of particular interest, since the applicants' claim was that their agreement helped attain the other three objectives of the Common Agricultural Policy, and the Court seems to have followed A.-G. Warner's view that the objectives of that policy 'are inseparable from each other'. By way of contrast, when assessing the validity of Community legislation in the light of these objectives, the Court has consistently held that priority may be given to one objective over the others,[63] and has upheld legislation serving only one of those objectives.[64]

The approach of the Commission to Regulation 26/62 when enforcing the competition rules may be illustrated by its Decision in the *Meldoc* case,[65] involving an agreement between Dutch dairy undertakings. The Commission pointed out that since Council Regulation 804/68[66] had replaced national market organizations in the dairy industry the agreement would not be justified as being an integral part of a national market organization. With regard to the attainment of the objectives of the Common Agricultural Policy, the Commission declared that the means to be employed in the dairy sector were stated in Regulation 804/68, whereas the agreement there at issue, which gave rise to a quota system, a compensation scheme, consultations on sales and prices, and measures designed to inhibit imports from other Member States, amounted to an attempt to set up a private intervention system very different from that for which the Regulation provided. Having, thus, concluded that the agree-

---

[59] Cases 40–8, 50, 54–6, 111, 113, and 114/73, *Suiker Unie and others* v. *Commission* [1975] ECR 1663 at pp. 1949–50.

[60] Ibid. at p. 1924.   [61] Ibid. at pp. 1948, 1951, 2020.

[62] [1975] ECR 563.

[63] Case 5/73, *Balkan* v. *HZA Berlin-Packhof* [1973] ECR 1091.

[64] e.g. Case 138/78, *Stölting* v. *HZA Hamburg-Jonas* [1979] ECR 713.

[65] Decision 86/596 of 26 Nov. 1986 (OJ 1986 L348/50).   [66] JO 1968 L148/13.

ment did not fall within the first sentence of art. 2(1) of Regulation 26/62, the Commission took the view that the second sentence of art. 2(1), stating, 'in particular', the agreements to which art. 85 did not apply, merely referred to a particular form of the arrangements exempted under the first sentence, and this could only be invoked in relation to agreements so exempted. By way of contrast, the Commission gave in effect a 'negative clearance' to the French national organization of the market in new potatoes.[66a]

With regard to practices claimed to form an integral part of a national market organization, there is the further problem of knowing what is a national market organization. In *Charmasson*[67] the European Court defined it as 'a totality of legal devices placing the regulation of the market in the products in question under the control of the public authority, with a view to ensuring, by means of an increase in productivity and of optimum utilisation of the factors of production, in particular of manpower, a fair standard of living for producers, the stabilisation of markets, the assurance of supplies and reasonable prices to the consumers'—in effect, therefore, an organization pursuing the same aims as those laid down by article 39 of the EEC Treaty for common organizations, albeit at the national level, and, hence, an entity which can hardly co-exist with a common organization unless expressly preserved or required.[68]

As an exception, art. 2 of Regulation 26/62 has been strictly construed, particularly with regard to the concept of agricultural products. Thus, an exclusive purchasing obligation with regard to rennet, which is not listed in Annex II to the EEC Treaty, despite being extracted from calves' fourth stomachs,[69] did not fall within the exception, even though it was used in the manufacture of cheese, which is listed in Annex II,[70] nor did a price fixing arrangement relating to cognac and the wine from which it was distilled, on the ground that spirits are expressly excluded from Annex II, despite its economic importance for agricultural producers in the area concerned.[71] Furthermore, it should be emphasized that Regulation 26/62 does not create an exemption from the prohibition of an abuse of a dominant position set out in art. 86 of the EEC Treaty. Thus, in Case 27/76, *United Brands* v. *Commission*,[72] which concerned an abuse of a dominant position in the market of bananas, the fact that an agricultural product was involved made no difference to the application of the normal competition rules.

On the other hand, in the matter of state aids, Regulation 26/62 does not apply the substantive Treaty rules to agricultural products. Art. 4 of the

[66a] OJ 1988 L59/25.   [67] [1974] ECR 1383 at p. 1396.   [68] See *infra*, pp. 130–2.
[69] See *supra*, p. 4.
[70] Case 61/80, *Co-operative Stremsel- en Kleurselfabriek* v. *Commission* [1981] ECR 851.
[71] Case 123/83, *BNIC* v. *Clair* [1985] ECR 402.   [72] [1978] ECR 207.

Regulation merely provides for the application of the first and third paragraphs of art. 93 of the Treaty, providing for the review of existing systems of aid by the Commission and requiring the notification of new aids. Hence, the application of the substantive state aids rules to trade in agricultural products depends on the terms of the Regulations establishing common organizations of the market for the products in question, although it should be borne in mind that the state aid relating to a product covered by a common organization may interfere with the operation of that common organization and, thus, infringe it, quite apart from the infringement of the state-aids rules as such.[73] In fact, most common organizations of the market do provide for the application of arts. 92–4 of the EEC Treaty within their scope and 'save as otherwise provided in this Regulation'.[74] While the Treaty provisions on state aids have themselves been held not to be of direct effect, in the sense of creating rights enforceable by individuals before national courts, it was argued in Case 78/76, *Steinike und Weinlig* v. *Germany*,[75] that their incorporation in a directly applicable Regulation did render them so enforceable. However, the Court, following A.-G. Warner, held that the inclusion of the state-aids rules in an agricultural Regulation did not alter their nature and scope; as A.-G. Warner pointed out, the effect was to lift the bar to their application which would otherwise have resulted from art. 42 of the Treaty. In the result, it is, therefore, for the Commission to enforce the state aids rules within common organization of agricultural markets, and this has for example led it to take decisions with regard to French aids to maintain farm incomes,[76] with regard to United Kingdom subsidies to users of fishing vessels,[77] and with regard to preferential tariffs charged to glasshouse growers for natural gas in the Netherlands.[78] So far as the notification of state aids is concerned, it is only the first sentence of art. 93(3) of the Treaty which is applied to trade in agricultural products by art. 4 of Regulation 26/62, and not the last sentence, which prohibits Member States from introducing the notified aid until the Commission has reached a decision, and has been held to be directly effective as establishing procedural criteria which a national court can appraise in a line of cases beginning with Case 6/63, *Costa* v. *ENEL*.[79]

On the other hand, much use is now made by the Commission of the principle laid down in Cases 15 and 16/76, *France* v. *Commission*,[80] that the European Agricultural Guidance and Guarantee Fund[81] may legitimately refuse to finance a Community aid provided under a common

[73] Case 177/78, *Pigs and Bacon Commission v. McCarren* (1979) ECR 2161 (see *infra*, p. 22).
[74] See e.g. Council Regulation 2727/75 on the common organization of the market in cereals art. 22.
[75] [1977] ECR 595.   [76] Decision 81/608.   [77] Decision 83/315.
[78] Decision 85/215.   [79] [1964] ECR 585.   [80] [1979] ECR 321.
[81] See *infra*, pp. 104–6.

organization, where a Member State supplements it with an illicit national aid. In that case, the French authorities added a supplementary national aid to the Community aid for the distillation of wines, and it was held that as it was impossible to determine the quantity of wine which would have been distilled in France if there had been no national aid, the Fund was not liable to reimburse France for any of the payments made.

On the other hand, it remains open to the Council, in the context of a common organization, to authorise a national aid. In Council Regulation 855/84, for example, which is largely concerned with adjustments to the system of monetary compensatory amounts,[82] art. 3(1) deems aids granted to German farmers to compensate for the revaluation of the German 'representative rate'[83] (the result of which would be to reduce guaranteed prices expressed in DM) to be compatible with the common market, and hence, not prohibited by the Treaty rules, in so far as those are incorporated into the relevant common organizations.

Where, however, there is no common organization, there is no general application of the state-aids rules to agricultural products, as was expressly recognized by the European Court in relation to the market in potatoes in Case 114/83, *Société d'initiatives* v. *Commission*.[84] Particular difficulties may, therefore, arise in so far as the free-movement-of-goods rules do apply to agricultural products not subject to a common organization but the state-aids rules do not. This was the background to the famous (or infamous) sheepmeat dispute with France, where France took the view that the United Kingdom system of deficiency payments constituted a state aid, yet the Court held that France could not prevent or restrict the import of sheepmeat which had benefited from the United Kingdom system.[85] A solution suggested by the Court was that nothing prevented the French authorities from adopting their own scheme of aids for the sheepmeat sector until a common organization of the market was established.

A more general solution has, however, been found in the continued use of art. 46 of the EEC Treaty. This provides that where an agricultural product is subject to a national market organization or equivalent rules in one Member State, which affect the competitive position of similar production in another Member State, a countervailing charge fixed by the Commission is to be applied by the other Member States to imports of the relevant product from that Member State, unless that State applies a countervailing charge on export. In effect, this allows for countervailing charges to be imposed where national support measures give rise to low-priced (and presumably subsidized) exports. Whilst the development of common organizations has obviously limited the scope of this provision, it continued to be used after the end of the transitional period in a series of

---

[82] See *infra*, pp. 108–13.   [83] See *infra*, p. 111.   [84] [1984] ECR 2589.
[85] Case 232/78, *Commission* v. *France* [1979] ECR 2729.

Commission Regulations fixing countervailing charges on the import into Germany and the Benelux countries of ethyl alcohol of agricultural origin produced in France—although the Commission made it clear, as in the recitals to Regulation 1407/78[86] in this series, that the real problem was the failure of the Council to legislate on the applicability of the state aids rules to this sector. This continued use of art. 46 was upheld by the European Court in Case 337/82, *St. Nikolaus Brennerei* v. *HZA Krefeld*,[87] where it was also held that art. 46 may be invoked not only where a national organization continues lawfully to exist, but also where the national support-measures may be incompatible with Community law. In that case, the imposition of countervailing charges to prevent distortion of competition could be coupled with enforcement proceedings against the Member State in question under art. 169 of the EEC Treaty.

Whilst at first sight art. 46 might appear to authorise the imposition of charges equivalent to customs duties on imports from other Member States, it should be observed that these charges are not fixed unilaterally by the Member States, but are fixed by the Commission to be applied by the Member States.[88] It was clearly held in the sheepmeat case[89] that France had no power unilaterally to impose such charges on allegedly subsidized mutton and lamb exported from the United Kingdom to France. It may, however, be suggested that the real solution is to extend the state aids rules (which do allow for social and regional considerations) to agricultural products in general.

(iv) Deficiency payments and common organizations

Under art. 40(3) of the EEC Treaty, a common organization of the market may provide for aids for production and marketing, and in some common organizations price support is provided through a system of subsidies, as in the case of oil-seeds under Council Regulation 136/66,[90] or durum wheat under the common organization of the market in cereals.[91] Where such subsidies apply universally throughout the Community, there is no particular problem for intra-Community trade, but difficulties may arise where subsidies and intervention purchase are alternative methods of support, since the market price in Member States operating the system of subsidies will tend to be lower. Hence, Council Regulation 1837/80,[92] on the common organization of the market in sheepmeat, which allows the United Kingdom to opt for a variable slaughter premium, and Council Regulation 1347/86[93] authorising the United Kingdom, by way of derogation

---

[86] OJ 1976 L170/24.   [87] [1984] ECR 1051.

[88] Cf. the discussion of the legitimacy of the system of monetary compensatory amounts, *infra*, 113.   [89] Case 232/78, *Commission* v. *France* [1979] ECR 2729.

[90] JO 1966 p. 3025.   [91] Reg. 2727/75 art. 10 (OJ 1975 L281/1).

[92] OJ 1980 L183/1.   [93] OJ 1986 L119/40.

from the usual method of support, to grant premiums for the slaughter of certain adult bovine animals, both require 'clawback' of the premium, or payment of an export levy, before the goods leave the Member State in which the subsidy was paid. In effect, therefore, the system of art. 46 is used even within the context of common organizations where distortions of competition would otherwise occur.

Nevertheless, practical problems may arise where different methods of support are used within the same common organization with regard both to cost and to overall price levels. Hence, whilst Council Regulation 1347/86 continued to allow the United Kingdom to grant premiums for the slaughter of adult bovine animals, it provided that only 40 per cent of the cost should be met by the European Agricultural Guidance and Guarantee Fund.[94] With regard to the latter problem, this would appear to form the background to Case 61/86, *UK* v. *Commission*,[95] in which the United Kingdom sought the annulment of two Commission Regulations, in so far as they imposed 'clawback' under the sheepmeat regime on sheepmeat products which did not themselves qualify for payment of the premium and on which it had not been paid, the Commission's view being that such products derived indirect benefit from the payment of the premiums.[96] However, in its judgment, the Court held that, in principle, a levy constitutes an obstacle to the free movement of goods, and that it could only be justified in relation to goods which had directly benefited from a premium.

(d) Status of special agricultural rules

Whilst art. 38(2) of the EEC Treaty, providing that the rules for the establishment of the common market shall apply to agricultural products 'save as otherwise provided in arts. 39 to 46', may generally be regarded as referring to derogations from the normal Treaty rules in favour of agricultural products, such as those resulting from art. 42 with regard to the competition rules, it has also been interpreted as meaning that the general rules of the Treaty must give way to any stricter rules laid down in specific agricultural legislation. This first clearly appeared in Case 83/78, *Pigs Marketing Board* v. *Redmond*.[97] In that case, which concerned the marketing system operated by the Northern Ireland Pigs Marketing Board, the United Kingdom argued that the Board was a 'state monopoly' within the meaning of art. 37 of the EEC Treaty, and that by virtue of art. 44 of the 1972 Act of Accession it would not require to be adjusted in

[94] See *infra*, pp. 104–6. [95] [1988] 2 CMLR 98.
[96] See the recitals to Commission Regulation 9/86 (OJ 1986 L2/14).
[97] [1978] ECR 2347.

accordance with that provision until 31 December 1977 (the facts giving rise to the action having occurred on 12 January 1977). The Court, however, pointed out that the production and marketing of pigs was governed by a common organization of the market, by then contained in Council Regulation 2759/75,[98] which applied in the United Kingdom from 1 February 1973 by virtue of art. 60(1) of the Act of Accession, and held quite simply that the provisions of the Treaty relating to the Common Agricultural Policy have precedence, by virtue of art. 38(2), over the other rules relating to the establishment of the common market, in case of any discrepancy, so that the longer period of grace allowed to state monopolies was not relevant. The rules of the common organization were interpreted as requiring every producer to have access to an open market regulated solely by the instruments provided for by that organization, with the result that any national provisions which prevented producers from buying and selling freely within the State in which they were established were incompatible with the principles of the common organization.

This principle of the precedence of agricultural legislation was repeated in Case 177/78, *Pigs and Bacon Commission* v. *McCarren*,[99] which concerned a levy raised by the Irish Pigs and Bacon Commission and used, inter alia, to finance an 'export bonus'. The same point about state monopolies arose, but, also in that case, an issue arose as to the provision in the Regulation establishing the common organization which provided for the application of arts. 92–94 of the Treaty on state aids[100] 'save as otherwise provided in this regulation'. It was held that the application of the general state aid rules (which permit certain aids, and are not substantively directly effective so as to be enforceable by individuals before national courts) was subordinate to the provisions governing the common organization. Although Council Regulation 2759/75[101] on the common organization of the market in pigmeat, and the provisions on the free movement of goods held to be an integral part of it do not appear expressly to prohibit the payment of bonuses, the Court, nonetheless, found that, according to the idea on which the regulation dealing with the common organization of the market in pigmeat is based, the products referred to therein are, in fact, required to move freely within the Community at the price-level resulting from the operation of the machinery for the common organization of the market, and neither Member States nor agencies on which they have conferred powers are entitled to create advantages for the marketing of national products as against those of other Member States by means of financial machinery such as the grant of bonuses. Hence, irrespective of the general state aids rules, national export subsidies may not be paid where there is a common organization of the market.

[98] OJ 1975 L282/1.   [99] [1979] ECR 2161.   [100] See *supra*, pp. 17–20.
[101] OJ 1975 L282/1.

(e) *Legal requirement for common organizations and policies*

It has already been observed that in the absence of a common organization agricultural products, whether or not covered by a national organization of the market, became subject to the general rules of the Common Market with regard to importation, exportation and movement within the Community.[102] Perhaps of greater practical importance, however, is the legal vacuum which may be created in so far as Member States are unable to take unilateral protective measures. Thus, in Case 68/76, *Commission* v. *France*,[103] which involved French restrictions on the export of potatoes, France claimed that in the absence of a common organization Member States could, under arts. 39–46 of the EEC Treaty, still take measures of a short term nature derogating from the basic Treaty rules on free movement. The Court held, however, that after the end of the transitional period, arts. 39–46 could not justify a unilateral derogation from (in this case) art. 34, forbidding measures having equivalent effect to quantitative restrictions on exports, even if no common organization had been introduced. It added that, far from there being a lacuna for Member States to fill, by reason of the transfer of power to a Community—and the reason for that transfer—problems such as, in this case, the potato shortage should from the end of the transitional period be settled by Community measures taken in the interest of all producers and consumers in the Community.

A similar view was expressed in the sheepmeat case,[104] where the Court, whilst recognising the difficulties involved, reaffirmed that after the expiry of the transitional period those matters and sectors 'specifically assigned to the Community' are the responsibility of the Community, so that a decision to adopt any necessary special measures could no longer be made unilaterally by the Member States concerned. It added that the fact that this had not been done did not justify the maintenance by a Member State of a national organization of the market features of which were incompatible with the Treaty requirements relating to the free movement of goods.

This inability of a Member State to act unilaterally except in accordance with the general Treaty rules was emphasized once more in Case 288/83, *Commission* v. *Ireland*,[105] where it was held that the Irish government could not prevent the import of Cyprus potatoes in free circulation in the United Kingdom. The strongest statement of a Member State's inability to act in the absence of a common organization or policy occurred, however,

---

[102] Case 288/83, *Commission* v. *Ireland* [1985]. ECR 1761 See *supra*, pp. 12–14.
[103] [1973] ECR 515.
[104] Case 232/78, *Commission* v. *France* [1979] ECR 2729.   [105] [1985] ECR 1761.

in the context of fisheries. Under art. 102 of the 1972 Act of Accession a common policy on fisheries conservation measures should have been adopted by the end of 1978, but, as is well known, the common policy was not adopted until January 1983.[106] The position after the end of 1978 came before the Court in Case 804/79, *Commission* v. *United Kingdom*,[107] It was there argued by the United Kingdom that, even after the expiry of the period laid down in art. 102 of the Act of Accession, Member States retained residual powers and duties until the Community had fully exercised its powers, but the Court firmly held that 'Member States are . . . no longer entitled to exercise any power of their own in the matter of conservation measures in the waters under their jurisdiction', at least with regard to resources to which the fishermen of the other Member States have an equal right of access (which left the question open with regard to exclusive zones). Furthermore, although the Council had not taken the relevant conservation measures, 'the transfer to the Community of powers in this matter being total and definitive, such a failure to act could not in any case restore to the Member States the power and freedom to act unilaterally in this field'; thus, repeating the view the Court had taken ten years earlier with regard to the supply provisions of the Euratom Treaty,[108] where it was said that the powers conferred could not be withdrawn from the Community except by virtue of an express provision of the Treaty. In the result, it was stated that, in principle, conservation measures must remain as they were at the end of 1978, subject to amendment to take account of biological and technological developments, but that Member States had no power to lay down new conservation policies; with regard to such amendments, or the introduction of necessary interim conservation measures, the Member States may only act as trustees of the common interest so that they became under a duty not only to undertake detailed consultations with the Commission and to seek its approval in good faith, but also not to lay down national conservation measures in spite of objections, reservations, or conditions which might be formulated by the Commission.

This approach may, perhaps, be explained by the fact that the Court has derived an exclusive external competence from the Community's internal competence with regard to fisheries,[109] and the internal and external aspect of fisheries policy are so interlinked that the exclusivity of the one must be reflected in the other. Be that as it may, the effective result is that where there is a legal requirement for a common organization or policy, there is also a practical need for such an organization or policy at least where protective or interventionist measures are regarded as desirable.

---

[106] See *infra*, p. 91.   [107] [1981] ECR 1045.
[108] Case 7/71, *Commission* v. *France* [1971] ECR 1003.
[109] Cases 3, 4, and 6/76, Kramer [1976] ECR 1279.

(ƒ) *Protection of health*

Measures taken to protect the health of humans, animals, and plants are self-evidently likely to be encountered in trade in agricultural products, and as a matter of law they represent an area where the general Treaty rules may be particularly relevant to trade in agricultural products, notably art. 36, permitting restrictions on the movement of goods justified on grounds of the protection of health. Some measure of the importance attached to the matter may be gleaned from art. 104 and 105 of the 1972 Act of Accession and art. 112 of the Greek Act of Accession. Art. 104 of the 1972 Act of Accession granted the United Kingdom, Ireland and Denmark derogations from Council Directive 64/432/EEC,[110] on veterinary-health-inspection questions in intra-Community trade in bovine animals and swine, enabling them to maintain certain national-safeguard measures. After the end of the Accession transitional period, an amendment was made to Directive 64/432 to enable Member States free of foot-and-mouth disease, and not practising routine vaccination, to impose certain conditions on the entry of animals upon their territory until a date which was extended until 1984, when Council Directive 84/643[111] was adopted, allowing such Member States to require certain listed guarantees. Art. 105 of that Act of Accession authorized Ireland and the United Kingdom, in respect of Northern Ireland, to retain their national rules relating to protection against foot-and-mouth disease with regard to the import of fresh meat, by way of derogation from Council Directive 64/433/EEC[112] on health-protection questions in intra-Community trade in fresh meat. After the expiry of the Accession transitional period, the derogation was also continued until 1984, when Council Directive 84/643 allowed until 30 September 1985 for the United Kingdom, in respect of Northern Ireland, and Ireland to substitute the general rules of the Directive for the previous special arrangements. Community measures specifically relating to the control of foot-and-mouth disease were in fact introduced by Council Directive 85/511,[113] which set out the minimum-control measures required of Member States as from 1 January 1987. At the same time a trio of Directives[114] was adopted amending earlier Directives on trade in live cattle and pigs, trade in meat products, and animals from which meat is obtained for intra-Community trade, with regard to rules concerning outbreaks of swine fever. By way of contrast, art. 112 of the Greek Act of Accession prohibited Greece from sending to other Member States any bovine animal or swine, or fresh meat from bovine animals, swine, goats,

---

[110] JO 1964 p. 1977.   [111] OJ 1984 L339/27.
[112] JO 1964 p. 2012.   [113] OJ 1985 L315/11.
[114] Directives 85/320, 85/321, and 85/322 (OJ 1985 L168/36, 39, and 41).

sheep or lambs from certain regions to be designated under a procedure therein laid down, until a period of twelve months had elapsed since the appearance of the last source of exotic virus foot-and-mouth disease or since the last vaccination against this disease.

In so far as Community health measures have been taken, they are not necessarily coterminous with the development of common organizations, generally taking the form of separate Council Directives issued under the dual authority of art. 43 of the EEC Treaty, relating to the Common Agricultural Policy, and art. 100, which is the general provision relating to the approximation of laws. However, some legislation, such as Council Directive 85/649,[115] prohibiting the use in livestock farming of certain substances having a hormonal action, has been adopted under art. 43 alone. This is a matter of more than technical importance, since under art. 43 the Council may act by qualified majority,[116] whereas under art. 100 it is required to act by unanimity, and it was for that reason that the United Kingdom sought the annulment of this Directive in Case 68/86, *United Kingdom* v. *Council*,[117] claiming that it should have been adopted under art. 100. The importance of the use of the correct authorising provisions has become even greater following the introduction of art. 100a into the EEC Treaty, by art. 18 of the Single European Act, allowing the Council to adopt measures for the approximation of laws by a qualified majority for the purpose of establishing the internal market by 31 December 1992. It is at first sight ironic that some of the Community health legislation which has been enacted relates to products not yet subject to common organizations, such as Council Directives 69/464 and 69/465,[118] respectively concerned with the control of potato wart disease and the control of potato cyst eelworm. However, the truth of the matter would appear to be that the real aim of much of this legislation is the protection of health rather than the development of common organizations as such.

It has generally been accepted by the Court that such Community measures are not a hindrance to intra-Community trade but are intended to achieve the gradual abolition of measures adopted unilaterally by the Member States which might be regarded as justified under the general Treaty rules despite their restrictive effect on trade between Member States.[119] It has been held that the Community measures themselves must have due regard to freedom of trade within the Community,[120] but the Court has accepted that it was justifiable for Council Directive 77/93, on protective measures against the introduction into the Member States of

---

[115] OJ 1985 L382/228.   [116] See *infra*, pp. 144–45.
[117] 23 Feb. 1988. It was held that such legislation falls within the objects of the CAP.
[118] JO 1969 L323/1 and 3.
[119] Case 37/83, *Rewe-Zentrale* v. *Landwirtschaftskammer Rheinland* [1984] ECR 1229.
[120] Ibid. at pp. 1248–9.

harmful organisms of plants or plant products, which, in principle, requires inspection to be carried out by the exporting Member State and allows only sampling in the importing Member State, to define sampling as inspections carried out on up to one third of the consignments introduced from a given Member State.[121]

Where the holding of inspections is governed by Community law, it would appear that Member States cannot claim that parallel inspections under national law may be justifiable under the general rules of the Treaty.[122] The consistent line of case law to this effect would appear, however, to be challenged in the new art. 100a of the EEC Treaty, introduced by art. 18 of the Single European Act. Under art. 100a harmonization of national legislation for the purposes of achieving the internal market by 31 December 1992 may be achieved by 'measures' (rather than simply Directives) adopted by a qualified majority, but where such measures are adopted by a qualified majority, art. 100a(4) provides that a Member State which 'deems it necessary to apply national provisions on grounds of major needs referred to in art. 36 [of the EEC Treaty— which include the protection of health] . . . shall notify the Commission of these provisions', and the Commission may confirm such provisions after having verified that they are not a means of arbitrary discrimination or a disguised restriction on trade between Member States, subject to being able to invoke an accelerated enforcement procedure against the Member State. Whilst it is clear that, within its limits, this provision does override the Court's case law, and empowers Member States to legislate on a matter covered by Community legislation, it gives rise to numerous questions: Does it apply whenever art. 100a is used or only if a qualified majority vote is taken? If, as appears likely, it only applies to the latter case, can it be invoked by any Member State or only by a Member State which voted against the Community legislation? The further problem then arises as to whether the Commission's confirmation is to be obtained before or after the entry into force of the national measures. Whatever the answers to these questions, art. 100a(4) may be seen as the price to be paid for the acceptance of a system of decision-making which may lead to the enactment of Community legislation in areas still subject to national measures. In any event, in Case 73/84, *Denkavit Futtermittel*,[123] it was held that where Directives regulated the composition and preparation of animal foodstuffs, but did not regulate health inspections of these products, Member States could still justify national health inspections under the general Treaty rules. Under these rules, total or partial restrictions on the import or export of goods and inspections carried out by reason of import or export are, in principle, prohibited as measures equivalent to quantitative

---

[121] Ibid. at p. 1249.
[122] Case 28/84, *Commission* v. *Germany* [1985] ECR.   [123] [1985] ECR 1019.

restrictions on imports and exports under arts. 30 and 34 of the EEC Treaty,[124] but they may be justified under article 36 if they are intended to protect the health and life of humans, animals, or plants, provided they do not constitute a means of arbitrary discrimination or a disguised restriction on trade between Member States.

Before turning to a detailed consideration of art. 36, however, attention should be drawn to its relationship to the 'mandatory requirements' recognized by the Court in its judgment in Case 120/78, *Rewe* v. *Bundes-monopolverwaltung für Branntwein*.[125] The Court there stated that, while a national trading rule applying equally to domestic and imported products (in this case, relating to the alcoholic strength of 'cassis de Dijon') could well have the effect of preventing the sale within a Member State of goods legitimately marketed in another Member State, 'obstacles to movement within the Community resulting from disparities between the national laws relating to the marketing of the products in question must be accepted in so far as those provisions may be recognised as being necessary in order to satisfy mandatory requirements relating in particular to the effectiveness of fiscal supervision, the protection of public health, the fairness of commercial transactions and the defence of the consumer'. However, a national trading rule constituting such an obstacle which is not necessary to satisfy a mandatory requirement may be categorized as a measure equivalent to a quantitative restriction on imports prohibited by art. 30 of the EEC Treaty. Hence, there is a potential overlap between this case-law and art. 36: under the *Cassis de Dijon* doctrine, a measure applying equally to domestic and imported products which is necessary for the protection of health will not constitute a measure equivalent to a quantitative restriction; on the other hand, the justification under art. 36 is only triggered if the measure is prima facie equivalent to a quantitative restriction; yet, for a measure relating to imports to be justified under art. 36 it has long been held that effective measures for the same purpose must be taken with regard to domestic production.[126]

However, although protection of health was considered in the *Cassis de Dijon* case itself, it would appear to be the current practice of the Court to consider whether measures are justified on health grounds in the light of art. 36 even if those measures are equally applicable to domestic products as well as to imports. Hence, in Case 97/83, *Melkunie*,[127] which was

[124] See e.g. Case 4/75, *Rewe-Zentralfinanz* v. *Landwirtschaftkammer Bonn* [1975] ECR 843.
[125] [1979] ECR 649. This case has given rise to a plethora of comments; see Dashwood, 'The Cassis de Dijon Line of Authority' in *In Memoriam J. D. B. Mitchell* (Sweet and Maxwell, London, 1983) p. 145 at p. 159 for a convenient list.
[126] Case 4/75, *Rewe-Zentralfinanz* v. *Landwirtschaftskammer Bonn* [1975] ECR 843; in the analogous area of public policy see Case 121/85, *Conegate* v. *HM Customs and Excise* (11 Mar. 1986).   [127] [1984] ECR 2367.

concerned with Dutch legislation relating to the presence of active coliform bacteria and active micro-organizms in milk products, the Fifth Chamber held that this 'equally applicable' legislation was prima facie a measure having equivalent effect to a quantitative restriction, in so far as it prohibited the marketing of goods lawfully produced and marketed in the exporting Member State, but that it was justified under art. 36. In the context of differing national views of what is needed to protect health, it would, in fact, appear to be the Court's practice to accept the more restrictive approach where there is shown to be scientific disagreement as to the safe levels of bacteria, additives,[128] or pesticides.[129] On this last aspect, the Council enacted in 1986 Directives 86/362 and 86/363[130] on the maximum levels of pesticide residue in cereals and foodstuffs of animal origin. To fall within the protection of art. 36, a national measure must constitute a 'seriously considered health policy', which was held not to be the case with regard to the British policy adopted in 1981 imposing a prohibition on imports into Great Britain of poultrymeat and eggs from all other Member States except Denmark and Ireland in Case 40/82, *Commission* v. *United Kingdom*.[131] The expressed aim of this prohibition was to enable Newcastle disease (of which the last outbreak in Great Britain had been in 1978, and the last outbreak in France in 1976) to be combatted by a slaughter policy, and the import restrictions were intended to ensure that imports could only be accepted from Member States (i.e. Denmark and Ireland) which were totally free from Newcastle disease, which prohibited the use of vaccine, and which imposed compulsory slaughter requirements in the event of an outbreak of the disease. The Court doubted that this was a seriously considered health policy, because it was introduced in a matter of days (whereas the previous change to a policy of vaccination in 1964 had been preceded by elaborate reports and studies), it followed domestic pressure to restrict the growing imports of French poultry products, it was timed to exclude French turkeys from the 1981 Christmas market, and because the prohibition on French imports was not lifted when the French changed their policy so as to accord with the three conditions stated by the British authorities. Furthermore, to avoid being categorized as arbitrary discrimination, measures with regard to imports must be matched by effective measures taken with regard to domestic products.[132]

Assuming it does fall within a seriously considered health policy, in order to be justified under art. 36 a measure must be reasonable, or

---

[128] Case 53/80, *Kaasfabriek Eyssen* [1981] ECR 409.
[129] Case 54/85, *Mirepoix* [1986] ECR 1067.   [130] OJ 1986 L221/37 and 43.
[131] [1982] ECR 2793. This judgment led to the action for damages in *Bourguoin* v. *MAFF* [1985] 3 All ER 585. See *infra*, p. 166.
[132] See *supra*. n. 126.

proportionate to the objective it pursues. Hence, in the poultrymeat case it was held that a total prohibition on imports could only be justified if the United Kingdom could show that it was the only possibility open to it, and the Court took the view that less stringent measures could have been used. A total ban may, however, be permissible in the case of prohibited additives, as in the Dutch rules prohibiting the addition of nisin to processed cheese for sale on the Dutch market, which were at issue in Case 53/80, *Kaasfabriek Eyssen*.[133] The proportionality rule was particularly considered in Case 124/81, *Commission* v. *United Kingdom*,[134] where it was held that the functions served by the United Kingdom requirement that an import licence be obtained to import UHT milk could equally well be met by declarations by importers, and that the functions served by the United Kingdom requirement that imported UHT milk be re-treated (which was effectively a prohibition on imports) could equally well be met by a requirement that importers produce certificates issued by the competent authorities of the exporting Member States, coupled with controls by means of samples. This particular matter has subsequently been regulated by Council Directive 85/397[135] on health and animal-health problems affecting intra-Community trade in heat-treated milk.

In general, the Court has taken the view, however, that for a Member State both to require a certificate from the exporting Member State and to carry out itself systematic inspection of the imported goods goes beyond what may be justified under art. 36.[136] It may also be noted that in Case 132/80, *United Foods* v. *Belgium*,[137] it was held that, although a Member State could still carry out health inspections of fish, it was a disguised restriction on trade to require twenty-four hours' notice to be given before imported fish could be inspected, given that fresh fish was a highly perishable commodity.

Where a health inspection is justified under art. 36, the further problem arises as to whether the Member State may charge for carrying it out. In trade between Member States, the European Court has consistently held that unless the charge falls within the general scope of internal taxation, or constitutes payment for a service to the particular importer or exporter (rather than a service in the general interest),[138] it will be prohibited as a charge equivalent to a customs duty under arts.13 and 16 of the EEC Treaty. This was confirmed in Case 158/82, *Commission* v. *Denmark*,[139] in relation to Danish inspections of groundnuts and groundnut products which were agreed to be justified under art. 36. On the other hand, charges

---

[133] [1981] ECR 409.   [134] [1983] ECR 203.   [135] OJ 1985 L226/13.
[136] Case 251/78, *Denkavit Futtermittel* [1979] ECR 3369.   [137] [1981] ECR 995.
[138] This was held with regard to quality controls in Case 63/74, *Cadsky* v. *INCE* [1975] ECR 781.
[139] [1983] ECR 3573.

may be levied where inspections are carried out by national authorities pursuant to requirements of Community law. The Court was faced with this problem in Case 46/76, *Bauhuis* v. *The Netherlands*.[140] This was a reference for a preliminary ruling from a Dutch court in proceedings brought by a cattle dealer to recover fees paid for the veterinary public-health inspections of certain animals carried out by the Netherlands authorities before the export of those animals. Basically, the question at issue was whether these fees constituted charges having equivalent effect to customs duties on exports. It would appear that certain of the fees were paid on the inspection of bovine animals and swine required by Council Directive 64/432,[141] on animal health-problems affecting intra-Community trade in bovine animals and swine. On the other hand, some of the fees related to inspections other than those laid down by the said Directive or on animals other than those referred to in the Directive, and carried out solely under national law. The Court dealt with these two situations separately.

With regard to the inspections carried out under the Directive, the Court pointed out that the Directive harmonized the animal-health measures in force in the Member States by making it obligatory for them to standardise domestic provisions in this field, in accordance with the requirements of the Directive. The harmonization or approximation required by the Directive would appear mainly to consist in imposing upon Member States exporting cattle the obligation to ensure compliance with certain veterinary and public health measures intended, amongst other things, to guarantee that the exported animals are not a source of contagious disease. Of course, to comply with the Directive, a Member State usually must introduce legislation of its own, but the Court pointed out that the measures in question are not prescribed by each Member State in order to protect some interest of its own, but by the Council in the general interest of the Community; and so, the Court deduced they cannot, therefore, be regarded as unilateral measures which hinder trade, but rather as operations intended to promote the free movement of goods; in particular, by rendering ineffective the obstacles to this free movement which might be created by national measures for veterinary and public-health inspections adopted pursuant to art. 36. The Court concluded that fees charged for inspections required by Community Law which are uniform and are required to be carried out before dispatch within the exporting country do not constitute charges having an effect equivalent to customs duties on exports, provided they do not exceed the actual cost of the inspection for which they were charged. Indeed, the Court went so far as to say that the reasons for the prohibition of any obstacle to intra-Community trade,

---

[140] [1977] ECR 5. [141] JO 1964 p. 1977.

whether such an obstacle takes the form of charges having an effect equivalent to customs duties or of measures having effect equivalent to quantitative restrictions, do not apply to this case. Similarly, in Case 89/76, *Commission* v. *Netherlands*[142] the Court applied the same criteria to hold that fees (not exceeding the actual cost) could be charged for phytosanitary inspections carried out under the 1951 International Plant Protection Convention, to which all the Member States were party, since these inspections were not unilateral measures but were intended to assist the free movement of goods.

On the other hand, with regard to the charges for the inspections carried out under Dutch law alone, the Court said that the reasons which render lawful the collection of appropriate duties for the carrying out of uniform Community inspections of general application cannot be applied to situations which continue to consist of obstacles set up unilaterally, even if the domestic inspections are measures for the promotion of exports. The Court, therefore, concluded that fees charged by the exporting State for inspections carried out by the authorities of that State which are not required by Community Regulation or Directive, but which have been prescribed for the purpose of checking whether the conditions to which the Member State of destination has made the importation subject have been complied with, constitute charges having an effect equivalent to customs duties.

Different considerations apply, however, where inspections are carried out at the external frontier of the Community on products imported directly from non-Member States. Regulations establishing common organizations of the market generally prohibit charges having an equivalent effect to customs duties in trade with third countries, such as art. 20(2) of Council Regulation 805/68[143] on the common organization of the market in beef and veal which was at issue in Case 84/71, *Marimex* v. *Italian Finance Administration*,[144] and which contains a proviso 'save as otherwise provided in this Regulation or where derogation therefrom is decided by the Council'. However, in Case70/77, *Simmenthal* v. *Italian Finance Administration*,[145] following the Opinion of A.-G. Warner, the Court held that the prohibition had a different aim and a different basis in internal and external Community trade. In internal trade it is intended to secure the free movement of goods, but in external trade the prohibition must be considered in the light of the requirements of the Common Commercial Policy and the Common Customs Tariff; notably, that imports from the third countries should be subject to uniform treatment. In particular, the Court held that the principle laid down in *Bauhuis* does not apply to trade with third countries. Although the Court did not say so in as many words,

---

[142] [1977] ECR 1355.   [143] JO 1968 L148/24.   [144] [1972] ECR 89.
[145] [1978] ECR 1453.

there is, of course, no Community policy in favour of the free movement of goods into the Community from third countries; indeed, the prohibition here is not so much on charges having equivalent effect to customs duties, as such, but on their imposition by Member States individually in such a manner as to upset the uniform external protection of the Community. The Court, in fact, held that the Council and Commission may create exceptions or derogations from the prohibition on such charges, provided that the ensuing charges have a uniform effect in all Member States in trade with third countries.

The question whether the *Bauhuis* principle applied arose because of the enactment of Council Directive 72/462[146] on health- and veterinary-inspection problems upon importation of bovine animals and swine and fresh meat from third countries. This required Member States to carry out certain health inspections on animals and meat, and to charge for such inspections. The charging provisions were drafted in a similar way and, if art. 23(4) might be taken as an example, provide that 'all expenditure incurred pursuant to this Article shall be chargeable to the consignor, the consignee or their agents, without repayment by the State'. The question of its effect did not finally prove relevant since the Court held that the charges it required to be imposed must be related to inspections carried out under the terms of the Directive. It was, however, found that the Community measures required to implement the Directive had not, in fact, been taken, with the result that it was not possible to carry out the inspections under the Directive, and the Directive could not justify the levying of any charges. This defect appears subsequently to have been rectified by the enactment of Council Directive 85/73,[147] in January 1985, on the financing of health inspection and controls of fresh meat and poultrymeat. This had the declared purpose of setting out common rules and criteria. It provided for the Council to take a decision on a standard level of fees by 1 January 1986, a target which would appear not to have been met, but would still allow Member States to exceed that level if the total fee collected by a Member State was lower than or equal to the real figure for inspection costs. This would hardly seem, therefore, to be much of an advance on the situation reached in the case-law. In the interim, legislation such as art. 9 of Council Directive 64/433[148] and art. 11 of Council Directive 72/461[149] on health problems affecting intra-Community trade in fresh meat, provided that in the absence of Community provisions relating to imports from third countries national provisions relating to such imports should not be more favourable than those governing intra-Community trade. In the event, the Court had to accept in *Simmenthal* that in such a case a Member State must hold and charge for inspections

---

[146] JO 1972 L302/28.   [147] OJ 1985 L32/14.   [148] JO 1964 p. 2012.
[149] JO 1972 L302/24.

where such inspections would be held and could be charged for in internal Community trade, and in Case 30/79, *Land Berlin* v. *Wigei*,[150] it even accepted that such charges could exceed those levied on inspections of Community products, provided they were not manifestly disproportionate. Although this may avoid reverse discrimination against Community products, it hardly aids the preservation of the uniformity of the Community's external stance, though the Court asserted in Case 1/83, *Intercontinentale Fleisch-handelgesellschaft*,[151] that there was no risk of diversion of trade if the charge for a health inspection did not exceed the cost of carrying it out. In that case it was further held that, at least where the amount of the charge corresponds to the cost of the controls, the legality of the levying of the charge for health controls on fresh meat cannot be subject to proof of the existence of comparable charges in all the other Member States of the Community—an open acceptance of different treatment in different Member States.

[150] [1980] ECR 15.   [151] [1984] ECR 349.

3

Characteristics of the Common Agricultural Policy

(a) Aims and beneficiaries

The first paragraph of article 39 of the EEC Treaty sets out five express objectives of the Common Agricultural Policy, and the second paragraph sets out three further matters of which account should be taken. The five express objectives are stated to be: firstly, to increase agricultural productivity by promoting technical progress and by ensuring the rational development of agricultural production and the optimum utilization of the factors of production, in particular, labour; secondly, to ensure a fair standard of living for the agricultural community, in particular by increasing the individual earnings of persons engaged in agriculture; thirdly, to stabilise markets; fourthly, to assure the availability of supplies; and, lastly, to ensure that supplies reach consumers at reasonable prices. As will be self-evident, in economic and political reality these objectives are not easy to reconcile, and, in fact, the Court recognized in *Balkan* v. *Hauptzollamt Berlin- Packhof*,[1] that the Community Institutions may allow any one of these objectives 'temporary priority in order to satisfy the demands of the economic factors or conditions in view of which their decisions are made'.

In practice most common organizations are based on a common price system, and, in general, the European Court has treated them as being intended to give certain guarantees of income to agricultural producers, thus fulfilling the second objective of art. 39(1), rather than for the benefit of those further down the distributive chain. An illustration of this is Case 2/75, *Einfuhr- und Vorratsstelle Getreide* v. *Mackprang*.[2] This was a reference for a preliminary ruling as to the validity of a Commission Decision of 8 May, 1969,[3] authorizing Germany to limit its intervention purchases of certain cereals to those harvested in Germany. The background to this was that the French franc had suffered a fall in its forward rate in the spring of 1969, and it became profitable to buy cereals in France and resell them in Germany to the intervention agency there, since the intervention prices expressed in French francs and German marks remained unaltered, despite their real value having changed; a problem, incidentally, which the current financial mechanisms are intended to

[1] [1973] ECR 1091.   [2] [1975] ECR 607.
[3] Decision 69/138 (JO 1969 L112/1).

prevent. The case arose from the refusal of the German intervention agency to accept from a cereal merchant certain French cereals which were in transit to Germany on 8 May. The Court held that the intervention system was set up with a view to guaranteeing to producers a market for their cereals at reasonable prices where there are no markets available providing normal profit margins. The Court accepted, however, that it was necessary to avoid any inducement to transport the goods with the sole purpose of obtaining more favourable intervention conditions, and, in fact, held that the decision was valid, pointing out that, in any event, it could not harm producers of cereals, because an offer to to sell intervention at the marketing centres of the Member State where the cereals were at the time remained perfectly possible.

In Cases 67–85/75, *Lesieur Cotelle and others* v. *Commission*,[4] the Court even held that the subsidy granted for oil-seeds harvested and processed within the Community, under Council Regulation 136/66,[5] is intended as a guarantee for growers of the seeds. The plaintiffs in that case were, in fact, oil millers and not seed growers. The Court said that in so far as Regulation 136/66 was intended to give guarantees, the latter related to colza-seed farmers and not processors, as appeared from art. 24 of the Regulation, according to which the derived intervention price[6] guaranteed that producers would be able to sell their produce at a price which, allowing for market fluctuations, was as close as possible to the target price.[7] The subsidies granted to seed processors were not intended to guarantee the latter a fixed payment for their processing, but to enable them to buy Community seed at prices close to the target price. The Court concluded that the oil millers could not claim any guarantee under Regulation 136/66.

However, it is only Community agricultural producers who are intended to benefit, so that the Protocol on German Internal Trade does not enable agricultural products of the German Democratic Republic to benefit from refunds payable under the Common Agricultural Policy, as was held in Case 14/74, *Norddeutsches Vieh- und Fleischkontor* v. *HZA Hamburg-Jonas*.[8]

If the five objectives might be considered individually,[9] the first is the aim of increasing productivity. Undoubtedly output has grown to an extent where persistent surpluses have been created, though there may be room for argument as to how far this is attributable to scientific progress and how far it is attributable to the common policy. From the legal point of view, the type of legislation giving effect to this objective was exemplified in

---

[4] [1976] ECR 391.

[5] JO 1966 p. 3025.

[6] See *infra*, p. 54.

[7] Ibid.

[8] [1974] ECR 899.

[9] A critical view of the degree to which they have been achieved may be found in ch. 7 of Hill, *The Common Agricultural Policy: Past, Present, and Future* (Methuen, London, 1984).

Council Directives 72/159–72/161,[10] respectively concerned with the modernization of farms, the encouragement of the cessation of farming and the reallocation of agricultural areas, and the provision of socio-economic guidance for persons engaged in agriculture; they were replaced in 1985 by Council Regulation 797/85,[11] on improving the efficiency of agricultural structures. It must be said, however, that, faced with the wine surplus, the Court upheld in Case 44/79, *Hauer* v. *Land Rheinland-Pfalz*,[12] the validity of legislation prohibiting the planting of new vines, holding such a restriction justified in the general Community interest.

The aim of achieving a fair standard of living for the agricultural community explains why the prices under common organizations of the market have historically been set at a level above world prices. However, the same price guarantees have usually been available both to small peasant farmers and to agricultural producers operating on an industrial scale, and differences in efficiency appear to have led to an increased divergence in agricultural incomes. Fundamental legal problems have, therefore, arisen as to whether prices may be reduced, and whether small scale producers could be offered income support rather than price support if it is regarded as desirable to retain them in farming.

With regard to the first problem, the Treaty obligation is to 'increase' individual earnings, and until 1985 no express reduction in common prices[13] was made, although some common prices were increased by less than the rate of inflation. It should, however, be observed that the rate at which common prices are converted into national currencies[14] may be of greater practical importance. A preferred method has been to maintain common prices but to impose a levy which will, effectively, reduce the guaranteed prices, for certain producers, or on the occurence of certain events. The milk co-responsibility levy introduced by Council Regulation 1079/77,[15] which has the effect of reducing prices for most milk producers, was upheld by the court in Case 138/78, *Stölting* v. *HZA Hamburg-Jonas*,[16] as a measure to stabilize markets, and Council Regulations 856 and 857/84[17] introduced an 'additional levy' on quantities of milk delivered beyond a 'guarantee threshold' (i.e. a limit beyond which the guaranteed price system will not operate). This levy is set at a level which may exceed the guaranteed support price, and, thus, constitute a penalty.[18] Furthermore, the version of the common organization of the market in sugar introduced by Council Regulation 1785/81[19] imposes a levy even on production within the basic quotas therein set out, to meet the cost of disposing of such of that production as is surplus to current requirements, and Council

---

[10] JO 1972 L96/1, 9 and 15.
[13] See *infra*, pp. 106–8.
[16] [1979] ECR 713.
[18] See *infra*, pp. 79–80.

[11] OJ 1985 L93/1.
[14] See *infra*, p. 111.
[17] OJ 1984 L90/10 and 13.
[19] OJ 1981 L177/4.

[12] [1979] ECR 3727.
[15] OJ 1977 L131/6.

Regulation 934/86[20] added an 'elimination levy' designed to eliminate the deficit which had accumulated by the end of 1986. The burden of this is to be borne over the five marketing years from 1986/7 to 1990/1 under a system differentiated according to production regions to take account of the extent to which producers had benefited, directly or indirectly, from the guarantees under the common organization of the markets. To this a 'special elimination levy' was added by Council Regulation 1914/87[21] designed to eliminate the loss actually recorded in the 1986/7 marketing year, a levy repeated for 1987/88 by Council Regulation 1108/88.[21a]

With regard to the second problem, the milk co-responsibility levy was softened by the introduction of a system of support for the incomes of small-scale milk producers under Council Regulation 1210/83,[22] which was continued to 1986 by Regulation 1206/84.[23] In 1986 the same model was followed for the cereals market. The principle of a co-responsibility levy was introduced by Council Regulation 1579/86[24] subject to the provision of direct aid for small producers, and by Council Regulation 1983/86[25] the principle was laid down that this aid should be paid to small producers who had borne the co-responsibility levy, the maximum level of the aid being equivalent to the levy on 25 tonnes of cereals. Of more general importance has been the structural legislation currently enacted in Council Regulation 797/85,[26] on improving the efficiency of agricultural structures, which provides for the payment of aid where the labour income per man-work unit in agriculture is less than a level not exceeding the average gross wage of non-agricultural workers in the relevant region, which develops a concept introduced originally in Directive 72/159,[27] on the modernization of farms.

The aim of stabilizing markets must in reality be read with the aim of assuring the availability of supplies. The underlying assumption of the Common Agricultural Policy appears to be that supplies can only be made continuously available if there is over-production, since crops and animals cannot be persuaded to grow exactly to numbers or quantities required by the planner's predictions. Hence, there has to be some system to ensure that agricultural producers do not lose out as a result of what might be termed 'desirable' over-production and then reduce their production the following years, creating shortages. With regard to products of which the Community can produce the bulk of its requirements, the common organizations have sought to avoid the cycle of glut and shortage through a system of guaranteed prices and guaranteed disposal for goods which cannot be sold on the open market. However, in so far as this guaranteed price system prevents over-production from reducing market prices, an

[20] OJ 1986 L87/1.   [21] OJ 1987 L183/5.   [21a] OJ 1988 L110/25.
[22] OJ 1983 L132/8.   [23] OJ 1984 L115/73.   [24] OJ 1986 L139/29.
[25] OJ 1986 L171/1.   [26] OJ 1985 L93/1.   [27] JO 1972 L96/1.

undesirable over-production has developed, resulting in remedies such as the milk co-responsibility levy. The common organization of the market in sugar, introduced by Council Regulation 1009/67,[28] and re-enacted in Regulation 3330/74[29] and Regulations 1785/81,[30] has on the other hand always imposed production quotas. The legal bases for such quotas are considered by the European Court in Case 250/84, *Eridania*,[31] where it was held justifiable to base the quotas on historic production (the method also used, by way of comparison, for steel-production quotas under the ECSC Treaty) rather than current consumption, so that it was lawful to allocate to Italian producers a quota which was lower than Italian consumption; therefore, necessarily, opening the way to imports from other Member States. Even in the cereals market, Council Regulation 1451/82[32] introduced the principle of a 'guarantee threshold' under which over-production may lead to a reduction in the intervention price, and in the milk market Council Regulation 856/84[33] introduced the principle that deliveries beyond the guarantee threshold would lead to the imposition of an additional levy. However, the guarantee threshold for cereals was short-lived, being replaced in 1986 by the general co-responsibility levy under Council Regulation 1579/86;[34] hence, a reversion to the system introduced in 1977 in the milk sector. Problems of over-production appear also to have occurred in markets where support to some extent takes the form of subsidies rather than price support, such as oil seeds under the common organization of the market in oils and fats. Here, Council Regulations 1413/82[35] and 1101/84[36] authorized the establishment of a guarantee threshold for colza-, rape-, and sunflower-seed, and the system was amended by Council Regulation 1454/86[37] so as to enable levels of aid and intervention prices for those products to be reduced in advance of actual over-production if the level of production as *estimated* before the beginning of the marketing year would exceed the maximum guaranteed quantities.

Little Community agricultural legislation appears to have been aimed specifically at ensuring reasonable prices for consumers, apart from legislation designed to remove surpluses, such as 'Christmas-Butter' allowances. More generally, consumers may benefit from the application of export levies when world prices are higher than Community prices.[38]

The three factors of which account should be taken under the second paragraph of art. 39 are the particular nature of agricultural activity resulting from the social structure of agriculture and from structural and natural disparities between the various agricultural regions, the need to effect appropriate adjustment by degrees, and the fact that agriculture

[28] JO 1967 no. 308 p. 1.
[31] [1986] ECR 117.
[34] OJ 1986 L139/29.
[37] OJ 1986 L133/8.

[29] OJ 1974 L359/1.
[32] OJ 1982 L164/1.
[35] OJ 1982 L162/6.
[38] See *infra*, p. 56.

[30] OJ 1981 L177/4.
[33] OJ 1984 L90/10.
[36] OJ 1984 L113/7.

onstitutes a sector closely linked with the economy as a whole. With regard to the first of these factors, many common organizations have, by their very nature, a regional impact, although it was only after the accession of the United Kingdom, Ireland and Denmark that Council Directive 75/268[39] on mountain and hill-farming, and farming in less-favoured areas, was enacted. The support provisions of the Directive have subsequently been incorporated into the general structural legislation currently enacted in Council Regulation 797/85[40] on improving the efficiency of agricultural structures. However, both regional interests and links with the economy as a whole can be seen in the Council Regulations on integrated development programmes, including Regulation 1939/81[41] in relation to the Western Isles, and in Council Decisions 84/70–84/82[42] on pilot action in preparation for integrated mediterranean programmes. These last have been replaced by Council Regulation 2088/85[43] on integrated mediterranean programmes. The relationship between the guidance section of the Agricultural Guidance and Guarantee Fund and the Regional Development Fund and the Social Fund is one of the basic concerns of the section of the Single European Act concerned with economic and social cohesion, which requires measures to be taken to increase their efficiency and co-ordinate their activities.[44]

With regard to the extent to which agricultural legislation, as such, should reflect regional considerations, the judgment of the European Court in Case 250/84, *Eridania*,[45] is of considerable importance. In upholding the validity of sugar quotas allocated to Italy on the basis of historic production rather than consumption, the Court stated expressly that regional specialization was a permissible *objective* of a common organization of the market. Hence, there would appear to be little difference in status between these 'factors to be taken into account' and the objectives of the Common Agricultural Policy strictly so called.

(b) *General principles derived from the Treaty*

The published view of the Commission is that the Common Agricultural Policy is based on the single market, Community preference, and financial solidarity.[46] The concept of the agricultural single market will be considered in the context of the structures of common organizations,[47] and

---

[39] OJ 1975 L128/1. See *infra*, pp. 137–8.   [40] OJ 1985 L93/1.
[41] OJ 1981 L197/6.   [42] OJ 1984 L44/1–61.   [43] OJ 1985 L197/1.
[44] Under the new art. 130d introduced by the Single European Act. See *infra*, p. 143.
[45] [1986] ECR 117.
[46] Commission of the EC: *The Agricultural Policy of the European Community* (3rd edn. 1982) pp. 14–15.
[47] See *infra*, pp. 53 ff.

the principle of financial solidarity will be considered in the context of the financial mechanisms of common organizations.[48] Community preference, whatever its political attractions, only appears expressly in the Treaty in art. 44(2), a provision which allowed Member States to introduce a non-discriminatory system of minimum prices during the transitional period. Article 44(2) refers to 'the development of a natural preference between Member States', and in Case 5/67, *Beus* v. *HZA München*,[49] the Court held it to be one of the underlying principles of the Treaty, effectively generalizing this very specific illustration of the principle; it will be seen that the price structure of most common organizations inexorably leads to Community preference. A particular illustration of the principle may, however, be found in Case 55/75, *Balkan* v. *HZA Berlin-Packhof*,[50] where an importer complained that monetary compensatory amounts, designed to compensate the difference between real rates of exchange and agricultural rates of exchange where there is a risk of disturbances in trade in agricultural products, were imposed on imports of Bulgarian cheese into Germany but not on imports of similar Italian cheese. It was held that with regard to the cheese coming from Italy the general principle of Community preference justified a different assessment of the possibilities of disturbance, according to whether the products involved came from another Member State or from a third State. With regard to the treatment of different third States, it was observed in Case 236/84, *Malt* v. *HZA Düsseldorf*,[51] in the context of the imposition of monetary compensatory amounts on beef imported into the Community under a tariff quota, that there was of course no obligation on the Community to offer the same treatment to different third countries or to products imported from different third countries.

It may, however, be suggested that the most important legal principle laid down expressly by the Treaty in relation to agricultural common organizations is the requirement in art. 40(3) that common organizations 'shall exclude any discrimination between producers or consumers within the Community'.[52] As interpreted by the European Court in Case 5/73, *Balkan* v. *HZA Berlin-Packhof*,[53] this refers to discrimination as between producers or as between consumers, the relationship between the two groups being the concern of art. 39 of the EEC Treaty, stating the objectives of the Common Agricultural Policy. Discussion of the precise scope of this provision, and, in particular, of the question whether it produces direct effects, has been overtaken by the fact that the Court has held that it is 'merely a specific enunciation of the general principle of

---

[48] See *infra*, pp. 104 ff.   [49] [1968] ECR 3.
[50] [1976] ECR 11.
[51] 24 June 1986.
[52] See Vajda, 'Aspects of Judicial Review Within the CAP' (1979) 4 EL Rev. 244 and 341.
[53] [1973] ECR 1091 at p. 113.

equality which is one of the fundamental principles of Community law',[54] a principle which is, hence, a touchstone against which the validity of any Community act may be assessed. On the other hand, there are a number of decisions holding that, in the particular circumstances, differences in treatment do not amount to discrimination, or are objectively justified. Examples which might be given are Case 8/78, *Milac* v. *HZA Freiburg*,[55] where the Court found that, on the material before it, the plaintiff had not shown what constituted the discrimination alleged to result from provisions applying a corrective amount to imports into Germany and the Benelux countries from other Member States of skimmed-milk powder but not to imports of whole-milk powder, and Case 2/77, *Hoffmann's Stärkefabriken* v. *HZA Bielefeld*,[56] where the Court held that there were objective grounds for the difference between the treatment accorded potato-starch producers and that accorded maize-starch producers by Regulations reducing the production refund on maize-starch and potato-starch but allowing special transitional measures with regard to potato-starch alone.

The fine dividing line between valid and invalid difference in treatment imposed upon another subgroup of starch producers, the manufacturers of isoglucose, is illustrated in Cases 103 and 145/77, *Royal Scholten Honig* v. *Intervention Board*,[57] in which isoglucose manufacturers challenged the validity of Council Regulations respectively freezing and eventually eliminating production refunds on maize-starch (and other agricultural starches) used for the manufacture of isoglucose, and introducing a system of production levies on the manufacture of isoglucose. With regard to the Regulation freezing and eliminating the production refund, the Court repeated that art. 40(3) was a specific enunciation of the principle of equality, which 'requires that similar situations shall not be treated differently unless the differentiation is objectively justified'. In the light of this, the Court went on to consider whether the situation of isoglucose was comparable to that of other products of the starch industry—and it is, perhaps, in itself interesting to note that it was the products rather than the producers which the Court considered. It was found that there was no competition between starch and isoglucose, or between isoglucose and other products derived from starch except possibly glucose, and that even there the two products had different applications so that they could not be in a comparable competitive situation. On the other hand, it was stated that as isoglucose was at least partially interchangeable with sugar, the maintenance of the production refund in favour of manufacturers of isoglucose might have constituted discrimination against manufacturers of

---

[54] Cases 117/76 and 16/77, *Ruckdeschel* v. *HZA Hamburg-St Annen* [1977] ECR 1753 at p. 1769; Cases 124/76 and 20/77, *Moulins Pont à Mousson* v. *ONIC* [1977] ECR 1795, at p. 1811.
[55] [1978] ECR 1721.   [56] [1977] ECR 1375.   [57] [1978] ECR 2037.

sugar. From this, although it had referred initially to the general principle of equality, the Court concluded that the Regulation did not infringe the rule of non-discrimination between Community producers set out in the second sub-paragraph of art. 40(3) of the Treaty.

In relation to the introduction of a production levy on isoglucose, the Court considered whether isoglucose and sugar were in comparable situations. It pointed out that the Council had recognized in the recitals to the Regulation that isoglucose was a direct substitute for liquid sugar, and, in the recitals to a Regulation amending that Regulation, that 'any Community Decision on one of those products necessarily affects the other'. Having found that isoglucose and sugar were, in effect, in a comparable position, the Court went on to state that isoglucose manufacturers and sugar manufacturers were, nevertheless, treated differently as regards the imposition of the production levy, in that it only affected sugar produced outside the basic quota but within the maximum one, whereas it applied to the whole of isoglucose production. It was also noted that sugar manufacturers benefited from the intervention system, whereas isoglucose manufacturers did not. The final question, however, was whether this difference in treatment could be objectively justified. On behalf of the Council and Commission, it was argued that, since the price of isoglucose tended to follow the intervention price of sugar, the high intervention price of sugar (stated to be 15 per cent higher than the price which would have been fixed by normal criteria) gave a notional 15 per cent advantage to isoglucose, which roughly corresponded to the five-units-of-account maximum levy. The Court rejected this argument, stating that a similar advantage, if it existed, could be enjoyed by a sugar manufacturer with a favourably situated modern factory. It was further argued that the levy roughly corresponded to the charges borne by sugar manufacturers on the whole of their production, if that produced outside the quotas was taken into account.

The Court rejected this argument also, pointing out that sugar manufacturers paid beet growers a reduced price for beet used for sugar produced outside the basic quota, and that sugar manufacturers could limit their charges simply by limiting their production—in effect, keeping to their quotas—whereas a limit on production by an isoglucose manufacturer would be without effect as regards the rate of levy per unit weight. The Court held, although this time it had commenced simply by a reference to art. 40(3) of the Treaty, that the provisions of the Regulation establishing the production levy system for isoglucose offended against the general principle of equality of which the prohibition on discrimination set out in art. 40(3) of the Treaty was a specific expression.

The isoglucose cases show very clearly the Court's methodology when dealing with an alleged breach of the principle of equality. The first step is to see whether the products or producers between which or whom there is said to be discrimination are, in fact, in a comparable situation, which in the present cases appears to have been synonymous with a competing position. If they are not, as was the case with isoglucose and other starch products, that is the end of the matter. If they are in a comparable situation, the next step is to see if there is a difference in treatment between them. If there is a difference in treatment, the third and final step is to see whether it is objectively justified—and the approach of the Court in the isoglucose cases appears to have been that it was for the institutions to show that the difference was objectively justified rather than for the producers affected to show that it was not justified.

Although, at first sight, art. 40(3) and the underlying general principle may seem only to govern the validity of Community legislation, the European Court has held in Cases 201 and 202/85, *Klensch* v. *Luxembourg Secretary of State for Agriculture*,[58] that it applies to any measure taken in the context of a common organization of an agricultural market, whether that measure is taken by the Community authorities or the national authorities. Hence, in that case, the exercise by the Luxembourg government of its discretion under the milk quota system[59] to choose the reference year from which quotas would be calculated was held to be subject to the principle of non-discrimination. Furthermore, the general principle of equality of treatment is applied not just to producers and consumers but also, for example, to importers, as in Case 165/84, *Krohn*,[60] where it was held that the principle was breached by legislation which did not allow importers of manioc from Thailand to cancel their licences, following the introduction of a quota regime, but did allow such licences to be cancelled by those importing manioc from any other country.

(c) *General principles derived from the laws of the Member States*

It is, in fact, in the field of agriculture that the European Court has developed and applied many of the general principles of Community law which may be regarded as being derived from the laws of the Member States.[61] Thus, it was in an agricultural dispute that Advocate-General Dutheillet de Lamothe in his Opinion in Case 11/70, *Internationale Handelsgesellschaft* v. *Einfuhr- und Vorratsstelle Getreide*,[62] defined the

---

[58] 25 Nov. 1986.   [59] See *infra*. p. 74.   [60] [1985] ECR 3997.

[61] See Usher: 'The Influence of National Concepts on Decisions of the European Court of Justice' (1976) EL Rev. 359; Neri, 'Principe de la proportionnalitē' dans la jurisprudence de la Cour relative au droit communautaire agricole' (1981) RTDE 442.

[62] [1972] ECR 1125.

principle of proportionality as being that 'citizens may only have imposed on them, for the purposes of the public interest, obligations which are strictly necessary for those purposes to be attained'. It was there held by the Court that the system of deposits required for export licences under the common organization of the market in cereals did not breach the principle of proportionality. An example of a breach of the principle of proportionality is to be found in Cases 114, 116, and 119–120/76, *Bela-Mühle etc.*,[63] a series of references for preliminary rulings. The Court there held that a Council Regulation effectively requiring manufacturers of animal foodstuffs to incorporate intervention skimmed-milk powder into their products at a price three times that of the soya husks for which it was substituted imposed an obligation which was disproportionate, and not necessary to attain the objective of reducing stocks of milk powder (and discriminatory within the meaning of art. 40(3) (2) of the EEC Treaty). Not surprisingly, it held the Regulation to be invalid. Similarly, in Case 181/84, *E.D. and F. Man v. Intervention Board*,[64] it was held that where the objective of a deposit was to ensure that sugar was exported it was a breach of the principle of proportionality to require the forfeiture of the whole deposit when the exporter was late (by a few hours) in applying for the formal export licence, when there was still enough time to carry out the export transaction. The basis of this decision was a distinction between the primary obligation to carry out the export transaction and the secondary obligation to apply for an export licence within a specific time, the Court taking the view that to penalise failure to comply with the secondary obligation as severely as failure to comply with the primary obligation would breach the principle of proportionality. The distinction between primary and secondary obligations would appear to underlie the judgment in Case 122/78, *Buitoni*,[65] and a further gloss was put on it in Case 21/85, *Maas v. Bundesanstalt für Landwirtschaftliche Marktordnung*,[66] where a deposit paid under the food-aid legislation had been forfeited because the exporter loaded the goods into ships a few days late and because the ships used were older than the fifteen years specified in the legislation. The Court held the obligation to load the goods within a fixed time limit was a primary obligation, but that in the context of sea transport a delay of a few days did not necessarily breach that obligation, and, since the goods, in fact, arrived at their destination on time, the loss of the deposit could not be justified. With regard to the use of ships less than fifteen years old, which was held not to be a primary obligation, particularly since it was not required under other similar legislation, it was decided that this requirement should be interpreted as including ships equated with ships less than fifteen years old for insurance purposes, and that even if the ships used did

---

[63] [1977] ECR 1211. [64] [1985] ECR 2889.
[65] [1979] ECR 677. [66] 27 Nov. 1986.

not fall within the requirement as so interpreted, it was disproportionate to require the whole deposit to be forfeited.

This may, however, be contrasted with the decision in Case 9/85, *Nordbutter*,[67] in the context of legislation granting a subsidy on skimmed milk used for feeding animals other than calves. This required a quarterly declaration of the number of calves on the holding, and, under Commission Regulation 188/83,[68] the subsidy was reduced by 10 per cent if the declaration was up to ten days late, and was lost totally thereafter. It was held by the Court that since this expressly allowed for minor infringements of the deadline it did not breach the principle of proportionality.

On the other hand, technical definitions may be strictly interpreted, so that to require grapes to be turned into must and the must into wine in the immediate vicinity of the region concerned, in order for a wine to qualify as a quality wine produced in a specified region (VQPRD), was held to be necessary, in order to achieve the objectives of the legislation and, therefore, not to breach the principle of proportionality.[69] Similarly, highly technical rules laid down for the payment of, for example, denaturing premiums may well be strictly applied. Case 272/81, *Ru-mi* v. *FORMA*,[70] involved a highly specific formula for the de-naturing of skimmed-milk powder so as to ensure it could not be used as a feed for young calves, the intention being that it could, however, be used as feed for pigs and poultry. The Court took the view that it was not disproportionate to withhold the whole of the special aid for denaturing if the formula was not strictly followed, because of the risk that the product might thereby be diverted from its intended use. On the other hand, Council Regulation 1300/84[71] introduced a legislative application of the principle of proportionality in the context of premiums for the non-marketing of milk and the conversion of dairy herds, so that a reduced premium could be paid where there were minor breaches of the rules, rather than the premium being entirely lost.

Perhaps the most frequent use of these general principles in relation to Community agricultural legislation is as a guide to interpretation, so as to ensure the validity of that legislation, rather than as a criterion for determining the validity of that legislation. The general principle of legal certainty was so used in the *Deuka* cases.[72] In the first of these the Court was asked whether a Commission Regulation was invalid in so far as it provided that an increased denaturing premium should be discontinued even in respect of wheat purchased by the denaturer before the Regulation came into force. Having found that a denaturing undertaking may well

---

[67] 8 Oct. 1986.   [68] OJ 1983 L25/14.
[69] Case 116/82, *Commission* v. *Germany* (18 Sep. 1986).
[70] [1982] ECR 4167.   [71] OJ 1984 L125/3.
[72] Case 78/74, *Deuka* v. *Einfuhr- und Vorratsstelle Getreide* [1975] ECR 421, Case 5/75, *Deuka* v. *Einfuhr- und Vorratsstelle Getreide* [1975] ECR 759.

arrange its programme on the basis of an entire crop year, for the sake of legal certainty the Regulation had to be applied in such a way that there might still benefit from the system those quantities of goods purchased before the coming into force of the Regulation, provided the request (for a premium) was made to the intervention agency before the expiry of the time-limit arising from the Regulation. Interpreted in this way, the Regulation was held to be valid. In the second case, similar questions arose concerning the validity of Regulations respectively reducing and abolishing the relevant denaturing premium, and a similar answer was given: the Court stated that where there had been a commitment to denaturing before the expiry of the periods stipulated in the Regulations, it was right to apply, in the interests of legal certainty, for the computation of the amount of the denaturing premium, the provisions in force at the time the application was lodged, even if the technical mixing was not done until a subsequent date.

Just as the general principles derived from the Treaty are held to be binding upon Member States when acting in the context of Community law,[73] so also are those general principles derived from the laws of the Member States. This is, perhaps, most clearly illustrated by the attitude of the European Court to claims that a restriction on the import of agricultural products is justified on health grounds under art. 36 of the Treaty,[74] where it has consistently been emphasized that the restriction must be proportionate to the objective it pursues, as in the cases involving United Kingdom restrictions on imports of poultry meat,[76] and UHT milk.[76]

Finally, it may be noted that it was in the context of a common organization of the market that the Court developed, in Case 5/71, *Zuckerfabrik Schöppenstedt* v. *Council*,[77] the theory that the Community could incur non-contractual liability in relation to harm caused even by legislation involving measures of economic policy, where it constitutes a sufficiently serious violation of a superior rule of law for the protection of the individual, so that, for example, legislation breaching a general principle of Community law such as the principle of the protection of legitimate expectation could give rise to a liability in damages, as was held in Case 74/74, *CNTA* v. *Commission*.[78] Whilst the simple fact that such a principle has been breached may not, in itself, be a sufficiently 'serious' violation,[79] it was a breach of the general principle of equality of treatment

[73] Cases 201 and 202/85, *Klensch* v. *Luxembourg Secretary of State for Agriculture* (25 Nov. 1986). See *supra*, p. 44.
[74] See *supra*, pp. 29–30.
[75] Case 40/82, *Commission* v. *UK* [1982] ECR 2793.
[76] Case 124/81 Commission v. *UK* [1983] ECR 203.
[77] [1971] ECR 975.   [78] [1975] ECR 533.
[79] Cases 83 and 94/76 etc. Bayerische HNL v. *Council and Commission* [1978] ECR 1209.

by a Regulation abolishing production refunds on quellmehl whilst retaining them for pre-gelatinized starch which gave rise to the first actual award of damages in Case 238/78, *Ireks-Arkady* v. *Commission*.[80]

(d) Techniques of interpretation

Whilst the general principles discussed above may serve as aids to interpretation—and the Court has developed a further general principle that where a provision of Community secondary legislation may be interpreted either in a way which conflicts with underlying principles of Community law or in a way which accords with those principles, preference should be given to the latter interpretation[81]—it is also in the field of agricultural law that the techniques of interpretation characteristic of the European Court have been particularly developed. In the United Kingdom, the European Court is perhaps most typically associated with a 'purposive' style of interpretation,[82] that is, that legislation is interpreted in the light of what, in its context, appears to be its purpose. It was on this basis, for example, that the Court refused to give a single meaning for 'agricultural holding'[83] and it is also on this basis that the Court has interpreted the legal mechanisms common to common organizations.[84]

Without entering into too detailed an analysis of the development of this technique,[85] it would appear, at least in part, to be linked to the fact that all the official Community languages are equally authentic, as was recognized by the Court itself in Case 61/72, *Mij. PPW International* v. *Hoofdproduktschap voor Akkerbouwprodukten*,[86] where the obligations of national authorities with regard to the dispatch of 'advance fixing certificates'[87] were at issue. The Court there stated that, 'No argument can be drawn either from any linguistic divergences between the various language versions, or from the multiplicity of the verbs used in one or other of those versions, as the meaning of the provisions in question must be determined with respect to their *objective*'. Looking at the objectives of the system of advance fixing certificates, the Court noted that they were only issued on payment of a deposit by the trader, and that payment of, in this

---

[80] [1979] ECR 2985.
[81] Case 218/82, *Commission* v. *Council* [1983] ECR 4063.
[82] See the judgment of Lord Denning MR in *Buchanan* v. *Babco* [1977] 1 All ER 518, 522.
[83] Case 85/77, *Santa Anna* v. *INPS* [1978] ECR 527, 540.
[84] e.g. Case 113/75, *Frecassetti* v. *Italian Finance Administration* [1976] ECR 983, and Case 6/77, *Schouten* v. *Hoofdproduktschap voor Akkerbouwprodukten* [1977] ECR 1291 on import levies. See *infra*, pp. 63–5.
[85] For an account of the development of this technique in the Community, see Pescatore, 'Les objectifs de la Communauté comme principes de l'interprétation dans la jurisprudence de la Cour de Justice' in *Miscellanea W. J. Ganshof van der Meersch*, vol. ii at pp. 326–328.
[66] [1973] ECR 301.   [87] See *infra*, p. 64.

case, export refunds, depended on the presentation of a certificate by the trader. From this, it held that the national authorities had a duty to ensure that such certificates actually reached applicants for them, and that this obligation was not fulfilled by sending them by ordinary post when they failed to reach the addressee. A rather more esoteric example of the same impetus to purposive interpretation came to light in Case 100/84, *Commission* v. *UK*.[88] It involved a joint fishing operation by British and Polish trawlers in the Baltic sea some forty to eighty miles off the Polish coast. The British trawlers cast empty nets into the sea which were taken over by Polish trawlers. The Polish trawlers then trawled the nets, but did not take them on board. After the trawl was completed, the ends of the nets were passed to the British trawlers by the Polish trawlers, and the fish were landed on to the British trawlers. The question at issue was whether the fish were to be treated as being British in origin, in which case no CCT duty was payable (the view of the United Kingdom government), or as being Polish in origin, in which case CCT duty was payable (the view of the Commission). Under the EEC legislation, fish were to be treated as wholly obtained in one country if they were 'taken from the sea' by vessels registered in that country and flying its flag.[89] After considering the different language versions of that provision, which it held not to be decisive one way or the other, the Court looked to its purpose and general scheme, concluding that the origin of the fish should depend on the flag or registration of the vessel which catches them, and that the vessel which locates the fish and separates them from the sea by netting them performs the essential part of that operation. Hence, the fish were of Polish origin.

Similarly, resort may be had to the purposive approach to apply Community law in a situation not precisely envisaged by the draftsmen, or where the terminology in any language may be capable of more than one interpretation. Hence, in Case 109/84 *Von Menges*,[90] in the context of a dairy conversion scheme designed to encourage farmers to leave milk production, it was held that a farmer who replaced his herd of dairy cows with a flock of sheep which he used for producing sheep's milk could not benefit from the scheme, since although his sheep's milk did not fall within the common organization of the market in milk it competed with products falling within that organization, so that his activity was not helping to reduce the surplus of dairy production, which was the aim of the scheme.

However, the Court looks only to the purpose of the published version of the legislation[91] and not to an underlying political purpose if that is not

[88] [1985] ECR 1169.
[89] Council Reg. 802/68 (JO 1968 L148/1) art. 4(2)f.
[90] [1985] ECR 1289.
[91] See Kutscher, 'Methods of Interpretation as Seen by a Judge at the Court of Justice', *Reports of the Judicial and Academic Conference 1976 (European Court of Justice)* (Luxembourg, 1976) p. I–21.

apparent. In Case 69/84, *Padovani*,[92] the Court, therefore, took at face value legislation which reduced the import levy[93] on cereals imported by sea into Italy, purporting to take account of high port charges and unloading costs in Italy: in that case it held that the reduced levy was only payable if the cereals were not only declared to the Italian authorities but also physically unloaded in an Italian port, so that the full levy was payable where the cereals were transhipped to the Netherlands. On the other hand, it has been suggested[94] that the reduced levy really served the purpose of reducing prices on the Italian market.

Linked with its purposive approach is a cautious willingness by the Court to apply legislation by analogy to situations not falling within its precise terms. The attitude of the Court may, however, most clearly be illustrated by a pair of cases in which it refused to apply legislation by analogy. The *Neumann*[95] and *Ludwig*[96] cases, which were both referred to the European Court by the Bundesverwaltungsgericht, raised the question of the application by analogy of provisions of Council Directive No. 72/462/EEC on health and veterinary inspection problems upon importation of bovine animals and swine and fresh meat from third countries,[97] requiring Member States to carry out health inspections on certain types of meat imported from third countries and to charge for such inspections. In the *Neumann* case, the respondent had imported game, notably venison and wild boar, from third countries into the Federal Republic of Germany in 1975. In the *Ludwig* case the appellant had imported tins of beef goulash from Hungary in 1974. In each case the meat was inspected by the local authorities, and in each case a charge was made for such inspection, and the Bundesverwaltungsgericht was satisfied in each case that these charges were prohibited as charges having equivalent effect to customs duties.

Both importers appealed to their local administrative courts against the imposition of charges. In the *Neumann* case, the Verwaltungsgericht of Frankfurt allowed the appeal, but in the *Ludwig* case, the Verwaltungsgericht of Hamburg held that Council Directive No. 72/462/EEC should be extended by analogy to importations of tinned meat from third countries, and that it authorized the imposition of charges for the inspection of such meat. The Bundesverwaltungsgeright indicated in the order for reference that it agreed with the Frankfurt court, but that since the Hamburg court had expressed a contrary view, there was sufficient doubt in the matter to justify a reference to the European Court, and in both cases it asked specifically whether the relevant provisions of the Directive were applicable

---

[92] [1985] ECR 1859.   [93] See *infra*, p. 55.
[94] See, for example, Neville-Rolfe, *The Politics of Agriculture in the European Community* (Policy Studies Institute, London, 1984), p. 230.
[95] Case 137/77, *City of Frankfurt* v. *Neumann* [1978] ECR 1623.
[96] Case 138/77, *Ludwig* v. *City of Hamburg* [1978] ECR 1645.
[97] JO 1972 L302/28.

by analogy 'with the result that the Member States are entitled or obliged to carry out health inspections and may impose charges for such inspections'.

In fact, before judgment was delivered in these cases, the Court decided in Case 70/77, *Simmenthal* v. *Italian Finance Administration*,[98] that the relevant provisions of the Directive could not be applied by Member States because the necessary Community implementing legislation had not been enacted. Hence, the Directive could not have justified the charges in question whether they fall within its scope expressly or by analogy. Nonetheless, both Advocate-General Warner and the Court did consider the question whether it was possible to apply the Directive by analogy. In the single Opinion he delivered in the two cases, A.-G. Warner analysed the earlier case-law on interpretation by analogy,[99] and concluded that the authorities established a general rule and an exception, the general rule being that 'the application of a provision of Community legislation may not be extended to a case that is outside the express scope of that provision', and the exception being that 'where legislation contains an obvious lacuna, which must needs be filled, resort may be had to an analogy in order to fill it'. He then considered the scope of the Directive, which in its art. 1(1) is stated to apply to imports of 'domestic bovine animals and swine for breeding, production or slaughter' and 'fresh meat of domestic animals of the following species: bovine animals, swine, sheep and goats and solipeds'. Fresh meat is defined in art. 2(o) as 'meat which has not undergone any preserving process; however, chilled and frozen meat shall be considered to be fresh'. In the light of these provisions, A.-G. Warner stated as his opinion that game and tinned beef had been deliberately excluded from the scope of the Directive, and that their omission could not be regarded as a lacuna that might be filled by judicial decision.

The Court reached the same result, but from a somewhat different angle, basing itself on the fact, which it had emphasized in the decision in *Simmenthal*, that the prohibition on charges having equivalent effect to customs duties on imports from third countries is intended to protect the Community's uniform external stance *vis-à-vis* third countries. The Court pointed out that the Directive was intended not to strengthen the protection of public health and safety, but to establish uniform systems of inspection so as to prevent competition being distorted and trade being diverted. It stated that the imposition of charges under the Directive was linked to the establishment of a uniform Community system of inspections corresponding to the needs of the Common Customs Tariff, and that to allow Member States unilaterally to impose charges could go against this aim; hence provisions allowing charges to be imposed could not be

[98] [1978] ECR 1453.   [99] [1978] ECR at pp. 1641–2.

extended beyond their specific scope. The Court added that the Directive was not an illustration of a general principle of Community law under which charges could be imposed for any inspection carried out at the external frontiers of the Community, but an example of the derogations from the basic prohibition on the imposition by Member States of charges having equivalent effect to customs duties on goods imported from third countries.

On the other hand, in its contemporaneous judgment in Case 6/78, *Union Française des Céréales* v. *HZA Hamburg-Jonas*,[100] which will be considered in the context of Accession compensatory amounts,[101] the Court held that a *force majeure* clause[102] in the basic regulation governing export refunds[103] could be read into a regulation governing accession compensatory amounts since accession compensatory amounts served the same purpose as export refunds in trade with new Member States.

Similarly, analogy may be used to remedy a breach of a basic principle, so that when, in Case 165/84, *Krohn*,[104] it was held to be a breach of the principle of equality of treatment not to allow importers of manioc from Thailand to cancel their licences when importers from other third countries could do so, the Court held that the parallel legislation governing imports from countries other than Thailand should be applied by analogy to imports from Thailand. Application of legislation by analogy has also been used to prevent a breach of a general principle: in Cases 201 and 202/85, *Klensch* v. *Luxembourg Minister of Agriculture*,[105] it was decided that where Council Regulation 857/84[106] did not provide expressly for the reallocation of the milk quota of a farmer who left dairy farming of his own volition, the rules which would have applied if he had left dairy farming under the special outgoers' scheme should apply by analogy, so that his quota should go to the national reserve. To allocate his quota to the purchaser to which he had made his deliveries, as the Luxembourg government had done, would in the Court's view, breach the principle of non-discrimination with regard to other producers, and would tie that producer to the one purchaser if he wanted to re-enter the market.

---

[100] [1978] ECR 1675.   [101] See *infra*, pp. 121–3.

[102] See Loyant, 'La force majeure et l'organisation des marchés agricoles' (1980) RTDE 256.

[103] See *infra*, p. 55.

[104] [1985] ECR 3997.   [105] 25 Nov. 1986.   [106] OJ 1984 L90/13.

4

Common organizations of the market: structures

(a) Cereals

(i) The overall system

In order to attain the objectives set out in art. 39, a common organization of agricultural markets is required to be established under art. 40. Three alternative forms of common organization are set out in art. 40. These are common rules on competition, the compulsory co-ordination of the various national market organizations; and a European market organization. In practice it is the third of these that has always been used. Art. 40 further provides that the common organization may in particular, include regulation of prices, aids for the production and marketing of the various products, storage and carry-over arrangements and common machinery for stabilizing imports or exports.

The most developed of these common organizations create an integrated market with a single Community-wide price structure, although since 1971 the practical realization of this ideal has been hampered by floating exchange rates, despite the existence of the requisite legal framework, as will be seen.[1] The common organization of the market in cereals is of pivotal importance, since the common organizations of the markets in pigmeat (under Council Regulation 2759/75),[2] eggs (under Regulation 2772/75),[3] and poultrymeat (under Regulation 2777/75)[4] are treated as ancillary to it, prices being based on the cereal input of the products concerned. The common organization of the market in cereals may also be taken as the basic model of a fully developed Community-market organization. A transitional scheme was established under Council Regulation 19[5] in 1962. This involved a system of levies in trade between Member States to compensate for the different price levels in different Member States pending the adoption of co-ordinated price levels.[6] It is ironic that since 1971 a system of charges and subsidies has had to be re-introduced in trade between Member States to compensate for differences

---

[1] See *infra*, p. 108.   [2] OJ 1975 L282/1.   [3] OJ 1975 L282/56.
[4] OJ 1975 L282/77.   [5] JO 1962 p. 933.
[6] For an account of the negotiations leading to the adoption of this Regulation, see Neville-Rolfe, *The Politics of Agriculture in the European Community* (Policy Studies Institute, London, 1984), ch. 7.

in price levels resulting from the collapse of the system of fixed exchange rates. It was replaced by a single market system in 1967, established under Council Regulation 120/67,[7] which indeed started the basis of the present form of the organization. The fact that the single market stage was reached for a large number of products between 1966 and 1968 has wider ramifications for the development of Community law. It may be argued that it was one of the factors which enabled the Common Customs Tariff,[8] with its concomitant removal of customs duties and quotas, as such, in trade between Member States, to be introduced eighteen months early in July 1968.[9] The 1967 Regulation suffered much amendment and it and its subsisting amendments were consolidated into Council Regulation 2727/75[10] which, in turn, has been amended on a number of occasions, notably by Council Regulation 1143/76[11] altering the pricing structure—in fact, the essential feature of the system—only a year later.

Leaving aside certain special provisions relating to common wheat of bread-making quality and durum wheat, the price structure rests essentially upon a 'target price' and an 'intervention price'. The target price is the price which it is hoped producers will be able to obtain. The intervention price is, in principle, the price at which national intervention agencies, such as the United Kingdom Intervention Board for Agricultural Produce, will buy in products subject to the organization; hence, it represents the minimum price. However, in 1987 the concept of the 'buying-in' price was introduced under Council Regulation 1900/87,[12] by virtue of which buying in was to take place at 94 per cent of the intervention price, and only if the market price for certain cereals in certain export ports fell below the intervention price. These prices are supported by a system of external protection. Under the current scheme,[13] a single Community intervention price is fixed for Ormes which is declared to be the production area having the greatest surplus of cereals. A single target price is fixed for Duisburg as being the centre of the area having the greatest deficit. In fixing the target price, account is taken, amongst other things, of the costs of transport from Ormes to Duisburg. It might be mentioned that under the original scheme both the target price and a so-called basic intervention price were fixed for Duisburg, and derived intervention prices were calculated from this basic price for the different production areas of the Community. For wheat of bread-making quality there was a 'reference price', which was effectively an increased intervention price. In 1986, however, this reference price was abolished by Council Regulation 1579/86,[14] but at the same time a special

[7] JO 1967 p. 2269.   [8] Council Reg. 950/68, JO 1968 L172/1.
[9] See, e.g. Neville-Rolfe, *The Politics of Agriculture*, p. 240.
[10] OJ 1975 L281/1.   [11] OJ 1976 L130/1.   [12] OJ 1987 L182/40.
[13] Reg. 2727/75 art. 3, as most recently substituted by Reg. 1579/86 (OJ 1986 L139/29).
[14] OJ 1986 L139/29.

premium was introduced for wheat and rye of higher bread-making quality, it being expressly declared in the recitals that the previous bread-making quality requirements 'were not sufficiently stringent' and had boosted the production of that type of wheat.

At the frontiers of the Community, a threshold price is applied. This is calculated so that the selling price for the imported product on the Duisburg market shall be the same as the target price, differences in quality being taken into account.[15] It would appear that the threshold price is calculated from the target price rather than the intervention price because, by definition, the target price is higher than the intervention price and so, allowing for vagaries of calculation and the factors which have to be used in calculating Community levies, the general result will always be that, in any event, imports do not come in below the intervention price, even though they might not always come up to the level of the target price. In practice, the threshold price is fixed for Rotterdam. In the case of imports, a levy is, in principle, charged which is equal to the threshold price minus the CIF price, which is expressly required to be calculated for Rotterdam on the basis of the most favourable purchasing opportunities on the world market.[16] In other words, the levy is intended to cover the difference, if any, between the world price and the Community price. In the case of exports, it is somewhat more vaguely provided that the difference between quotations or prices for products on the world market and prices in the Community 'may' be covered by an export refund. Subject to certain safeguards, importers or exporters may obtain an advance-fixing certificate, fixing either an import levy or export refund in advance.[17]

In the Community internal market, a role is also played by subsidies. For producers of durum wheat, art. 10 of Regulation 2727/75 provides for the payment of a fixed aid per hectare sown and harvested, which could be regarded as a form of regional support. Indeed, it is payable only for the production of durum wheat in zones of the Community where this production constitutes a traditional and important part of agricultural production. The 'production refunds' for the manufacture of starch from, inter alia, maize and common wheat are also authorized under this common organization,[18] the aim being to enable starch manufacturers to buy the raw materials at common-agricultural-policy prices and still to be able to compete with substitute chemical products. In so far as it may be desirable to encourage retention of stocks from one marketing year to the next, 'carry-over' payments may be granted under art. 9, but, in fact, under art. 6 the basic

---

[15] Reg. 2727/75 art. 5 as amended.   [16] Ibid. art. 13.   [17] Ibid. art. 15.
[18] Ibid. art. 11. However, under Council Regs. 1006–1010/86 (OJ 1986 L94/1–9) such refunds are limited to the situation where import arrangements provide insufficient protection.

prices are themselves subject to monthly increases phased over part or all of the marketing year, effectively, to provide for storage costs and, thus, encourage orderly marketing. Provision may also be made, as required, for, for example, private storage aid or denaturing premiums, in addition to the basic system. Two further types of subsidy were introduced by Regulation 1579/86.[19] As a correlative to the introduction of a co-responsibility levy[20] in the cereals market, it provided for direct aid for small producers, up to the amount of the co-responsibility levy on producers marketing not more than twenty-five tonnes; and, as part of the more general effort to achieve (or restore, in the terms of the recitals) balance in the market, it provides for the payment of aid for cereals harvested in the Community that are put to new industrial uses, up to the limit of what would have been the export refunds on those cereals if they had been exported.

This price structure rests to a very large degree on the premise that the product is one in which the Community is largely self-sufficient and of which Community production is to be encouraged, and that imports will be the exception and must not be allowed to disturb Community prices. It also assumes, in the systems of import levies and export refunds, that world prices will be lower than Community prices. However, this assumption has not always been justified, and by virtue of art. 19 export levies may be imposed so as to prevent Community producers taking advantage of higher world prices. This for example was the background to Case 95/75, *Effem* v. *Haupzollamt Lüneberg*,[21] in which the Court held that no less than five regulations fixing flat rate export levies on compound animal feeding stuffs, containing differing percentages of cereals, were invalid.

The basic criticism which may be made of the common organizations of which that governing the market in cereals is a basic model, is that in their original form they involved an open ended commitment to intervention buying and hence encouraged over-production. To a certain degree it could be suggested that this must have been deliberate in a consumer society. Consumers expect to be able to have supplies of what they want continuously available. However, a situation of structural surplus developed in some sectors, and in the cereals market, Council Regulation 1451/82[22] introduced an art. 3a into Regulation 2727/75, setting a 'guarantee threshold'. Under this system, production beyond the guarantee threshold over a period of three years would have led to a graduated reduction in the intervention price. However, in 1986 this system was repealed and replaced by a general co- responsibility levy under Council Regulation 1579/86,[23] to be collected on cereals that undergo first processing or intervention buying or export in the form of grain. It is perhaps, ironic to

---

[19] Introducing art. 4a and 11a into Reg. 2727/75, OJ 1986 L139/29.
[20] See *infra*.   [21] [1976] ECR 361.
[22] OJ 1982 L164/1.   [23] OJ 1986 L139/29.

note that in the milk sector, where a guarantee threshold was also introduced in 1982,[24] a co-responsibility levy had been in operation since 1977,[25] and the current effort to curb production takes the form of a quota system linked to an additional (effectively confiscatory) levy.[26]

Nevertheless, the agreement on 'stabilizers' reached in theEuropean Council meeting in Brussels in February 1988[27] as part of the overall compromise on the Community's future financing and new 'own resources' represents a mixture of guarantee threshold and co-responsibility levy. Under this system a guarantee threshold of 160 million tonnes has been set for cereals for each marketing year from 1988/9 to 1991/2, and a provisional additional co-responsibility levy of up to 3 per cent is to be levied at the beginning of each marketing year to keep expenditure on the management of the market within predetermined budgetary limits. If it transpires at the end of the marketing year that the guarantee threshold has not been exceeded, or has been exceeded by less than 3 per cent, the provisional co-responsibility levy is to be proportionately reimbursed, but if the guarantee threshold is exceeded, the actual intervention price is to be reduced by 3 per cent at the beginning of the next marketing year—an operation which could have dramatic effects if repeated each year. The agreement further provided for both the basic co-responsibility levy and the additional co-responsibility levy to be paid by the first buyer, and for exemption for a defined category of small producers. On the other hand, in the market in oils and fats, Council Regulation 1454/86[28] provided that where it was anticipated that the 'maximum guaranteed quantities' for colza, rape, and sunflower would be exceeded, even before the beginning of the marketing year, the intervention prices (and Community aid) might be reduced by up to 5 per cent pro rata to the excess. This principle was taken further by Council Regulation 1915/87[29] providing for a reduction in the aid payable for rape- and sunflower-seed where over-production is anticipated, equal to the effect of the over-production on the target price.

Under the terms of the European Council compromise reached in February 1988[30] it was further provided that the institutional prices for 1988/9 would be reduced by 0.45 per cent for each 1 per cent excess over the guarantee threshold in that year, and that for 1989/1 the reduction would be 0.50 per cent for each 1 per cent excess. In order to enforce this reduction, the payment of Community aid is treated as provisional until it has been established whether the maximum quantity has been exceeded.

---

[24] Council Reg. 1183/82, OJ 1982 L140/1.
[25] Council Reg. 1079/77, OJ 1977 L131/6.   [26] See *infra*, pp. 72–81.
[27] Implemented by Council Reg. 1097/88, OJ 1988 L110/7.
[28] OJ 1986 L133/8.   [29] OJ 1986 L139/29.
[30] Implemented by Council Reg. 1098/88, OJ 1988 L110/10.

Finally, a financial limitation on the previously open-ended commitment to intervention buying was imposed under the February 1988 compromise: it was agreed to set a reference base for agricultural expenditure (27,500 million ECU in 1988), and to limit the growth of the Guarantee Section of the European Agricultural Guidance and Guarantee Fund, [31] i.e. the Community fund used to finance intervention, to 80 per cent of the growth in GNP.

(ii) Fixing the prices

The basic prices are set by the Council for a whole marketing year, the dates of which have changed with surprising frequency, partly as a reflection of the changing geographical balance of the Community. Under the scheme introduced by Council Regulation 1579/86,[32] the marketing year for all cereals and for all Member States runs from 1 July to 30 June of the following year, whereas the immediately preceding system effectively allowed for three different marketing years, distinguishing durum wheat from other cereals and distinguishing Greece, Italy and certain *départements* in the South of France from the rest of the Community. The Council is required to set the target and intervention prices before the beginning of the marketing year. Hence, when, in 1985, the Council failed to reach a decision on the relevant prices by the due date, the Commission took it upon itself to issue a Decision[33] setting-out 'precautionary measures' with regard to the buying-in of cereals, eventually adopting its own Regulation 2124/85,[34] which remained in force, unchallenged, for the whole year. The legal basis for the Commission's action was, essentially, that the Member States were in breach of their duty under art. 5 of the Treaty, to attain the objectives of the Treaty and that it was the Commission's duty under art. 155 to ensure that the provisions of the Treaty were observed.[35]

The only guidance given as to the calculation of prices relates to target prices under art. 3(5) and threshold prices under art. 5(4). Target prices comprise the intervention price, together with an element for the cost of transport between Ormes and Duisburg, and a market element. This market element is supposed to represent the difference between the intervention price and the level of market prices 'to be expected in a normal harvest and under natural pricing conditions on the Community market, in the area having the greatest surplus'. While a lawyer may wonder how a group of politicians may determine this economic ideal, in practice target prices for cereals would appear to be in the range of twenty

---

[31] See *infra*, p. 104.   [32] OJ 1987 L183/7.
[33] Commission Decision 85/329 (OJ 1985 L169/94).
[34] OJ 1985 L198/31.   [35] See *infra*, p. 146.

per cent to thirty per cent higher than the intervention price. With regard to both target and threshold prices, very precise criteria are laid down as to the calculation of transport costs respectively between Ormes and Duisburg and Rotterdam and Duisburg, and in Cases 131 and 150/78, *Becher* v. *Bundesanstalt für Landwirtschaftliche Marktordnung*,[36] the applicant tried unsuccessfully to argue that the transport costs taken into account in determining the threshold price were too low, with the result that the price itself and the correlative import levies were too high.

(iii) Legal nature of the prices

Target and threshold prices

Target and threshold prices in the above scheme essentially serve a function of calculation and are not in themselves available to producers. Nevertheless, it is clear that Member States may not legislate, notably in price-control legislation, so as to deprive producers of the opportunity of obtaining the target price.[37] Similarly, it was held in Case 60/75, *Russo*,[38] that a Member State could not buy cereals on the world market and sell them in the Community for less than the target price, on the basis that the producer should not be prevented from having the opportunity of obtaining a price approximating to the target price. On the other hand, a producer who had actually obtained more than the target price for his products could not claim to have suffered harm.

Intervention price

The intervention price, on the other hand, is the price guaranteed to the producer, albeit only to the producer.[39] Under art. 7 of Council Regulation 2727/75,[40] the intervention agencies designated by the Member States are obliged to buy in cereals complying with quality and quantity requirements which are offered to them. Whilst until 1987 buying in was at the intervention price itself, Council Regulation 1900/87[41] introduced the concept of a 'buying-in price', set at 94 per cent of the intervention price, to be operative only if the market price for certain cereals fell below the intervention price in certain export ports. The cereals and ports concerned were defined in Commission Regulation 2232/87,[42] which listed Rouen for common wheat of bread-making quality, Southampton for common wheat not of bread-making quality, Naples and Bari for durum wheat, Bayonne for maize, and Rouen and Southampton for barley; this Regulation also provided that the market price must remain below the intervention price

---

[36] [1979] ECR 1421.
[38] [1976] ECR 45.
[40] OJ 1975 L281/1.

[37] Case 31/74 *Galli* [1975] ECR 47.
[39] Case 2/75 *Mackprang* [1975] ECR 607.
[41] OJ 1987 L182/40.
[42] OJ 1987 L206/16.

for two weeks before buying in may commence. Traditionally, the common organization of the market in cereals has provided for intervention to be available throughout the marketing year, but under the system introduced in 1986 by Council Regulation 1581/86[43] intervention agencies were required to buy in cereals only from 1 October to 30 April in each marketing year, although cereals could, however, be offered under deferred-payment terms from 1 August in Portugal, Italy, Greece and Spain, and from 1 September in the rest of the Community, including the United Kingdom. It was stated openly in the recitals to this Regulation that the fact that cereals could at all times be sent to intervention was very often, even at the beginning of the marketing year, seen as an outlet in its own right by many operators, with the result that such operators did not have to seek to market their grain. The period for buying in was changed again in 1987 by Council Regulation 1900/87,[44] being, in principle, extended from 1 October to 31 May for most of the Community and from 1 August to 31 May for Italy, Spain, Greece, and Portugal, but with no provision for earlier offers on deferred payment terms.

Until the enactment of Regulation 1581/86, intervention in the cereals market had retained a format more appropriate to the pre-1976 pricing structure with different, regional-derived intervention prices, in that offers for intervention had to be made to an intervention agency in respect of a marketing centre chosen from among the three centres nearest to the place the cereals were when the offer was made.[45] This condition was hardly relevant to a single price system when the same price will be paid throughout each Member State, and any differences arising from conversion and exchange rates will for most practical purposes be eliminated by the system of monetary compensatory amounts.[46] Under the system introduced in 1986, the cereals may be offered to any intervention agency (except that cereals offered on deferred payment terms in Portugal, Italy, Greece, and Spain from 1 August must be harvested in these countries). However, the intervention agency may decide where the cereals are to be taken over, although the offeror is required only to meet the transport costs to the intervention centre to which the cereals can be transported at least cost,[47] the agency being liable for any additional costs if it decides to take the goods over elsewhere. The intervention centres are determined by Commission Regulation 2006/80,[48] pursuant to Council Regulation 1145/76,[49] and in the United Kingdom are at Aberdeen, Ashford, Avonmouth, Belfast, Berwick-upon-Tweed, Brighton, Cambridge, Cowes, Darlington, Doncaster, Driffield, Exeter, Glasgow, Hartlebury, Inverness, Ipswich,

---

[43] OJ 1986 L139/36.   [44] OJ 1987 L182/40.
[45] Council Reg. 2738/75 (OJ 1975 L281/49).   [46] See *infra*, pp. 108–13.
[47] Council Reg. 1581/86 art. 1(2); OJ 1986 L139/36.
[48] OJ 1980 L197/1.   [49] OJ 1976 L130/8.

King's Lynn, Leith, Liverpool, Locharbriggs, Londonderry, Manby, Newcastle, Northampton, Old Dalby, Oxford, Perth, Prees Heath, Ripon, Southampton and Tilbury. With the exception of Cambridge, which is also an intervention centre for rye, they are considered to be intervention centres only for common wheat and barley.

On the other hand, the intervention agency may agree with the offeror that it will take over the goods at the place where they are located when the offer is made, but in this case the costs which would have been incurred in taking the cereals to the centre to which they could have been transported at least expense are to be deducted from the intervention price; furthermore, the Commission is empowered to authorise the agency to *require* the goods to be stored in the warehouse where they are located at the time the offer is made.[50]

The fundamental legal concept underlying intervention is that a binding obligation for the intervention agency can be created by the receipt of an offer from a person holding Community cereals.[51] It was clearly established in Case 49/71, *Hagen* v. *Einfuhr- und Vorratsstelle Getreide*,[52] that 'it is important that the concept of a valid offer and the conditions thereby involved shall apply throughout the Community' so that the terms 'offer' and 'offered' had to be uniformly interpreted. The Court then held that, given the consequences of an offer in this context, it could only be regarded as having been made when it came to the knowledge of the intervention agency; that is, it was received in writing by the intervention agency. It was further held that the offer would not be complete if it did not indicate the location of the cereals at the time, but that was in the context of the old requirement that the goods should be offered to one of the three nearest intervention agencies, at a time when there were regional price differences. Whilst, however, the location of the cereals is no longer important in that perspective, it is still very relevant in so far as the intervention agency has to decide at which centre to take over the goods or whether to require them to stay where they are. It was, nevertheless, held that an incomplete offer could be later completed, but that it would only be effective once it had satisfied all the conditions. In the light of this, it is of particular note that Council Regulation 1579/86[53] empowers the Commission to authorise the submission to intervention agencies of offers which include a cancellation clause. The practical explanation would appear from the recitals to be a desire to encourage producers to seek a more advantageous outlet for their grain whilst guaranteeing that it can, as a last resort, be bought in.

Under art. 3(1) of Commission Regulation 1569/77,[54] on the procedure and conditions for the taking over of cereals by intervention agencies, as

---

[50] Council Reg. 1581/86 art. 2(2); OJ 1986 L139/36.
[51] Council Reg. 2727/75 art. 7 as amended; OJ 1975 L281/1.
[52] [1972] ECR 23.   [53] OJ 1986 L139/29.   [54] OJ 1977 L174/15.

amended by Regulation 2134/86[55] the offer must be made in writing, but it may be made by telegram or telex to the intervention agency. The offer may be made[56] by any holder of a homogeneous batch of not less than 80 tonnes of common wheat, rye, barley, maize, or sunflower, or 10 tonnes of durum wheat, harvested within the Community. Since intervention is meant to provide an outlet for cereals which cannot be sold because of market conditions, rather than for cereals which are intrinsically unsaleable, the intervention agency is only required to purchase cereals which are sound, fair, and of marketable quality,[57] and the quality standards for cereals laid down by Council Regulation 2731/75[58] were raized by Council Regulation 1580/86,[59] notably with regard to the criteria for common wheat and with regard to the moisture content of cereals in general. Reflecting this, the Annex to Commission Regulation 1569/77,[60] as amended by Regulation 2134/86,[61] sets out a maximum moisture content of 14 per cent, and, under art. 2, from 1987–88 a request to increase this to 15 per cent may only be made in the event of unfavourable weather conditions.

The original version of Regulation 1569/77 provided for payment to be made as soon as possible.[62] However, in the 1985–6 marketing year, it would appear for budgetary reasons, an amendment was made by Regulation 2180/85[63] to provide for payment to be made only between the 90th and 120th day after the goods were taken over by the intervention agency, although a relaxation was made by Regulation 2262/85[64] to allow payments to small producers to be made after the 60th day, the Member States being left to determine the concept of the 'small' producer. This change to payment between the 90th and 120th day was made permanent, and without derogation, by Commission Regulation 2134/86.[65]

Cereals acquired by the intervention agency may be sold by tender either back on to the Community market 'at prices enabling disturbance of the market to be avoided';[66] that is, at a price above the intervention price (which is highly unlikely in market characterized by large-scale intervention purchases, unless there is a bad harvest), or with a view to export.[67] On the other hand, the Council may establish other selling procedures, and if a comparison may be taken from the milk sector, the sale of cheap intervention 'Christmas butter' is well known, and has been upheld by the Court as being justified as a method of ensuring that stocks are rotated and

---

[55] OJ 1986 L187/23.
[56] Art. 1 of Commission Reg. 1569/77 as amended by Commission Reg. 2134/86.
[57] Art. 2 of Commission Reg. 1569/77.
[58] OJ 1975 L281/22.   [59] OJ 1986 L139/34.   [60] OJ 1977 L174/15.
[61] OJ 1986 L187/23.   [62] Art. 3(4).   [63] OJ 1985 L203/62.
[64] OJ 1985 L211/23.   [65] OJ 1986 L187/23.
[66] Council Reg. 1581/86 art. 3(1)a; OJ 1986 L139/36.
[67] Ibid. art. 3(1)b.

reduced and that consumption is increased.[68] Indeed, in the early part of 1987, following exceptionally cold weather, intervention stocks of certain agricultural products were given away free to be distributed to those in need.[69] and later that year the Council enacted Regulation 3730/87,[70] laying down general rules for the supply of food from intervention stocks to designated organizations for distribution to the most deprived persons in the European Community.

In conclusion, it may be said that the concept of intervention has undergone a profound change. From being a year-round, open-ended guarantee to producers it has become restricted in time, it has been made subject to more restrictive quality standards, some prices have been reduced in real terms in both 1985–6 and 1986–7,[71] payment may be delayed by up to 4 months, and buying in is no longer at the intervention price itself. It remains to be seen whether a reduction in production will ensue.

Import levies and export refunds

The legal nature of import levies has given rise to some contention. As far as the external protection afforded by the levies is concerned, they must, in their objectives, be distinguished from customs duties. The Court pointed out in Case 17/67, *Neumann* v. *Haupzollamt Hof*,[72] that, whatever similarities import levies may have to customs duty, a levy is a charge regulating external trade connected with a common price policy and not a customs duty, as such.

In case 113/75, *Frecassetti* v. *Italian Finance Administration*,[73] the question arose whether a Commission Recommendation relating to customs duties[74] could also be applicable in the case of import levies. This Recommendation set out a general rule subject to certain exceptions, one of which was that where the rate of customs duty was lowered in the period between the goods being declared for customs purposes and finally cleared and released from customs, then the person declaring the goods was entitled to ask for the lower rate of duty to be applied. The Court held that the Recommendation could not be applied to agricultural levies. It was pointed out that the levy is primarily intended to protect and stabilise the Community market; in particular, by preventing price fluctuations on the

---

[68] Case 27/85, *Vandermoortele* v. *Commission* (11 Mar. 1987).

[69] See, e.g., Council Reg. 220/87, on the free supply of intervention stocks of processed cereals to charitable organizations (OJ 1987 L25/2).

[70] OJ 1987 L352/1.

[71] See the recitals to Council Reg. 1584/86, fixing the prices applicable to cereals for the 1986/87 marketing year (OJ 1986 L139/41).

[72] [1967] ECR 441.　　　　　　　　　　[73] [1976] ECR 983.

[74] Commission Recommendation of 25 May 1962 (JO 1962 p. 1545).

world market from affecting prices within the Community. The increase in prices on the world market resulting in a reduction in the levy after the date of acceptance by the customs of the import declaration should, therefore, have no influence on the determination of the rate of levy, since the rate of levy is in principle determined in relation to the purchase price of goods. Consequently, if the authorities concerned were able to put back the dates to be taken into consideration for the determination of the levy, they would risk abusing the levy system to the detriment of Community produce. On the other hand, there is no requirement or, indeed, authorization for the levy to do more than to cover the gap between the world price and the Community price.

This particular problem was faced by the Court in connection with the advance-fixing procedure for levies in Case 6/77, *Schouten* v. *Hoofprodukt-schap voor Akkerbouwprodukten*.[75] Normally the levy to be charged is that applicable on the day of importation. However, an applicant may request advance fixing,[76] and in this case the levy applicable is the one in force on the day on which the licence is applied for, adjusted on the basis of the threshold price which will be in force during the month of importation, and to this levy is added a premium. The premium takes account of world prices or, at any rate, future trends in world prices. In principle, where the current CIF price is higher than the CIF forward delivery for the same product the rate of the premium is equal to the difference between the two prices. Under normal circumstances it does not much matter whether this premium is added to the levy before or after it has been adjusted to take account of the threshold price in the month of importation, because during any given marketing year a threshold price can only go upwards together with the target and intervention prices, the aim being to encourage producers to store some of their harvest. Likewise, on the change-over from one marketing year to the following marketing year it has normally been the case that the basic threshold price fixed for the new marketing year is higher than the highest threshold price fixed for the old marketing year.

However, on the change-over from the 1973/4 to the 1974/5 marketing year the basic threshold price fixed for the new marketing year was lower than the combination of the basic threshold price and the last monthly increases at the end of the previous marketing year. In the *Schouten* case the fall in the threshold price was, in fact, greater than the initial amount of levy, and it is easiest to illustrate the problem on the actual figures involved in that case. In Dutch currency, the current levy at the time the advance fixing was applied for was 0.45 florins per metric ton and the premium for the month envisaged for importation was 4.85 florins, producing a total of

---

[75] [1977] ECR 1291.
[76] Council Reg. 2727/75 art. 15(2); OJ 1975 L281/1.

5.3 florins. The fall in the threshold price was, in fact, the equivalent of 2.9 florins. Since a levy cannot be a negative sum, if the adjustment to the levy was to be carried out before the premium was added to it, then the plaintiffs would still have to pay 4.85 florins. If, however, the initial levy and the premium were lumped together to form a single whole, and then adjusted to take account of the threshold price applicable in the month of importation, then there would be a total of 5.3 florins, from which 2.9 florins could be deducted, leaving the importer to pay a net sum of 2.4 florins per metric ton.

Looking at the purpose served by the levy system, the Court said that, in view of its objective and the function which it fulfils within the system of levies, it is impossible for the correcting factor of the premium to be applied so as to increase the levy fixed in advance beyond what is necessary to cover the difference between the prices ruling outside and within the Community. The Court held that adding the premium after the levy has been adjusted could lead to importations at a level higher than the threshold price, which was incompatible with the principles of the Common Agricultural Policy. The Court therefore deduced that the levy to which the premium is added is not the levy which has been adjusted, but the levy calculated on the day on which the application for the certificate was lodged. The Court ended by stating that the wording of the articles of the regulation in question 'does not necessitate a contrary conclusion'. However, although the Court may have indicated in *Schouten* that the price of imports should not be raised above the threshold price, it has, nevertheless, consistently held that the basic, flat-rate import levy must be applied irrespective of the actual price of the cereals being imported. An extreme example of this came to light in Case 58/86, *Co-opérative agricole des Avirons*,[77] in the context of the importation of South African maize into the French overseas *département* of La Réunion at a price higher than the Community threshold price. The Court stated here that the levy was designed to ensure Community preference[78] and to achieve the objectives of the Common Agricultural policy, and that it did not relate to the prices of individual transactions—indeed, in the view of the Court, traders should arrange import transactions in the light of the Community rules, rather than the other way round.

Conversely, with regard to export refunds, in Case 62/83, *Eximo*,[79] it was held that a trader opting for advance fixing of a refund cannot complain that he would have obtained a higher rate by claiming the refund at the time of export. In practice, differential export refunds may be encountered, calculated so as to take account of the particular characteristics of the market of importation. The European Court has consistently

---

[77] 26 Mar. 1987.   [78] See *supra*, p. 41.   [79] [1984] ECR 2295.

held, as in Case 89/83, *Dimex Nahrungsmittel*,[80] that such refunds, given
their specific nature, are payable only on proof that the goods have been
put into free circulation in the importing state. It is, in fact, a basic feature
of the system of export refunds under art. 16 of Council Regulation 2727/75[81]
that while the refund is the same for the whole Community (in so far as that
is possible under the system of agricultural conversion rates used in the
Community)[82] it may be varied according to use or destination. So far as
the concept of export is concerned, particular problems may occur where
the goods are trans-shipped within the Community. However, in Case 337/85,
Commission v. *Ireland*,[83] it was held that, for the purpose of payment of
export refunds, goods are exported from the first European Community
port in which the customs export formalities are carried out, even if they
are later trans-shipped in another European Community port.

The detailed implementing legislation on export refunds was codified in
1987 in Commission Regulation 3665/87,[84] and, correlative to the
introduction of the new nomenclature for customs purposes in 1988,
Commission Regulation 3846/87[85] established an agricultural product
nomenclature for export refunds.

It would appear to be the system of export refunds that has given rise to
the greatest number of complaints from the Community's trading partners.
However, under GATT rules, even if the refunds are categorized as
subsidies (which the Community would deny) they would be prohibited
only if they could be shown to cause a serious disturbance of trade. It
seems that so far no report of a GATT panel against the EEC has been
formally adopted by the GATT Council or Codes Committees. In the
result, the United States, in particular has tended to take unilateral
retaliatory measures.[86]

Licences and deposits

The system of import and export in the common organization of the
market in cereals is inextricably interlinked with the issue of import and
export licences and their concomitant system of deposits. art. 12 of
Regulation 2727/75[87] requires all imports into the Community or exports
therefrom to be subject to the issue of import or export licences, this issue
being itself conditional upon the lodging of a deposit guaranteeing that
importation or exportation will be effected during the period of validity of
the licence. Although the licences are issued by the national authorities,

---

[80] [1984] ECR 2815.   [81] OJ 1975 L281/1.   [82] See *infra*, pp. 111 ff.
[83] 22 Oct. 1987.   [84] OJ 1987 L351/1.   [85] OJ 1987 L366/1.
[86] See Garcia Bercero, 'Trade Laws, GATT, and the Management of Trade Disputes
between the US and the EEC' (1985) *Yearbook of European Law 149* at pp. 164–71.
[87] OJ 1975 L281/1.

they are Community licences and, in principle, may be issued to any applicant irrespective of the place of his establishment in the Community; in the terms of art. 12, they are valid throughout the Community. This system of import and export licences is widely used in other common organizations, and common detailed rules are contained in Commission Regulation 3183/80,[88] as amended. The core of the system is to be found in art. 8 of that Regulation, providing that the licence comports both an authorization to carry out the transaction and an obligation to carry it out. The use of deposits to ensure that the obligation is performed is widely used in other common organizations, and the method has been adopted for transactions other than import and export. Common detailed rules for the application of the system of securities for agricultural products were consolidated in Commission Regulation 2220/85.[89]

It is in this area that much of the case-law on the principle of proportionality has arisen,[90] the validity of the licence and deposit system being upheld in Case 11/70, *Internationale Handelsgesellschaft* v. *Einfuhr- und Vorratsstelle Getreide*,[91] where the principle of proportionality was raized as a matter of German law, and the Court took account of it as a general principle of Community law. The system was there justified largely on the basis of the need for the Community and the Member States to have precise knowledge of intended transactions:

This knowledge, together with other available information on the state of the market, is essential to enable the competent authorities to make judicious use of the instruments of intervention, both ordinary and exceptional, which are at their disposal for guaranteeing the functioning of the system of prices instituted by the regulation, such as purchasing, storing and distributing, fixing denaturing premiums and export refunds, applying protective measures and choosing measures intended to avoid deflections of trade. This is all the more imperative in that the implementation of the common agricultural policy involves heavy financial responsibilities for the Community and the Member States.

It is necessary, therefore, for the competent authorities to have available only statistical information on the state of the market but also precise forecasts on future imports and exports.

In particular, deposits were needed because licences had to be issued to any applicant:

Since the Member States are obliged . . . to issue import and export licences to any applicant, a forecast would lose all significance if the licences did not involve the recipients in an undertaking to act on them. And the undertaking would be ineffectual if observance of it were not ensured by appropriate means.

[88] OJ 1980 L338/1. [89] OJ 1985 L205/5.
[90] See Barents 'The System of Deposits in Community Agricultural Law: Efficiency v. Proportionality' (1985) EL Rev. 239.
[91] 18 Nov. 1987.

The choice for that purpose by the Community legislature of the deposit cannot be criticized in view of the fact that that machinery is adapted to the voluntary nature of requests for licences and that it has the dual advantage over other possible systems of simplicity and efficacy.

The Court took the view that a mere declaration of transactions effected would not be adequate, and that a system of fines imposed after the event would pose administrative and legal complications, particularly since the traders involved would not necessarily be resident in the Member State seeking to enforce the obligation arizing from the issue of the licence. It also strongly asserted that the system of deposits itself could not be equated with a penal sanction, since it was merely the guarantee that an undertaking voluntarily assumed would be carried out. However, where a trader is required to reconstitute a deposit because the transaction has not been carried out in time, it was held by the 6th Chamber in Case 137/85, *Maizena*,[92] that this was a sanction rather than a guarantee, the sanction being the counterpart of the anticipated release of the deposit.

With regard to the amount of the deposit, the Court held that account should be taken not so much of the deposit itself, which was repayable, but of the costs and charges involved in lodging it, finding that they did not, in that case, constitute an amount disproportionate to the total value of the goods in question and of the other trading costs. However, in its judgment given the same day in Case 26/70, *Einfuhr- und Vorratsstelle* v. *Henck*,[93] the Court did look at the size of the deposit: the case involved advance fixing of an export refund, and the deposit required was several times greater than that required where the refund was not fixed in advance. Nevertheless, the Court again held it to be justified:

It cannot be denied that as a principle it is necessary to fix the amount of the deposit required in the case of 'advance fixing' of the refund at a higher level than in the case of a transaction giving rise to the application of the refund applicable on the day of exportation. As the system of advance fixing was created in the interests of trade, it was necessary to provide at the same time, in the scheme of the regulation, for adequate guarantees to eliminate the possibility that machinery of the common organization of the markets might be upset by speculation made possible by the introduction of this option.

To that end, the deposit was fixed in such a manner as to take into account price trends and consequently the variation in refunds during the period of validity of the export licence. The amount of the deposit must be sufficient to take away from exporters any interest, as the prices on the external markets vary, in changing their export plans as they are apparent from the licences applied for and issued. It appears, therefore, that the requirement of a higher deposit in cases of advance fixing of the refund is a method necessary to guarantee compliance on the part of

_____
[92] [1970] ECR 1125.
[93] [1970] ECR 1183.

exporters with the obligation attached to the issue of the licence and thereby to ensure the accuracy of the forecasts of future market trends.

Taking into account the size of price fluctuations which can occur on the markets in question, this amount in no way appears excessive. Furthermore, determination of the amount of the deposit falls within the discretion of the authority having the power to adopt regulations in the matter.

With regard to the release of the security, art. 29 of Commission Regulation 3183/80[94] provides that the obligation or right arizing from the licence is regarded as having been respectively fulfilled or excised when the customs formalities are completed, subject to the product being put into free circulation. This reflects the Court's earlier case-law which, for the purpose of determining whether the transaction had been completed within the time set by the licence, was prepared to take account of the time at which the goods were submitted to the customs authorities of the importing state, but would only do so if proof was adduced of the fact that the goods had later been put into free circulation.[95]

Regulation 3183/80 does expressly exclude forfeiture of the deposit in cases of *force majeure*.[96] In the *Internationale Handelsgesellschaft case*[97] it was stated that this concept was not limited to absolute impossibility but must be understood in the sense of 'unusual circumstances, outside the control of the importer or exporter, the consequences of which, in spite of the exercise of all due care, could not have been avoided except at the cost of excessive sacrifice'. This could appear to have been slightly relaxed in a pair of judgments in 1974[98] where reference was made to 'abnormal circumstances, outside the control of the importer, and which have arisen in spite of the fact that the titular holder of the licence has taken all the precautions which could reasonably be expected of a prudent and diligent trader'. However, the application of the principle to a particular set of facts in a dispute between a trader and a national agency falls within the jurisdiction of the national court, as was made clear in Case 158/73, *Kampffmayer* v. *Einfuhr- und Vorratsstelle Getreide*,[99] where it was claimed that loss of the import licence in the post constituted *force majeure*. The question, therefore, arose as to whether sending the licence by ordinary post constituted the fulfilment of the duty of care owed by a reasonably diligent trader, and the European Court held that that was a

---

[94] OJ 1980 L338/1.

[95] Case 186/73, *Norddeutsches Vieh- und Fleischkontor* v. *Einfuhr- und Vorratsstelle Schlachtvieh* [1974] ECR 533, 543; Case 3/74 *Einfurh- und Vorratsstelle Getreid* v. *Pfutzenreuter* [1974] ECR 589, 597–8.

[96] Art. 32. More generally, see Loyant, 'La force majeure et l'organization des marchés agricoles' (1980) RTDE 256.

[97] [1970] ECR 1125 at pp. 1137–38.

[98] The cases mentioned in n. 95 at pp. 544 and 599 respectively.

[99] [1974] ECR 101.

matter of the application of the law rather than its interpretation, so that it was for the national court to decide whether the licence holder had acted as a prudent and diligent trader. However, the Court itself has held that to act in reliance upon an assurance of a national customs official that the period of validity of a licence could be extended does not in itself constitute *force majeure*.[100] Most importantly, it was held in Case 109/86, *Theodorakis*,[101] that non-performance by the other contracting party does not constitute *force majeure*.

A legislative version of the distinction the Court has made in its case-law on proportionality between primary and secondary obligations[102] is found in art. 20 of Regulation 2220/85,[103] which distinguishes between primary, secondary and subordinate requirements which a security is intended to guarantee, in so far as the relevant specific Regulation has defined the primary requirement. In this context, secondary requirements are time-limits, and subordinate requirements are any other requirement. Under this scheme, if a primary requirement is not fulfilled the security is forfeited in full, if a secondary requirement is breached, but the primary requirement is fulfilled, 15 per cent of the sum secured is forfeited plus a further percentage for each day by which the time-limit is not met, and if just a subordinate requirement is breached, just 15 per cent of the sum secured is forfeited.

(b) Other products

Other common organizations may use some or all of the techniques noted in the common organization of the market in cereals. A relatively complete combination of internal support and external protection is used for milk, beef and veal, sheepmeat, and sugar, but less comprehensive intervention systems are used for pigmeat, certain fruit and vegetables, and table wine, the last named more often being supported by storage and distillation aids. Other markets rely virtually entirely on external protection alone, notably eggs and poultry, wine other than table wine, and other fruit and vegetables. For some products, such as oil-seeds under Council Regulation 136/66,[104] the Community has made GATT concessions leading to low rates of duty, and, although a target- and intervention-price structure is provided for these seeds, the basic method of ensuring that Community prices are paid is that whenever the target price is higher than the world market price a subsidy is granted for such seeds harvested and processed within the Community, this subsidy being equal to the difference between the target price and the world-market price. It may be observed, however,

---

[100] Case 125/83, *Corman* [1985] ECR 3039.　　　[101] 27 Oct. 1987.
[102] See *supra*, p. 45.　　　[103] OJ 1985 L205/5.　　　[104] JO 1966 p. 3025.

that even here, where it may be suggested that it was anticipated that imports would be the norm, it was found necessary to introduce a 'guarantee threshold' for colza-, rape-, and sunflower-seed in Council Regulations 1413/82[105] and 1101/84.[106] Indeed, Council Regulation 1915/87[107] introduced a system whereby the aid on rape- and sunflower-seed could be reduced, where over-production was anticipated, by an amount equal to the effect of overproduction on the target price. Lastly, there are some products for which flat-rate aids are granted, and in 1988, following agreement in the European Council, a system of automatic reduction of the institutional prices, proportionate to over-production during that marketing year, was introduced.[108] In the case of durum wheat, this is combined with an intervention system,[109] but it is the sole system of support for products such as peas and field beans, dried fodder, hops, flax and hemp, silkworms, and seeds for propagation. Quality standards are of particular importance in some markets, notably fruit and vegetables and eggs, and are the prime concern of the market in live trees and other plants, bulbs, roots, and the like, cut flowers, and ornamental foliage. However, even where intervention exists it will be seen that more restrictive conditions have been imposed, notably in the milk market, and that there has been a move away from open-ended price support for agricultural products. It remains to be seen how far this trend will go, and whether the Community will turn to a system of income support for selected farmers, rather than the general price support for their produce. In April 1987 the Commission did put forward proposals for a Community system of aids to agricultural income and for a framework system for national aids to agricultural income,[110] and under the February 1988 agreement in the European Council on the Community's future financing and new 'own resources',[111] the Council was requested to take a decision on this matter by 1 July 1988. It might, finally, be observed that with regard to products processed from agricultural products the pattern exemplified in Council Regulation 3033/80[112] is to impose, at the external frontiers of the Community, a system of external protection which is a hybrid of customs duties and agricultural levies, comprising a customs duty referred to as the 'fixed component' and an agricultural levy referred to as the 'mobile component', which reflects the Community price of the quantity of the basic agricultural product regarded as being included in the processed product. Similar proportionate export refunds are also envisaged.

[105] OJ 1982 L162/6.
[106] OJ 1984 L113/7.
[107] OJ 1987 L183/7.
[108] See *supra*, p. 57.
[109] See *supra*, p. 54.   [110] OJ 1987 C236/4 and 8.
[111] Agence Europe Special Edition (no. 4722) 14 Feb. 1988
[112] OJ 1980 L323/1.

(i) Milk

Under Council Regulation 804/68[113] a target price is set for milk, but intervention prices are set, with the exception of certain Italian cheeses, only for skimmed-milk powder and butter; that is, forms in which milk may be stored. Hence the 'mountains' of skimmed milk powder and butter. External protection is achieved by setting threshold prices for 'pilot products' representing particular groups of products, other products in that group being termed 'assimilated products', and by charging a levy which is in principle equal to the difference between the threshold price and a free-at-Community-frontier price determined on the basis of the most favourable purchasing opportunities in international trade. Conversely, export refunds may be paid to enable Community milk products to be exported to world markets. As well as this basic system, various aids have from time to time been offered to aid the consumption of surplus butter in particular. Insofar, as such, aids are linked to a particular use of the butter, a consistent case-law has developed to the effect that a successful tenderer remains bound by the obligation to use the butter for that purpose, and cannot assign that obligation to the person who purchases from him, so that the tenderer will be liable to forfeit his security if a subsequent purchaser does not comply with the obligation.[114] There was also a system of premiums for the non-marketing of milk and the conversion of dairy herds, governed by Council Regulation 1078/77,[115] as amended, though this would now appear to be subsumed in the general scheme of compensation for discontinuance of milk production linked to the system of quotas.[116]

As a result of a political agreement reached in the Council of Ministers on 16 December 1986, hailed by the Commission as 'probably one of the most important reached since the inception of the CAP'[117] and as being of importance indirectly for the other common policies, the system of intervention support in the dairy sector has been not only limited in time, as in the cereals market,[118] but also limited in quantity. Under Council Regulation 773/87,[119] art. 7(1) of Regulation 804/68[120] has been amended so that intervention agencies are obliged to purchase skimmed milk powder complying with the relevant conditions only between 1 March and 31 August in each year, and the Commission was given power to modify the intervention arrangements for both butter and skimmed milk under the management-committee procedure, on the basis of criteria laid down by the Council. Such criteria were laid down in Council Regulation 777/87

---

[113] JO 1968 L148/13.   [114] Case 20/84, *De Jong* [1985] ECR 2061.
[115] OJ 1977 L131/1.   [116] See *infra*, pp. 74 and 80.
[117] Introd. to 'Green Europe Newsflash' no. 38.
[118] See *supra*, p. 60.   [119] OJ 1987 L78/1.   [120] JO 1968 L148/13.

modifying the intervention arrangements for butter and skimmed milk-powder,[121] under which intervention buying of butter could be suspended once quantities offered for intervention after 1 March 1987 exceed 180,000 tonnes, and following an amendment by Council Regulation 1112/88[121a] intervention buying of skimmed milk powder could be suspended once the quantities offered in the period from 1 March to 31 August each year exceeded 100,000 tonnes. It was, however, envisaged[122] that buying might be continued on the basis of a standing invitation to tender, that measures might be applied to avoid erratic changes in prices, and that particular account should be taken of the situation in Ireland (also singled out for special treatment under the quota system)[123] and Spain.

If intervention buying is suspended, a safety net is, nevertheless, maintained for butter, in that if the market prices for butter fall to 92 per cent of the intervention price or less for a representative period buying in may be resumed, but subject to a further restriction: if actual stocks of butter (including those dating from before 1 March 1987) exceed 250,000 tonnes, buying in will be resumed only if market prices for butter fall to 90 per cent of the intervention price or less. There is, however, no such safety net for skimmed-milk powder; indeed, it may not be wholly without relevance that the Commission's original proposals for the dairy sector in the early 1960s envisaged intervention only for butter, and the Commission endeavoured to resist intervention buying of skimmed milk powder.[124]

Whilst cynics might see in these changes an explanation for the willingness to subsidise the giving away of certain milk products to the needy in the early part of 1987,[125] later generalized under Council Regulations 3730/87,[126] it would appear that the Commission regarded them as indicating the way forward in other market sectors.[127] Be that as it may, the Commission introduced a further technical restriction of intervention in the dairy sector at the end of 1986, by extending the distance which butter or skimmed-milk powder may be required to be transported without the transport costs being borne by the intervention agency (that is, the offeror simply receives the intervention price) from 100 km. to 350 km.;[128] no doubt, because of the difficulties of finding suitable storage space.

[121] OJ 1987 L78/10. [121a] OJ 1988 L110/32. [122] Ibid. art. 1(3).
[123] Ibid. art. 1(3)c and d. [124] See Neville-Rolfe, *The Politics of Agriculture* p. 242.
[125] See Commission Reg. 246/87, on emergency measures for the free distribution of milk and certain milk products to the most deprived persons (OJ 1987 L25/27).. This followed an amendment of the basic Council Reg. 804/68 by Council Reg. 231/87 (OJ 1987 L25/3).
[126] OJ 1987 L352/1.
[127] As reflected in its proposals for the 1987/8 marketing year, where, for example, it proposed reducing intervention in the cereals sector to the period Feb.–May, and to the rice sector only from Apr.–July.
[128] Commission Reg. 3996/86 (OJ 1986 L339/16) for butter and Commission Reg. 3711/86 (OJ 1986 L342/8) for skimmed milk.

It is also in the milk market that surplus production has given rise to other drastic remedies, albeit not in the form of a general reduction in the level of Community prices. Rather, a system of levies has been used, the first being a milk co-responsibility levy introduced by Council Regulation 1079/77.[129] This, as has been observed, was upheld by the European Court as a measure intended to stabilise markets in Case 138/78, *Stölting* v. *HZA Hamburg-Jonas*,[130] even though it has the effect of reducing prices for most producers; for small-scale milk producers, however, Council Regulation 1210/83[131] introduced a system of income, rather than price, support. This levy did not, in itself, achieve the desired reduction in production, and in 1982, the year that the principle of a guarantee threshold[132] was introduced into the cereals market, Council Regulation 1183/82[133] amended the basic Regulation 804/68[134] so as to introduce a guarantee threshold for milk and milk products, derived from the 1981 production figures plus a margin of 0.5 per cent. However, the passing of this threshold triggered not a reduction in price as envisaged for the cereals market, but the introduction in 1984 of a production quota system linked to an 'additional levy' on deliveries and sales exceeding the quotas, fixed at such a level as to be virtually confiscatory and imposed for a period of eight[134a] years from 1st April 1984. The quotas were originally based on the guarantee threshold plus a further 0.5 per cent (i.e. the 1981 production figures plus 1 per cent[135]), but this figure itself constituted a basis for continued surplus production, and Council Regulation 1335/86[136] provided for it to be reduced by 3 per cent in two stages by March 1988. Following the political agreement in December 1986 to restrict production even more,[137] a further proportion of the quota was 'temporarily withdrawn' by Council Regulation 775/87:[138] 4 per cent of the quota laid down for the third period of twelve months (1986–7) in the fourth period (1987–8), rising to 5.5 per cent of that quota in the remaining periods. Following the extension of the quota system to eight years by Council Regulation 1109/88,[138a] this additional withdrawal has been continued to the end of that period. On the other hand, provision was made to compensate producers for the quantities temporarily withdrawn under Regulation 775/87 at the rate of 10 ECU per 100 kg.,[139] payable in the first three months of the following marketing year; a somewhat higher rate than the level of annual compensation fixed under the general scheme for the permanent discontinuance of milk production under Council Regulation 1336/86,[140] originally

---

[129] OJ 1977 L131/6.　　　　　　[130] [1979] ECR 713.　　　　　　[131] OJ 1983 L132/5.
[132] See *supra*, p. 56.　　　　　　[133] OJ 1982 L140/1.　　　　　　[134] JO 1968 L148/13.
[134a] Extended to eight years by Council Reg. 1109/88 (OJ 1988 L110/27).
[135] Council Reg. 804/68 art. 5c(3) as inserted by Council Reg. 856/84 (OJ 1984 L90/10).
[136] OJ 1986 L119/19.　　　　　　　　[137] 'Green Europe Newsflash' (EC Commission) no. 38.
[138] OJ 1987 L78/5.　　　　　　[138a] OJ 1988 L110/27.
[139] Reduced to 8, 7 and then 6 ECU for the sixth, seventh and eighth years by Reg. 1111/88. Art. 2(1).　　　　　　　　　　　　　　　　　　[140] OJ 1986 L119/21; see *infra*, p. 80.

fixed at 4 ECU per 100 kg., but raised to 6 ECU per 100 kg. by Regulation 776/87,[141] although provision was made in both cases for national supplementation of this compensation within certain limits.[142] By way of contrast with this system of quotas, it may be observed that when faced with surplus production in the cereals sector, the Council in 1986 repealed the concept of a guarantee threshold for cereals and replaced it by a general co-responsibility levy of the type introduced in the milk market in 1977, under art. 1(3) and (4) of Regulation 1579/86.[143] However, in 1988, following the European Council compromise on the Community's future financing and new 'own resources', guarantee thresholds were reintroduced for cereals,[144] coupled with a provisional additional co-responsibility levy of up to 3 per cent, and the possibility of reducing the intervention price by 3 per cent in the marketing year following that in which the guarantee threshold had been exceeded.

Quite apart from its substantive importance, this system shows clearly the problems involved in controlling an 'administered market' at the Community level, and its implementation in the United Kingdom has given rise to the creation of a new type of administrative tribunal, the Dairy Produce Quota Tribunals.[145] At the Community level, as has been noted, the system was introduced by Council Regulation 856/84,[146] inserting the quota and levy provisions into the basic Regulation 804/68, and Council Regulation 857/84,[147] setting out the details of the levy system. The Community implementing rules were established by Commission Regulation 1371/84,[148] which achieved the distinction of being amended ten times in the first fifteen months after its enactment—chiefly, however, to accommodate the inability of certain Member States to collect the levy by the due date. These Community rules were implemented in the United Kingdom by the Dairy Produce Quotas Regulations 1984,[149] revoked and replaced by the Dairy Produce Quotas Regulations 1986.[150]

Essentially, the scheme requires that the levy be imposed in each region of a Member State under one or other of two specific formulas.[151] Under 'Formula A', the levy is payable by the producer on milk delivered to a purchaser which exceeds the reference quantity for the twelve months in question, and under 'Formula B', the levy, is in principle, payable by the purchaser on quantities delivered by producers which exceed the reference quality for that period, the purchaser being under a duty to recover the levy through the price paid by him or it to the producers. However, under

---

[141] OJ 1987 L78/8.   [142] Art. 2(2) of Reg. 775/87; art. 2(2) of Reg. 1336/86.
[143] OJ 1986 L139/29. See *supra*, p. 56.   [144] See *supra*, p. 57
[145] Dairy Produce Quotas Reg. 1984, SI 1984/1047 Reg. 6, Sch. 5, continued by the Dairy Produce Quotas Regs. 1986, SI 1986/470, Reg. 37, Sch. 18.
[146] OJ 1984 L90/10.   [147] OJ 1984 L90/13.   [148] OJ 1984 L132/11.
[149] SI 1984/1047.   [150] SI 1986/470.
[151] Reg. 804/68 art. 5c as inserted by Council Reg. 856/84 (OJ 1984 L90/10).

an amendment introduced by Regulation 773/87,[152] even if overall deliveries do not exceed the purchaser's reference quantity, a Member State may, nevertheless, provide that the levy is due in its entirety from all producers who exceed their production quotas by more than 10 per cent or 20,000 kg., the declared aim being to increase the deterrent effect of the levy. The Member States are required to indicate the regions into which their territory is divided and the formula chosen for each of these regions; considerable flexibility is, however, retained in the United Kingdom, where the statutory instrument enables the Minister (in Scotland, the Secretary of State) to announce the regions into which the United Kingdom is divided by advertisement published in the Gazette and farming press, and similarly to announce the formula chosen for each region.[153] Whichever formula is chosen, there is also provision for levy to be payable on excess quantities sold for direct consumption, and the same producer may, where appropriate, be subject both to a direct-sales quota and a delivery quota (or wholesale quota, to use the United Kingdom terminology).

The reference quantities, or quotas, were, in principle, based on production in the 1981 calendar year plus a margin of 1 per cent,[154] that is, the original 1982 guarantee threshold but with a further 0.5 per cent margin, but for Ireland and Italy the 1983 figures were used. In the Irish case, this was stated to be because of the proportion of the gross national product involved, and in the Italian case because production in 1981 was the lowest for ten years and because Italian yields per cow are relatively low. However, the other Member States could also use suitably weighted 1982 or 1983 figures, and in the United Kingdom, although the 1981 calendar year was chosen for direct sales quotas, the 1983 calendar year was chosen for wholesale quotas. The European Court has held that in exercising this choice the Member States remained subject to the general principle underlying the Common Agricultural Policy, notably art. 40(3) of the EEC Treaty prohibiting discrimination between producers, so that it was not open to the Luxembourg government to choose the year 1981 when, under local conditions of the market, that would have the effect of favouring one particular dairy at the expense of the others.[155] In the United Kingdom, the wholesale quotas were in general determined by reducing the 1983 figures by 9 per cent,[156] though other weightings were used for particular areas, such as Scottish area B (defined as Kintyre, south of Tarbet, and the islands of Arran, Bute, Coll, Gigha, Great Cumbrae, Islay, Little Cumbrae and Orkney) where they were reduced by 5.8135 per

[152] OJ 1987 L78/1.
[153] Dairy Produce Quotas Reg. 1986, Reg. 6.
[154] Reg. 804/68 art. 5c(3) as inserted by Council Reg. 856/84 (OJ 1984 L90/10).
[155] Cases 201 and 202/85, *Klensch* v. *Luxembourg Secretary of State for Argiculture* (25 Nov. 1986).
[156] Dairy Produce Quotas Regs. 1984 Sch. 2 para. 4(c).

cent, thus reflecting the provision of Commission Regulation 1371/84[157] under which the weighting may take account of the trend of deliveries in a region in relation to the average in that Member State.[158] Purchaser quotas are simply the aggregate of the relevant wholesale quotas,[159] and, therefore, may be correspondingly increased or reduced when the wholesale quotas are increased or reduced in accordance with the Community legislation.[160] As has already been noted,[161] these quotas have been reduced by a further 3 per cent under Community legislation,[162] and 5.5 per cent has been 'temporarily withdrawn'.[163]

In addition to the basic reference quantities, at the level of individual producers, the Community legislation envisages that special reference quantities may be made available where milk production development plans were made under the structural Directive 72/159[164] before March 1984 (referred to as a 'development claim' in the United Kingdom legislation),[165] for certain young farmers (not implemented in the United Kingdom), and where 'exceptional events' have occurred in the reference year (referred to as a 'base year revision claim' in the United Kingdom legislation).[166] The Community legislation further permits additional reference quantities to be granted where certain small-scale development plans are approved after the entry into force of the system, and for producers undertaking farming as their main occupation. This last possibility has been taken up in several ways in the United Kingdom legislation: in the context of wholesale quotas, a claim may be made in cases of exceptional hardship, and the Minister may make a general wholesale provision,[167] and with regard to both quotas, the Minister may make a 'small producer provision'.[168] Both of these additional provisions are, however, dependent on the existence of adequate reserves within the relevant quotas at the regional or national level, and the small producer provision (a small producer being essentially one whose aggregate quota is less than 200,000 litres)[169] does not apply to a producer entirely within a remote area (i.e. Scottish Area B and any area outside the scope of a milk marketing board)[170] who has no wholesale quota. However, such producers benefit from additional remote-areas direct-sales provision and remote-areas wholesale provision, again subject to available reserves.[171]

---

[157] OJ 1984 L131/11.   [158] Art. 2.
[159] Dairy Produce Quotas Regs. 1984 Sch. 3 para. 1(a); Dairy Produce Quotas Regs. 1986 Reg. 2.
[160] Dairy Produce Quotas Regs. 1986 Reg. 7(1).
[161] See *supra*, p. 74.   [162] Council Reg. 1335/86 (OJ 1986 L119/19).
[163] Council Reg. 775/87 (OJ 1987 L78/5).   [164] See *infra*, p. 134.
[165] Dairy Produce Quotas Regs. 1986 Reg. 17.
[166] Dairy Produce Quotas Regs. 1984 Sch. 1(9).
[167] Dairy Produce Quotas Regs. 1985 Regs. 16 and 19.
[168] Ibid. Regs. 20 and 21.   [169] Ibid. Sch. 12 para. 1(2).
[170] Ibid. Reg. 2.   [171] Ibid. Regs. 23 and 24.

From the outset, a producer in a region subject to Formula A or B could exchange direct sales quota for wholesale quota with any other producer in that region, but a greater degree of reallocation and redistribution was introduced by Council Regulation 590/85,[172] amending Regulation 857/84. This enabled a producer with both a direct-sales and a delivery (wholesale) quota to increase one at the expense of the other: as expressed in the United Kingdom legislation, the quantity to be converted is limited to the unused element of the relevant quota. More importantly, this amendment, continued for a further twelve months by Regulation 1305/85,[173] also provided generally for the reallocation of unused quotas. As implemented in the United Kingdom, the total amount by which direct sales by sellers who had not used all their quotas fell short of those direct sellers' quotas could be allocated pro rata to those direct sellers who have exceeded their quotas. A similar exercise could be carried out with regard to wholesale and purchaser quotas within a particular region, and an overall shortfall within a region could be allocated to another region with an overall excess of production and used for producers there on a pro-rata basis, and any residual wholesale shortfall could, finally, be distributed between holdings subject to both direct-sales and wholesale quota which had exceeded their aggregate quota. However, the system of reallocation of wholesale quota was made more restrictive in 1987. Under Council Regulation 773/87,[174] the quantities available for redistribution may be reallocated as a matter of priority to producers meeting certain objective criteria rather than proportionately among those who have exceeded their quota, and Member States may provide for the levy to be payable by producers who exceed their quotas by more than 10 per cent or 20,000 kg., even if the overall quantities delivered to the purchaser do not exceed the purchaser's reference quantity. Nevertheless, Council Regulation 2998/87[175] has permitted Member States to authorize the temporary transfer in advance for a period of twelve months of the quota which a producer does not intend to use for that period, so that reallocation need no longer always take place after the event.

At the United Kingdom level, the national direct sales quota and the national wholesale quota are derived from the Community Regulations. Within the national direct-sales quota, a national direct-sales reserve has been created, which comprises any unallocated element of the national quota and any surrendered quotas.[176] The national wholesale quota is divided into regional wholesale quotas, aggregated from producer wholesale quotas, and, apart from an initial, regional wholesale reserve used

---

[172] OJ 1985 L68/1.   [173] OJ 1985 L137/12.   [174] OJ 1987 L78/1.
[175] OJ 1987 L352/1.
[176] Dairy Produce Quotas Regs. 1984 Reg. 7 and Sch. 1 para. 16, to which Reg. 2 of the 1986 Regs. refers back.

effectively to iron out differences between estimated and actual quotas and to allow for development and base-year revision claims, there is a running regional reserve comprising any quantity of wholesale quota not allocated, any surrendered wholesale quotas, and any increase in the regional quota compared with the previous quota year.[177] These reserves are used for the additional provisions described above[178] and as the mechanism for the conversion of direct sales quotas into wholesale quotas and vice versa.[179] Until 1987, there was no specific Community legislation regulating the surrender of quotas by a producer giving up milk production of his own volition, but the European Court held in Cases 201 and 202/85, *Klensch* v. *Luxembourg Minister of Agriculture*,[180] that it would breach the principle of non-discrimination to allocate the quota to the purchaser to which that producer used to deliver, and that it should, rather, be allocated to a national reserve. However, Council Regulation 1899/87[181] introduced a scheme for the reallocation of quotas released by those discontinuing milk production without taking advantage of the EEC schemes of compensation.[182] In such circumstances, the outgoing producer may receive compensation equivalent to the sum paid for the additional quota by the purchaser thereof, provided it is less than the amount which would be payable under the general compensation scheme laid down by Council Regulation 1336/86[183] for the permanent discontinuance of milk production. Transfers between running, regional wholesale reserves may also be used to reallocate the national quota among the regions. At the Community level, there is also a Community reserve, intended to supplement the quotas in Member States in which implementation of the levy system raises particular difficulties liable to affect supply or production structures; until 1986, this was used only to benefit Ireland, Northern Ireland, and Luxembourg. It has subsequently, however, also been used for the benefit of Spain.[184]

The rate of levy where the quotas are exceeded was fixed by Council Regulation 857/84. Under Formula A (where it is paid by the producer) and in direct sales it was originally fixed at 75 per cent of the target price, the target price being higher than the guaranteed intervention prices;[185] under Formula B (where it is paid by the purchaser) it has always been fixed at 100 per cent of the target price, on the basis that the levy will not in practice, necessarily cover all the excess quantities delivered by each producer. For similar reasons, Council Regulation 1305/85[186] introduced levy at the rate of 100 per cent even under Formula A where reference

---

[177] Dairy Produce Quotas Regs. 1984 Reg. 7(2)b and 5(9), to which Reg. 2 of the 1986 Regs. refers back.

[178] See *supra*, p. 77.   [179] See *supra*, p. 76.   [180] 25 Nov. 1986.

[181] OJ 1987 L182/39.   [182] See *infra*, p. 80.   [183] See *supra*, p. 74.

[184] For the 1987/8 marketing year, see Commission Reg. 3331/87 (OJ 1987 L316/18).

[185] See *supra*, p. 54.   [186] OJ 1985 L137/12.

quantities were allocated to producer groups rather than to individual producers, and eventually Council Regulation 774/87[187] introduced the levy at 100 per cent for Formula A as a whole, though it was left at 75 per cent for direct sales. The proceeds of the levy are allocated to the financing of expenditure in the milk and milk-products sectors, and by virtue of Council Regulations 1298/85[188] and 1305/85,[189] Member States could use the income from the levy to grant compensation to producers undertaking definitively to discontinue milk production; that is, in the United Kingdom to make payments under the Milk (Cessation of Production) Act 1985, although a specific Community-funded scheme for the payment of such compensation was introduced by Council Regulation 1336/86[190] and extended by Regulation 776/87.[191] At the same time (and, perhaps, bowing to reality), the levy was declared to be payable annually rather than quarterly, as was initially provided, although statements are required to be made half-yearly. In the United Kingdom, the Intervention Board for Agricultural Produce is responsible for the collection of the levy, but it is empowered to enter into an agreement with any milk marketing board providing for the discharge by the milk marketing board of its functions in this respect.[192]

In the United Kingdom, the Minister (in Scotland, the Secretary of State) is responsible for allocating the various quotas and for maintaining the relevant registers.[193] In this context. it may be observed that. whilst the system of reference quantities, or quotas, relates basically to *producers*, art. 7(1) of Council Regulation 857/84[194] provided for the transfer of a corresponding reference quantity when the *undertaking* was sold, leased, or transferred by inheritance, and, in implementation of this, art. 5 of Commission Regulation 1371/84[195] provides that where part of a holding is transferred the corresponding reference quantity shall be distributed among the producers operating the holding in proportion to the 'areas used for milk production' or according to other objective criteria laid down by the Member States. This phrase, as reproduced in the United Kingdom statutory instrument,[196] was at issue in *Puncknowle Farms* v. *Kane*,[197] wherc it was held that an area used for milk production was not limited to an area used to support cows which are actually lactating but included areas used to support the dairy herd by the maintenance of animals between one lactation and another, and to support the animals which are

[187] OJ 1987 L78/3.
[188] OJ 1985 L137/5.
[189] OJ 1985 L137/12.
[190] OJ 1986 L119/21.
[191] OJ 1987 L78/8.
[192] Dairy Produce Quotas Regs. 1986 Reg. 26.
[193] Ibid. Reg. 6.
[194] OJ 1984 L90/13.
[195] OJ 1984 L132/11.
[196] Dairy Produce Quotas Regs. 1984 Sch. 2 para. 6(3)e; see now Dairy Produce Quotas Regs. 1986 Sch. 4 paras 1 and 2.
[197] [1985] 3 All ER 790.

destined for inclusion in the dairy herd, even, it would appear, if used concomitantly for other purposes.

The problem of the allocation of quotas to tenants was regulated in the United Kingdom by the Agriculture Act 1986,[198] under which a tenant is entitled to a payment calculated under that legislation from the landlord on the termination of his tenancy, unless he has assigned his tenancy or certain defined new tenancies have been granted, in which case the quota is treated as allocated to the assignee or the new tenant (in Scotland, the successor to the right to the lease of the tenancy). The minister also determines the various special claims and additional provisions described above; however, like the Intervention Board,[199] he may enter into an agreement with any milk marketing board providing for the discharge by the milk marketing board of his functions. It is hardly, therefore, surprising that new administrative tribunals were established in the form of three Dairy Produce Quota Tribunals, respectively for England and Wales, Scotland, and Northern Ireland.[200] The Scottish Tribunal differed from the other two as originally established in that it was not assisted by local panels responsible for specific localities; however, its members may sit in separate panels, but as the Tribunal itself, the pattern adopted for the rest of the United Kingdom in 1986. The Tribunal could hear objections to refusals of basic quotas, and in the context of special-case claims could act both as what was termed a further-examination body and as a rejection review body. The 1984 scheme for special case claims was, essentially, that the minister might either reject the claim, which gave rise to the possibility of review, or reserve it for further examination if he accepted it. In jurisdictions with local panels, a further examination resulting in rejection or variation of the claim could be reviewed by the Tribunal. However, this further review would not appear to have been possible in Scotland, where the Tribunal itself was the further-examination body. On the other hand, the pattern established in 1986 for claims in special cases involves the minister simply referring the matter to the Tribunal for determination.

The position of the United Kingdom Milk Marketing Boards was raised in a Declaration on Liquid Milk (and Pigmeat, and Eggs) annexed to the 1972 Act of Accession, and was clarified by Council Regulation 1421/78,[201] enabling certain exclusive rights to be granted to organizations representing 80 per cent in number and 50 per cent of production of milk producers in the relevant area. Council Regulation 1422/78,[202] as implemented in Regulation 1565/79,[203] provided that such special rights were accorded to the five United Kingdom Milk Marketing Boards. Given the historic role of the Milk Marketing Boards as equalization bodies, paying producers a

---

[198] S. 12 and Sch. 1 (England) and Sch. 2 (Scotland).
[199] Dairy Produce Quotas Regs. 1986 Reg. 28.   [200] Ibid. Reg. 27 and Sch. 18.
[201] OJ 1978 L171/12.   [202] OJ 1978 L171/14.   [203] OJ 1979 L188/29.

single price based on aggregate profits made in all markets, the fundamental exclusive right conferred on them[204] is an exclusive right to purchase, coupled with a right to equalise prices paid to producers irrespective of the use for which the milk purchased from them is intended. However, art. 9 of Council Regulation 1422/78, setting out the general rules governing the exercise of these special rights, does allow differentiation of the prices at which milk is resold by the Boards on the basis of the use intended by the buyer, subject to a general prohibition on discrimination between buyers, but this provision was very strictly interpreted by the European Court in Case 23/84, *Commission* v. *UK*.[205] It was there held that this scheme requires the Boards to be subject to very strict control, so that 'differentiation of prices is excluded if it is found to entail risks of distortion or of discrimination, even if it is in conformity with the criterion of intended use or other objective criteria which in theory ought themselves to ensure that such differentiation is compatible with Community law'. Hence, for example, to charge different prices for whole milk depending on whether the butter manufactured therefrom was to be sold as bulk butter or as packet butter was held to be in breach of Community law. Nevertheless, the Court did expressly find that the milk-marketing-board system was 'of indisputable benefit to consumers'.

Protocol No. 18 to the 1972 Act of Accession also laid down conditions for the access of New Zealand butter and cheese to the United Kingdom market. The Protocol itself expired on 1 January 1978, but special arrangements have continued for the importation of specific quantities of New Zealand, the procedures to be followed until the end of 1988 eventually being laid down in Council Regulation 2007/84.[206]

(ii) Beef and veal

The common organization of the market in beef and veal established under Council Regulation 805/68[207] takes as its pivotal point a 'guide price' fixed for calves, and a 'guide price' fixed for adult bovine animals. These guide prices represent the target price in cereals terminology, but also have a role as an activating mechanism. Internally, the guide price was used to determine whether market prices had fallen sufficiently for regional or Community-wide intervention measures to be activated, and the guaranteed intervention price was itself calculated as a percentage of the guide price. As in the cereals and dairy sectors, however, the operation of this system has been altered in an attempt to reduce production and intervention stocks. Hence, since 1985, the intervention price has been lower than that

---

[204] Reg. 1421/78 art. 25.   [205] 2 Dec. 1986.
[206] OJ 1984 L187/6.
[207] JO 1968 L148/24.

which would normally result from the basic legislation,[208] and for the period 6 April 1987 to 31 December 1988 the system was changed[209] so that intervention buying would be authorized only when average Community market prices were less than 91 per cent of the intervention price, and the national or regional average market prices were less than 87 per cent of the intervention price, the buying-in price being calculated from a weighted average of the market prices; in other words, intervention was no longer at the intervention price. To ease the transition, provision was made for payment of a special premium to beef and veal producers, but this was not payable in the United Kingdom, where a system of premiums has been authorized as the standard system of price support. Under this derogation from the normal pattern of price support, a system remarkably similar to the pre-Accession deficiency-payments scheme may be operated. By virtue of this system, where the market price falls below a specified percentage of the guide price, a premium is paid on the slaughter of certain adult bovine animals, to make up the difference, but the meat is not brought into intervention. This premium is subject to 'clawback', however, if the beef is exported,[210] and under the version introduced in 1986,[211] only 40 per cent of the cost is to be met by the European Agricultural Guidance and Guarantee Fund.[212]

External protection is achieved by a combination of customs duties and levies. Imports both of live cattle and of carcas beef are subject to the relevant Common-Customs-Tariff duty, and a variable levy is added to the duty-paid price. This levy is calculated so as to cover the difference between the duty-paid import price and the relevant Community guide price; the basic import price used in calculating the levy, like other world prices used in common organizations, is itself calculated from prices on markets in third countries, and does not relate to individual transactions.[213] How much of this levy is actually payable depends on the price of the products in question on the representative markets of the Community, the levy being lower when this price is above the guide price, and higher when this price is below the guide price.

(iii) Sheepmeat

The sheepmeat regime was established ten years after the expiry of the time-limit for the introduction of common organizations by Council Regulation 1837/80,[214] following, in particular, the dispute between the

[208] See, e.g. Council Reg. 1345/86 (OJ 1986 L119/37).
[209] Council Reg. 467/87 (OJ 1987 L48/1).   [210] See *supra*, p 21.
[211] Council Reg. 1347/86 (OJ 1986 L119/40).   [212] See *infra*, p. 104.
[213] For the complications to which this can give rise, see Case 7/76, *IRCA* v. *Italian Finance Administration* [1976] ECR 1213.
[214] OJ 1980 L183/1.

United Kingdom and France which gave rise to Case 232/78, *Commission v. France*.[215] It has several distinctive features, notably its use both of aid and intervention systems, with further aid permitted from the outset as an alternative to intervention. However, a particular characteristic when it was introduced was that the 'basic price', on which the organization essentially rests, was to be converted into different 'reference prices' for specified regions of the Community, determined originally from previous local prices, with the aim that these prices should converge over a period of four years. These rather belated transitional arrangements for sheepmeat were, nonetheless, held to be valid by the European Court in Case 106/81, *Kind* v. *EEC*.[216] The separate reference prices were, in fact, abolished under Council Regulation 871/84[217] when a single-price system was introduced.

The general system of aid instituted under the common organization has become known in English as the annual ewe-headage payment. The 'maximum guaranteed level' of 63.4 million head of ewes was introduced as a stabilizer by Council Regulation 1115/88.[217a] It is paid, under art. 5, in so far as the average market price in a region is below the basic price per 100 kg.; this difference is, in principle, multiplied by a coefficient representing the normal average production of lamb meat per ewe expressed per 100 kg. of carcas weight. Following Greek accession, Council Regulation 3523/85[218] extended this system of aid to goatmeat producers, at a rate of 80 per cent of the sheepmeat premium, and also provided for its extension, at the same rate, to certain mountain breed ewes which would not otherwise be 'eligible'.[219] In the United Kingdom, the only relevant mountain-breed ewes originally mentioned were Lake District Herdwicks,[220] but subsequent amendments[221] have added Blackface sheep in Lewis and Harris and Cheviots in Sutherland, parts of Caithness, and Ross and Cromarty. A payment on account may be made for producers in 'less-favoured farming areas'[222] where a revenue loss is foreseeable. The intervention system may be activated where the average market price falls below a specified percentage of the seasonally adjusted basic price, intervention purchase being possible where market prices are at or below a seasonally adjusted intervention price of 85 per cent of that basic price, and at or below a seasonally adjusted derived intervention price for the relevant region.

As an alternative to intervention, the amended art. 9 enables the United Kingdom to pay a variable slaughter premium in *Great Britain* where

---

[215] [1979] ECR 2729.   [216] [1982] ECR 2885 at p. 2920.   [217] OJ 1984 L90/35.
[217a] OJ 1988 L110/36.   [218] OJ 1985 L336/2.
[219] Under Council Reg. 872/84 (OJ 1984 L90/40) as amended by Council Reg. 3524/85 (OJ 1985 L336/5), an eligible ewe is a female sheep which, as it is delicately stated, 'has been put to the ram for the first time' or has lambed at least once, but is not a cull ewe.
[220] Annex to Council Reg. 872/84 as amended by Council Reg. 3524/85 (*supra*, n. 464).
[221] See Council Reg. 1970/87 (OJ 1987 L184/23).   [222] See *infra*, p. 137.

market prices fall below a 'guide level' of 85 per cent of the basic price, seasonally adjusted, the amount of the premium being the difference between the guide level and the market price. This premium is, however, subject to 'clawback' when the products are exported from *that region*, so as to ensure the harmonization of prices in trade with other Member States and with the other region of the United Kingdom, Northern Ireland. This was held to be a valid objective in the *Kind* case,[223] at least with regard to trade with other Member States, which was there at issue. However, while the Commission took the view that 'clawback' could be imposed on sheepmeat products not directly benefiting from the premium,[224] on the basis that the premium affected the overall level of prices, this view was successfully challenged by the United Kingdom in Case 61/86, *United Kingdom* v. *Commission*.[225]

Whichever method of support is used, however, the annual ewe-headage payment must be adjusted to take account of intervention purchase or payment of the variable slaughter premium.

External protection with regard to both live sheep and goats (except pure-bred breeding animals) and sheepmeat and goatmeat (except for offals and fat) is achieved by an import levy which is, essentially, based on the difference between the seasonally adjusted basic price and the free-at-Community- frontier offer price, calculated on the basis of 'most representative' purchasing possibilities, with the possibility of a special levy being imposed where the relevant products are exported from a third country at abnormally low prices.[226] There is, however, an overall limit on the levy on meat in respect of which the rate of duty has been bound under GATT, so that the levies are limited to the amount resulting from that binding or to that resulting from voluntary-restraint agreements.[227] Conversely, export refunds, which must be the same for the whole Community but may be varied according to end use or destination, may be paid to enable the relevant products to be exported.[228]

(iv) Pigmeat, poultry and eggs

These products may be considered together to the extent that they are treated as ancillary to the common organization of the market in cereals, and that the legislation governing them, currently Council Regulations 2759/75[229] on pigmeat, 2771/75[230] on eggs, and 2777/75[231] on poultrymeat, has always been enacted in parallel with the legislation governing the common organization of the market in cereals. This parallelism was

---

[223] [1982] ECR 2885 at p. 2922.
[224] See, for example, Commission Regs. 3451/85 (OJ 1985 L328/23) and 9/86 (OJ 1986 L2/14).
[225] [1988] 2 CMLR 98. [226] Reg. 1837/80 arts. 10 and 12 as amended.
[227] Ibid. art. 15 as amended. [228] Ibid. art. 17.
[229] OJ 1975 L282/1. [230] OJ 1975 L282/49. [231] OJ 1975 L282/77.

however, broken in arts. 99–101 of the Greek Act of Accession, where accession compensatory amounts[232] were calculated from the prices of the products themselves, rather than from the prices of feed grain, which was the method used in the 1972 Act of Accession. However, a return was made to the traditional pattern in the Spanish and Portuguese Act of Accession,[233] under which the accession compensatory amounts on pigmeat, poultrymeat and eggs were once again derived from the compensatory amounts applicable to the relevant quantities of feed-grain. Nevertheless, it would appear from the judgment in Cases 71 and 72/84, *Surcouf* v. *Council and Commission*,[234] that *monetary* compensatory amounts[235] on pigmeat were from the outset calculated from the lowest intervention price for pork itself and that it was only in 1984[236] that the system was introduced of deriving these monetary compensatory amounts from those imposed on cereals; it was held by the Court that since under the general system of monetary compensation[237] compensatory amounts could be imposed on products subject to intervention, and since pigmeat was, at least in theory, subject to intervention, then monetary compensatory amounts could be calculated for and imposed on pigmeat, as such.

The most developed of these three common organizations, all of which rest, essentially, on external protection, relates to pigmeat. The pigmeat organization is founded on a 'basic price' which, as a matter of express legislation, must not lead to structural surpluses (and does not appear to have done so), and is calculated from the 'sluice-gate' price and levy on pig carcasses.[238] The sluice-gate price is calculated from the cost, primarily in feed grain, of producing one kilogram of pigmeat on the world market from world market price cereals, and imports of pig carcasses are subject to a levy basically comprising one variable and two fixed elements. The variable element arises insofar as the free-at-frontier price falls below the sluice-gate price, and makes up the difference between them, but does not apply to exports from countries which undertake to respect the sluice-gate price. The fixed elements are a component representing the difference between Community prices and world market prices for the relevant quantity of feed grain, and a component (giving preference to Community products) equal to 7 per cent of the previous year's sluice-gate prices. The internal basic price is calculated, therefore, from this system of external protection, and, although intervention purchasing may be authorized if the market price falls below the basic price, the Commission has a discretion whether to introduce such measures; furthermore, intervention prices may

---

[232] See *supra*, p. 121.   [233] Arts. 114–16, and 325, 327 and 329.
[234] [1985] ECR 2925.   [235] See *infra*, p. 108 ff.
[236] Council Reg. 855/84 (OJ 1984 L90/1).
[237] At that time art. 1(2)a of Council Reg. 974/71 (JO 1971 L106/1).
[238] Reg. 2759/75 art. 4.

range from 78 per cent to 92 per cent of the basic price.[239] Indeed, it would appear from the judgment in Cases 71 and 72/84, *Surcouf* v. *Council and Commission*,[240] that at the date of that judgment (September 1985) no buying in had been authorized by the Commission since 1971,[241] and that the usual method of support had consisted of aids for private storage. However, intervention purchase has subsequently been used as an exceptional support measure for areas hit by African swine-fever.[242]

For eggs and poultrymeat, a similar system is used to calculate sluice-gate prices and levies, but there is no internal guaranteed price support. That the criteria used in these calculations are not immutable is shown by Council Regulations 3232/86[243] and 3233/86,[244] altering the levy and sluice-gate prices respectively for eggs and poultrymeat as a result of changing the quantities of feed grain taken into account and modifying other standard feeding costs in the light of available data. However, all three products may benefit from export refunds where appropriate.

(v) Sugar

The legal interest of the common organization of the market in sugar lies in the fact that, apart from its use of the usual mechanisms of intervention, import levies and export refunds, it has from the outset been subject to a system of production quotas, now copied to some extent in the 'guarantee thresholds' imposed in other common organizations, even though the quota system was intended only to last until 1975.[245]

Under the original version of the sugar market established by Council Regulation 1009/67[246] and continued in Regulation 3330/74[247] a basic quota was allotted to each undertaking for each marketing year, and from this a maximum quota was calculated. Production outside the maximum quota was not to be disposed of on the internal market, and was subject to a levy if it was so disposed of. Even production within the maximum quota but outside the basic quota could be subject to a production levy to help cover the costs of its disposal. Under the current Regulation 1785/81,[248] the basic and maximum quotas are renamed 'A' and 'B' quotas, and the surplus is referred to as 'C' production, and even production within the 'A' quota may be subject to a levy to help meet the costs of disposing of the surplus

---

[239] Council Reg. 1423/78 (OJ 1978 L171/19).

[240] [1985] ECR 2925.

[241] Commission Reg. 641/71 (JO 1971 L73/10).

[242] Commission Reg. 1231/86 (OJ 1986 L112/6).

[243] OJ 1986 L301/1.

[244] OJ 1986 L301/2.

[245] Under art. 22 of Council Reg. 1009/67 (JO 1967 308/1). It was extended to 1990/91 by Reg. 934/86 (OJ 1986 L87/1).

[246] JO 1967 308/1.

[247] OJ 1974 L359/1.

[248] OJ 1981 L177/4. This regulation also incorporated the rules governing isoglucose into the common organization of the market in sugar.

within the 'A' and 'B' quotas, whilst an additional levy may be imposed on the 'B' production. This levy is, of course, only relevant when world prices are lower than Community prices, which has not always been the case with regard to sugar.

Nevertheless, by 1986 the accumulated deficit was such that Council Regulation 934/86[249] introduced an 'elimination levy' designed to eliminate the deficit which had built up to the end of that year, and Council Regulation 1914/87[250] introduced a 'special elimination levy' in the sugar sector for the 1986/7 marketing year, intended to ensure the marketing system was self-financing by multiplying the production levy by a coefficient derived from the relationship of the proceeds of that levy and the loss actually recorded in that year. This was repeated for the 1987/8 marketing year by Council Regulation 1108/88.[250a]

The legal basis of the system of quotas was considered by the Court in Case 250/84 *Eridania*[251] in relation to the Italian market in sugar, with regard to which the Court concluded that it was legitimate to base the quotas on historical production rather than current consumption, so that the Italian production quota could be less than Italian consumption. The underlying rationale appears to be that it is a legitimate Community objective to encourage regional specialization, and that the quota system is not intended to benefit the least efficient producers. Most important of all, the Court stated that Italian producers could not complain about being required to co-finance the disposal of the Community surplus when they did not even meet Italian consumption, on the basis that to claim that producers should be able to limit their liability to surpluses for which those producers were themselves responsible was incompatible with the very concept of a common market. This clear affirmation that quotas serve the interests of Community, rather than national, policy, even when historically derived, may be regarded as being of particular importance given the extension of the quota system to the milk sector.

Under Protocol No. 17 to the 1972 Act of Accession, the United Kingdom was permitted to continue imports under the Commonwealth Sugar Agreement until the end of February 1975, when the first Lomé Convention was signed. This allowed guaranteed access to the Community for specified annual quantities of sugar from named developing countries, and has been reproduced in successive Lomé Conventions, despite the Community's own surplus production.

---

[249] OJ 1986 L87/1.   [250] OJ 1987 L183/5.   [251] [1986] ECR 117.
[250a] OJ 1988 L110/25.

(vi) **Special features of other organizations**[252]

The basic features of a number of the other common organizations have already been described.[253] The market in fruit and vegetables[254] is characterized by the important role entrusted to producers' organizations, which may organize the withdrawal of products from the market and, following the amendments made by Council Regulations 3284/83 and 3285/83,[255] may extend their marketing rules in certain circumstances to non-members, provided they are compatible with Community Law.[256] Provision is also made for classic intervention, but at a buying in price fixed as a percentage of a 'basic price' calculated from market prices, and in 1986[257] the lower end of the range of buying in prices was reduced to 30 per cent of the basic price for cauliflowers, tomatoes, and aubergines, 40 per cent for apples and pears, and 50 per cent for the other products subject to intervention (peaches, table grapes, sweet oranges, mandarins, and lemons). In 1987, Council Regulation 1926/87[258] introduced a system of proportionate reduction of the basic and buying in prices for tomatoes if more than a fixed quantity became subject to intervention.

Whilst, traditionally, the common organization of the market in wine might seem to have been of interest in the United Kingdom from the point of view of the consumer rather than of the producer, the consolidated text in Council Regulation 822/87[259] expressly includes the United Kingdom in Zone A along with German areas other than Baden, Luxembourg, and such well-known wine-producing countries as Belgium and the Netherlands. It is not perhaps, too much of a surprise to note the enactment of Commission Regulation 3713/86,[260] authorizing the United Kingdom to permit an additional increase in the alcoholic strength of English wines to compensate for the bad summer. It has already been observed[261] that the basic system of support involves storage aid and distillation, but for products of Zone A (and the German area of Zone B) there is an overall limit of 1,000,000 hectolitres on the quantity eligible for distillation.[262] The long-term method of restricting surplus production is a prohibition on the planting of new vines currently in force until the end of 1990;[263] the original version of this prohibition was upheld by the European Court in Case 44/79, *Hauer* v. *Land Rheinland Pfalz*,[264] after observing that in all the Member

---

[252] For a more detailed account of the structure of each common organization, see Halsbury's *Laws of England* Vol. 52 ch. 13 (also published as *Law of the European Communities* ed. Vaughan (Butterworths, London, 1986) Vol. 2 ch. 13).
[253] See *supra*, p. 70.   [254] Council Reg. 1035/72 (OJ 1972 L118/1) as amended.
[255] OJ 1983 L325/1.   [256] Case 218/85, *Le Campion* (25 Nov. 1986).
[257] Council Reg. 1351/86 (OJ 1986 L119/46).   [258] OJ 1987 L183/24.
[259] OJ 1987 L84/1. See Annex iv (1).   [260] OJ 1986 L342/18.
[261] See *supra*, p. 70.   [262] Art. 43 of Reg. 822/87.   [263] Ibid. art. 6.
[264] [1979] ECR 3703. See n. in (1980) 5 EL Rev. 209.

States property ownership may be subjected to the requirements of the common good, and that all the wine-producing countries of the Community themselves imposed restrictions on the planting of vines, on the basis that the Community measure was not an undue restriction on the exercise of property rights, being justified by the aims the Community was pursuing in the general interest. By way of contrast, new plantings may be permitted of quality wines in specific regions,[265] with regard to which, because of the quality requirements, production is stated to be far below demand.

A novel development was proposed by the Commission in 1987 with regard to the market in oils and fats, in the form of a 'consumer price stabilization mechanism'.[266] As has been noted,[267] support in this sector rests, in particular, on subsidies; on the premiss that it is when consumer prices for oils and fats are lowest that the cost to the Community budget of maintaining Community production becomes unacceptable but that it is in the interest of consumers that Community production is maintained, this mechanism would have provided for a levy to be charged on any vegetable or marine oil or fat released in the Community for human consumption, or used for the production of food, in so far as the average prices of the preceding year were lower than a reference level calculated from the average of ex-refinery refined-soya-oil prices over the previous five years. Conversely, a consumer subsidy could be paid where the average prices exceeded that reference level. This would have been the first example of a levy imposed on consumers rather than producers, but, taken in the context of oils and fats, it would appear to be intended to meet the problem that where support is by subsidy and there is relatively free access for the products of third countries there will be no 'floor' prices within the Community, and the effect of the levy would appear to be to raise the prices to a particular reference level, an effect not very different in practical terms from that achieved by the traditional intervention system. However, it can hardly escape attention that the effect of such a levy would also be to raise the price of margarine as against that of butter, and the United States took the view that it would to a large extent affect products exported from that country. In the event, the proposal was not accepted by the Council.

(c) *Products not subject to common organizations*

The general principles governing agricultural products which are not

---

[265] See, for example, Council Decision 87/833 allowing new plantings of quality wines in specified regions of France, Spain and italy (OJ 1987 L102/27).

[266] As published in 'Agence Europe' Documents no. 1443 (4 Mar. 1987).

[267] See *supra*, p. 70.

subject to common organizations have been considered in the context of the application of the general rules of the EEC Treaty to agricultural products[268] and in the context of the legal requirement for common policies.[269] However, products which are not subject to a common organization may, nevertheless, still be regulated to some extent by legislation made under arts.38 to 47 of the EEC Treaty. Hence, art. 11 of Council Regulation 2727/75,[270] on the common organization of the market in cereals, provides for a production refund[271] not only on maize and common wheat used in the Community for the manufacture of starch but also on potato starch, even though potatoes themselves are not subject to a common organization. Similarly, although potatoes are not, therefore, subject to Community intervention arrangements, monetary compensatory amounts[272] may be imposed not only on products subject to intervention but also on products whose price depends on the price of intervention products, so that if a monetary compensatory amount (m.c.a.) is imposed on maize starch to reflect the incidence of the m.c.a. on maize (which is subject to intervention), then insofar as potato starch competes with maize starch it may be subjected to the system of m.c.a.'s, provided the m.c.a. on potato starch does not exceed that on maize starch, as was held in Case 145/79, *Roquette* v. *Administration des Douanes.*[273]

(d) The special problems of fisheries

By its very nature, fisheries legislation gives rise to problems not encountered in land-based agriculture, requiring not only the organization of a market in goods, but also the resolution of questions of territorial competence and of external relations. Hence, the Community's Common Fisheries Policy can only be regarded as having been completed on the enactment in January 1983 of Council Regulation 170/83,[274] establishing a Community system for the conservation and management of fishery resources.

(i) Marketing of fish products

A common organization of the market in fishery products was originally introduced by Council Regulation 2142/70[275] as part of the Common Agricultural Policy, and the current version is contained in Council Regulation 3796/81.[276] Inter alia, this common organization comports a price system, involving a guide price and a 'withdrawal' price, at or around

[268] See *supra*, pp. 12 ff.   [269] See *supra*, pp. 23 ff.   [270] OJ 1975 L281/1.
[271] See *supra*, p. 55.   [272] See *infra*, pp. 108 ff.   [273] [1980] ECR 2917.
[274] OJ 1983 L24/1.   [275] JO 1970 L236/5.   [276] OJ 1981 L379/1.

which products may be withdrawn from the market. Externally, the basic Common-Customs-Tariff duties are reinforced by a reference-price system, although the Commission has a number of alternative remedies to choose between if import prices remain below the reference price. The particular feature of the system, however, is the role played by producer organizations, which are empowered to operate the withdrawal system. Non-members may be required to abide by the rules of such organizations and to pay fees covering their administrative costs, and the organizations may levy contributions to finance their intervention measures. On the other hand, aid may be granted to new producer organizations, and Member States are required, within strict limits, to grant compensation for intervention measures. The fundamental limit is that Community reimbursement of this expenditure is on a degressive system as the proportion of fish withdrawn increases.

(ii) Territorial competence

Before accession to the EEC, Council Regulation 2141/70 was adopted,[277] laying down a common structural policy for the fishing industry, setting out the basic principle that rules applied by each Member State in respect of fishing in 'the maritime waters coming under its *sovereignty* or within its jurisdiction' should not lead to differences in treatment of other Member States, and that there should be equal conditions of access to fishing grounds situated in these waters, subject to a five year exemption for certain zones within a three-mile limit. However, one of the few derogations from established Community policy was given in arts. 100 and 101 of the 1972 Act of Accession, which permitted Member States until 31 December 1982 to restrict fishing within a six-mile limit to vessels which traditionally fished in these waters, with an extension to twelve miles in certain defined zones. These provisions were drafted as a derogation from Regulation 2141/70, which was, following the expiry of the five-year period for which it provided, replaced by Regulation 101/76,[278] which repeated the basic principles. However, it may be suggested that the importance of arts. 100 and 101 of the Act of Accession was considerably diminished by the decision of the Council[279] that the Member States should act in concert to extend their fishing zones to 200 nautical miles with effect from 1 January 1977 along their North Sea and North Atlantic coastlines, with the result that thereafter most Community waters were not subject to the Accession derogations. In Case 812/79, *Burgoa*,[280] A.-G. Capotorti suggested, with regard to third country rights in the six-to-twelve-mile zone,

---

[277] JO 1970 L236/1.   [278] OJ 1976 L20/9.
[279] Council Res. of 6 Nov. 1976.
[280] [1980] ECR 2787.

that it was 'wholly untenable' to argue that such rights should apply by analogy in the 12–200 mile zone.

Although the deadline of the end of December 1982 may, therefore, seem to have been of little relevance for the greater part of the fishing zones of the Member States, art. 103 of the Act of Accession enabled the Council to examine the provisions which could follow the derogations in force until the end of 1982. In fact, Council Regulation 170/83[281] provided in its art. 6(1) for the generalization of the exclusive zone up to a limit of twelve nautical miles rather than six, subject to the other conditions of art. 100 of the 1972 Act of Accession. That Regulation was not enacted until 25 January 1983, however, and for the intervening period the Commission purported to authorise the Member States to continue their exclusive zones under the Act of Accession. The validity of this authorization came before the European Court in Case 63/83, *R.* v. *Kirk*,[282] which arose from the prosecution of the Danish MEP, Kent Kirk, for fishing in United Kingdom coastal waters in January 1983, before the enactment of Regulation 170/83. The European Court held that, following the expiry of the derogation under the Act of Accession, the basic principle of equal access re-enacted in Council Regulation 101/76 was fully applicable, so that there was no legal vacuum which the Commission could authorise the Member States to fill, even as trustees of the Community interest.

A further territorial problem arises from the fact that certain of the territories of the Member States are excluded from the Community,[283] or at least excluded from the scope of the Common Agricultural Policy.[284] The problem then arises whether the fishery zones calculated from baselines in the excluded territories are themselves excluded from the scope of the Common Fisheries Policy. Such a view would appear, with one exception, to be supported by Community-Treaty practice: the exclusion of the Faroes under art. 26(3) of the 1972 Act of Accession, introducing art. 227(5)(a) into the EEC Treaty appears to have been accepted as excluding also the fishery limits measured from the Faroes, since in 1977 the Community negotiated an Agreement with the Danish Government acting on behalf of the Faroese Home Government, in order to obtain access for Community vessels to Faroese waters and vice versa.[285] Similarly, the Treaty amendment taking Greenland out of the Community must have been accepted as also taking out Greenland waters, since a contemporaneous agreement was negotiated again to allow Community access to Greenland waters.[286] The exception is that Faroese waters are

---

[281] OJ 1983 L24/1.   [282] [1984] ECR 2689.

[283] EEC Treaty art. 227(5) and 1972 Act of Accession Protocol No. 2 (Faroes).

[284] EEC Treaty art. 227(5) and 1972 Act of Accession Protocol No. 3 (Channel Islands and Isle of Man).

[285] OJ 1980 L226/12.   [286] OJ 1985 L29/9.

expressly included in art. 101 of the 1972 Act of Accession as benefiting from the twelve-mile exemption from equal access, which would not have been necessary if Faroese waters were not within the Community. However, since, conversely, the 1977 Agreement would not have been necessary if Faroese waters were within the Community, the better view may be either to regard the provision in art. 101 as redundant, or as a precaution in anticipation of Faroese accession.

With regard to the Isle of Man and the Channel Islands, art. 227(5) of the EEC Treaty provides that that Treaty shall apply 'only to the extent necessary to ensure the implementation of arrangements for those islands' set out in the 1972 Act of Accession. Protocol No. 3 to that Act, on the Channel Islands and the Isle of Man, provides in art. 1(2) that 'in respect of agricultural products and products processed therefrom which are the subject of a special trade regime' the islands shall apply the levies and other import measures applied by the United Kingdom under Community Law in trade with third countries and also shall apply 'such provisions of Community rules, in particular those of the Act of Accession, as are necessary to allow free movement and observance of normal conditions of competition in trade in these products'. It being now indisputable that sea fish and sea fisheries fall within the scope of the Common Agricultural Policy,[287] the basic legal situation of the Isle of Man and the Channel Islands may be summarized as being that they are in principle excluded from the Common Agricultural Policy, subject to this exclusion being disapplied in the specific instances mentioned in the Protocol.

That the old twleve-mile limits round the Isle of Man were excluded in principle from Community law was accepted—indeed urged—by the United Kingdom Government in Case 32/79, *Commission* v. *United Kingdom*,[288] which involved the legitimacy of United Kingdom fisheries legislation part of which purported to apply to Isle-of-Man waters. Such a view appears also to have been accepted by the Commission in that case, since the Commission argued that Community rules applied by virtue of Protocol No. 3,[289] which is only relevant if the waters in question are not prima facie subject to Community Law. It appears, similarly, to have been accepted by A.-G. Reischl.[290] The Court itself recognized that the twelve-mile belt round the Isle-of-Man was 'subject to special rules',[291] but after having had Protocol No. 3 drawn to its attention the Court expressly asserted that it was not necessary 'to consider the constitutional position of the Isle-of-Man and the relationship of that territory to the Community',[292] so that its judgment can hardly be of authority on that point. Rather, the Court decided the case on mechanical requirements of consultation and the

---

[287] Case 141/78, *France* v. *UK* [1979] ECR 2923.
[288] [1980] ECR 2403. [289] Ibid. at p. 2420. [290] Ibid. at pp. 2472–3.
[291] Ibid. at p. 2439. [292] Ibid. at p. 2444.

principle of non-discrimination, no doubt bearing in mind the Commission's submission[293] that even if Isle-of-Man waters were not subject to the CFP, the United Kingdom was still in breach of its Treaty obligations.

Whilst the legal problem, therefore, remains undecided, it would appear that in practice, the island authorities have co-operated in the administration of the system of log-books, landing declarations and inspections introduced to enforce the system of total allowable catches and quotas by Council Regulation 2057/82[294] and Commission Regulation 2807/83[295] with regard to fishing boats flying the flag of a Member State.

(iii) Internal community competence

Although Regulation 2141/70[296] had foreseen the enactment of measures 'to encourage rational use of the biological resources of the sea', art. 102 of the 1972 Act of Accession specifically provided that 'from the sixth year after Accession at the latest, the Council, acting on a proposal from the Commission, shall determine conditions for fishing with a view to ensuring protection of the fishing grounds and conservation of the biological resources of the sea', thus laying down a time-limit which expired on 31 December 1978.[297] The argument has been put forward that art. 102 conferred a new competence on the Community,[298] but in the view of the European Court fisheries, as such, fall within the Common Agricultural Policy as defined in the EEC Treaty.[299] So far as Community legislation is concerned, there existed skeletal legislation even before the end of 1978, but comprehensive legislation was not adopted until 1983, as has been noted; on the question of competence, however, the situation may be summarized as being that, in principle, Member States could enact their own measures until the end of 1978, subject to their being compatible with such Community legislation as existed, but that thereafter competence has resided in the Community.

The position during the first period was considered by the Court in a group of references from Dutch courts concerned with the application of Dutch catch quotas.[300] The approach of the Court was to see if the Dutch catch quotas jeopardized the objectives and functioning of the system established by the Regulations laying down a common structural policy for

---

[293] Ibid. at p. 2420.

[294] OJ 1982 L220/1; repealed and replaced by Council Reg. 2341/87 (OJ 1987 L207/1).

[295] OJ 1983 L276/1.   [296] JO 1970 L236/1.

[297] Case 185–204/78 Van Dam [1979] ECR 2345.

[298] Hiester: 'The Legal Position of the European Community with Regard to the Conservation of the Living Resources of the Sea' (1976) *Legal Issues of European Integration* LIEI 55.

[299] Case 141/78, France v. *UK* [1979] ECR 2923.

[300] Cases 3, 4, and 6/76, *Kramer* [1976] ECR 1279.

the fishing industry and the common organization of the market in fishery products, and pointed out that the Regulations themselves and art. 102 of the Act of Accession provided for comparable measures and that, indeed, a Regulation adopted after the questions were referred to the Court, Council Regulation 811/76,[301] expressly authorized Member States to limit the catches of their fishing fleets. It concluded that measures for the limitation of catches of fish and the possibility of taking such measures formed an integral part of the general system established by the Regulations.

Similar Dutch catch quotas were again at issue in the *Van Dam*[302] case, and the Court repeated that during the year 1978 (in that instance) the Member States had the right and duty to adopt, within their respective spheres of jurisdiction, any measure compatible with Community law to protect the biological resources of the sea and, in particular to fix fishing quotas. Further, in Case 61/77, *Commission* v. *Ireland*,[303] the Court had said that the Member States were entitled to take appropriate conservation measures 'so long as the transitional period laid down in art. 102 of the Act of Accession has not expired and the Community has not yet fully exercized its power in the matter'. However, this position of principle was affected by the 1976 Hague Resolution, it having been held that the Member States must in enacting new fisheries measures comply with the requirements of the Resolution adopted by the Council at The Hague in November 1976 pending implementation of a Community fisheries policy, on the grounds that that Resolution made specific the duties of co-operation imposed on Member States under art. 5 of the EEC Treaty. Annex VI to that Resolution required a Member State taking unilateral fisheries measures to consult the Commission and seek its approval, and in Case 141/78, *France* v. *UK*,[304] the United Kingdom was held to be in breach of its Treaty obligations by bringing into force the Fishing Nets (North-East Atlantic) Order 1977 without so doing. Hence, even from November 1976, any new, national fisheries measure would appear to require Community approval. If, however, such approval was sought and obtained, then a Member State could set total allowable catches, and divide them among other Member States, at least where it followed the Commission's proposals, as was held in Case 287/81 *Kerr*,[305] with regard to Danish catch quotas.

The position after the end of 1978 had to be considered by the European Court in Case 804/79, *Commission* v. *UK*,[306] where, as has already been observed in the context of the legal requirement for common policies,[307] it was held that Member States were no longer entitled to exercise any power

301 OJ 1976 L94/1. 302 [1979] ECR 2345. 303 [1978] ECR 417.
304 [1979] ECR 2923. 305 [1982] ECR 4053. 306 [1981] ECR 1045.
307 See *supra*, pp. 23 ff.

of their own in the matter of conservation measures in the waters under their jurisdiction, at least with regard to resources to which the fishermen of the other Member States had an equal right of access (which left the question open with regard to exclusive zones), and that, although the Council had not taken the relevant conservation measures, the transfer to the Community of powers in this matter was total and definitive, so that such a failure to act could not in any case restore to the Member States the power and freedom to act unilaterally in this matter. Hence, conservation measures must, in principle, until Community rules were enacted, remain as they were at the end of 1978, subject to amendment to take account of biological and technological developments, but Member States had no power to lay down new conservation policies; with regard to such amendments, or the introduction of necessary, interim conservation measures, the Member States might only act 'as trustees of the common interest' so that they became under a duty 'not only . . . to undertake detailed consultations with the Commission and to seek its approval in good faith, but also . . . not to lay down national conservation measures in spite of objections, reservations or conditions which might be formulated by the Commission'. This approach may, perhaps, be explained by the fact that, as will be seen, the Court has derived an exclusive external competence from the Community's internal competence, and the internal and external aspect of fisheries policy are so interlinked that the exclusivity of the one must be reflected in the other.

Be that as it may, this principle was at issue in the first reference for a preliminary ruling to be ordered by a Scottish court, Case 24/83, *Gewiese and Mehlich* v. *Scott Mackenzie*,[308] which concerned the prosecution of German fishermen for fishing for herring off the west coast of Scotland in 1981 under a 1981 Order which re-enacted a 1978 Order forbidding herring fishing in the relevant area. It was held that no fresh consultation of the Commission was required in the case of the re-enactment, without substantive amendment, of a national measure for the conservation of fishery resources which had previously been adopted in conformity with the procedural and substantive conditions laid down by Community law.

It would appear that, until the enactment of Council Regulation 170/83,[309] the system prescribed in Case 804/79, *Commission* v. *UK*,[310] was applied in practice, the Commission from time to time publishing lists of national conservation measures which had been the subject of Decisions by it.[311] Certain relatively limited Community measures were enacted, such as Council Regulation 2527/80[312] on technical measures for the conservation of fishery resources dealing with such matters as net mesh sizes, which, in turn, enabled the issue of specific measures such as Commission Regulation

---

[308] [1984] ECR 817.   [309] OJ 1983 L24/1.   [310] [1981] ECR 1045.
[311] e.g. OJ 1981 C218/2.   [312] OJ 1980 L258/1.

2962/81[313] regulating the use of trawls, Danish seines, or similar nets off the west of Scotland for the period 1 October 1981–31 March 1982. More generally, the Commission put forward proposals for a general policy, from time to time amending them, and, failing its adoption of these measures, as such, the Council at regular intervals issued Decisions[314] on fisheries activities 'in waters under the sovereignty or jurisdiction of Member States' (sovereignty here being of a rather titular nature) requiring Member States, *inter alia*, to observe the total allowable catches (TAC's) laid down in the Commission's proposals. The Commission itself even issued a declaration to the effect that it considered these proposals to be legally binding on the Member States.[315]

How far this declaration accurately stated the law seemed unlikely to be determined, following the adoption of a Community policy in Council Regulation 170/83,[316] the basic function of which is to enable total allowable catches to be set and to be distributed among the Member States 'in a manner which assures each Member State relative stability of fishing activities for each of the stocks considered'.

However, the point was directly raised before the Court in Case 346/85, *UK* v. *Commission*,[317] arising out of the refusal of the European Agricultural Guidance and Guarantee Fund[318] to finance United Kingdom fishery activities which were alleged to contravene the Commission's proposals. In its judgment, the Court stated categorically that unilateral proposals by the Commission were not rules of Community law, emphasizing, in particular, that legislation having financial consequences should be certain and of foreseeable applications.

Regulation 170/83 is, essentially, a framework regulation[319] enabling the Council by qualified majority to enact catch quotas, in the light of the advice of a Scientific and Technical Committee for Fisheries set up under the auspices of the Commission,[320] these quotas being calculated on a Community basis[321] and then distributed among the Member States.[322] The total allowable catches are normally set on an annual basis.[323] One practical problem which emerged was that over-fishing by vessels of certain Member States could lead to the closure of a fishery where other Member States had not yet used up their quota. Whilst Regulation 170/83 itself enabled Member States to exchange quotas by mutual arrangement,[324] a

[313] OJ 1981 L297/13.   [314] e.g. Council Decision 82/807 (OJ 1982 L339/57).
[315] OJ 1981 C224/1.   [316] OJ 1983 L24/1.   [317] 15 Dec. 1987.
[318] See *infra*, p. 104.
[319] For the history of the development of the Common Fisheries Policy, see Wise, 'The Common Fisheries Policy of the European Community' (1984).
[320] Reg. 170/83 arts. 2 and 12.   [321] Ibid. art. 3.   [322] Ibid. art. 4.
[323] See, e.g. Council Reg. 4034/86 (OJ 1986 L376/39), setting the total allowable catches for 1987.
[324] Art. 5(1).

Commission implementing Regulation enacted in 1987 provided an administrative mechanism for compensation between 'over-fishing' and 'prejudiced' Member States.[325]

(iv) External Community competence

That exclusive implied external competence may derive from the exercise of internal Community competence is a concept first enounced by the European Court in 1971 in the context of the European Road Traffic Agreement (AETR).[326] That exclusive implied external competence may arise once the time for implementing the internal policy has expired is a concept which has largely developed in the context of fisheries policy.

The point arose in Cases 3, 4, and 6/76, *Kramer and Others*.[327] These were references from Dutch courts in the context of criminal proceedings brought against fishermen accused of having breached Dutch legislation aimed at ensuring the conservation of stocks of sole and plaice in the north-east Atlantic in pursuance of the Netherlands' obligations under the North-East Atlantic Fisheries Convention of 1959 (NEAFC). Summarizing the questions which are here relevant, the Court was asked, in effect, whether the Community alone had authority to enter into commitments such as the Convention.

It was found that, in the absence of specific provisions of the Treaty authorizing the Community to enter into international commitments in the sphere of conservation of the biological resources of the sea, it was necessary to look at the general system of Community law in the sphere of external relations of the Community. The Court then considered the relevant Treaty provisions and also the Regulations then in force laying down a common structural policy for the fishing industry and the common organization of the market in fishery products. From this it deduced that the Community had at its disposal, on the internal level, the power to take any measures for the conservation of the biological resources of the sea, including the fixing of catch quotas. It also said that the only way to ensure the conservation of the biological resources of the sea, both effectively and equitably, was through a system of rules binding on all the States concerned, including non-Member States. In these circumstances, it followed from the very duties and powers which Community law had established and assigned to the institutions of the Community on the internal level that the Community had authority to enter into international commitments for the conservation of the resources of the sea. However, the Court then turned to the question whether the Community had, in fact, rather than as a possibility, assumed the functions and obligations

[325] Commission Reg. 493/87 (OJ 1987 L50/13).
[326] Case 22/70, *Commission* v. *Council* [1971] ECR 263. [327] [1976] ECR 1279.

arising from the Convention and from decisions taken thereunder. The Court found that at the time the Convention was entered into, in 1959, the Community had not issued any Regulations relating to the sea fishing industry and also those Regulations which had eventually been made limited themselves to providing the Community institutions with the power to take measures similar to those the Member States concerned had committed themselves to taking and did take, and that, so far, the institutions had not made use of that power. The Court concluded that, since the Community had not yet fully exercized its functions in the matter at the time the question arose, the Member States had the power to assume commitments within the framework of the North-East Atlantic Fisheries Convention and, consequently, had the right to ensure the application of those commitments within the area of their jurisdiction. However, it added a rider that this authority of the Member States was only of a transitional nature and that the Member States concerned were, by the time of that judgment, bound by Community obligations in their negotiations within the framework of the Convention and other comparable agreements. The Court, in fact, pointed out that the authority of the Member States should end from the sixth year after Accession at the latest, because under art. 102 of the Act of Accession the Council must by then have adopted measures for the conservation of the resources of the sea.

It has, in fact, been widely accepted by academic commentators that thereafter the Community has exclusive external authority with regard to fisheries,[328] and, more importantly, this has also been accepted by other negotiating parties. So, the Community, as such, is a party to the North West Atlantic Fisheries Convention 1978 and to the North East Atlantic Fisheries Convention 1981, the latter replacing the old NEAFC.

So far as bilateral relations are concerned, the Council adopted a series of Regulations laying down interim measures for the conservation and management of fisheries resources applicable to vessels flying the flags of various non-Member States, which, in turn, were followed by formal agreements with such states, including neighbours with a particular interest in fisheries such as Norway[329] and Spain,[330] as well as more distant countries such as Canada.[331] It may be observed that these agreements were based on the total-allowable-catch system, even though they antedated any overtly binding internal Community measure giving effect to TAC's. Bilateral agreements have also been made to enable Community

---

[328] Koers, 'The External Authority of the EEC in Regard to Marine Fisheries' (1977) CML Rev. 269. Baumann, 'Common Organizations of the Market and National Law' (1977) CML Rev. 303. Churchill, 'Revision of the EEC's Common Fisheries Policy' (1980) EL Rev. 3.
[329] OJ 1980 L226/48.
[330] OJ 1980 L322/4.
[331] OJ 1981 L379/54.

fishermen to fish off developing countries, such as Senegal[332] and Guinea Bissau,[333] paying compensation to those countries for the privilege.

(v) Relationship to previous international arrangements[334]

Under art. 234 of the EEC Treaty, rights and obligations arising from agreements concluded before the entry into force of that Treaty between one or more Member States, on the one hand, and one or more third countries, on the other, are not to be affected by the provisions of that Treaty, and under art. 5 of the 1972 Act of Accession this protection applies to agreements or conventions concluded by the United Kingdom, Ireland and Denmark before accession. Hence in Case 812/79, *A.-G.* v. *Burgoa*,[335] it was held that this provision applied to the 1964 London Fisheries Convention with regard to the relationship between Ireland and Spain; however, the case involved a Spanish vessel caught fishing twenty miles off the Irish coast, and the European Court, acting on the basis that it was accepted that the London Convention applied only to the zone up to twelve miles from the Irish coast, held that the 12–200-mile zone was governed by the relevant Council Regulation applying interim measures for the conservation and management of fishery resources applicable to vessels flying the flag of Spain, which was 'superimposed' on the regime previously applied in that zone, as to which the Court did not commit itself.

Although it has now been overtaken by Spanish Accession, the Community did enter into a formal agreement with Spain,[336] which contained an express declaration to the effect that 'the purpose of this Agreement is to establish the principles and rules which will govern, in all respects, the fishing activities of vessels of either Party within the fishing zones falling under the jurisdiction of the other Party' subject to one defined exception. On the other hand, the Agreements with Norway[337] and Sweden[338] (arts. 4 and 5 respectively) are expressed to be without prejudice to other existing agreements concerning fishing by vessels of one party within the area of fisheries jurisdiction of the other. Whatever the latter may mean, it was held that the effect of the Spanish Agreement was to replace earlier international agreements, so that Spanish fishermen could no longer rely on the London Convention in EEC waters.[339] However, more contentious, and possibly of wider relevance, is the

---

[332] OJ 1980 L226/17 and OJ 1985 L361/86.

[333] OJ 1980 L226/34 and OJ 1983 L84/2.

[334] See Churchill and Foster, 'European Community Law and Prior Treaty Obligations of Member States: The Spanish Fishermen's Cases' (1987) ICLQ 504.

[335] [1980] ECR 2787.   [336] OJ 1980 L322/1.   [337] OJ 1980 L226/48.

[338] OJ 1980 L226/2.

[339] Cases 50–8/82, *Administrateur des Affaires Maritimes* v. *Dorca Marina* [1982] ECR 3949.

attitude taken to the status of agreements not protected by art. 234 of the EEC Treaty within the twelve mile zone (but outside the six mile exclusive zone) as against EEC Regulations imposing interim measures with regard to vessels flying the flag of a relevant non-Member State. This was the problem faced in Case 181/80, *Procureur général Pau* v. *Arbelaiz-Emazabel*,[340] which involved a Spanish vessel caught fishing in 1977 between six and twelve miles from the French coast off Bayonne, without being in possession of the licence required by the relevant Council Regulation laying down interim measures for vessels flying the Spanish flag. It was argued on behalf of the Spanish skipper that under a 1967 Agreement between France and Spain, concluded within the framework of the 1964 London Fisheries Convention, Spanish nationals were entitled to fish in the area in question. Although these agreements clearly did not fall within the protection of art. 234, the European Court accepted, on the basis of its Kramer[341] judgment, that since the Community had not at that stage exercized its powers in the matter and its competence had not then become exclusive, France could validly enter into the agreements in question. It was also clear that the new Agreement between the EEC and Spain was not signed until 1980; however, the Court took account of the fact that the interim measures were expressed to be adopted 'pending the conclusion of the fishing agreements currently being negotiated' and of the fact that the Spanish authorities collaborated in the implementation of the Community interim measures, passing lists of licence applications to the Commission, and distributing the licences granted, so that they fell 'within the framework of the relations established between the Community and Spain in order to resolve the problems inherent in conservation measures and the extension of fishery limits'. The Court, thus, concluded that these relations 'replaced' the prior international obligations existing between certain Member States, such as France and Spain.

Whether a different view would have been taken if the Community's negotiating partners had been less co-operative remains a matter of speculation, although it must be said that in the context of general commercial policy the Court has held that measures of commercial policy of a national character are only permissible after the end of the transitional period by virtue of specific authorization by the Community;[342] transposed to fisheries, this would appear to mean that previous arrangements made at the national level must, at least after 1978, give way to Community measures, unless protected by art. 234 or specifically authorized. It has, indeed, been suggested that the situation could have arisen where the Member State would have been in breach of its EEC Treaty obligations if it had not applied the Community interim measures, but would have been in

---

[340] [1981] ECR 2961.   [341] [1976] ECR 1279.

[342] Case 41/76, *Donkerwolcke* v. *Procureur de la République, Lille* [1976] ECR 1921.

breach of its Treaty obligations to the non-Member State under general international law if it had applied these measures.[343]

The continuing importance of the fisheries issue may be evidenced by the fact that the Act of Accession of Spain and Portugal[344] lists by name the Spanish boats entitled to their, initially very limited, right of access to the waters of the older Member States. However, the basic criteria of nationality used under the Community fisheries legislation are the flag flown by a vessel or the Member State in which it is registered, so that catches by a vessel flying the flag of a Member State and/or registered in it count against the quota allocated to that State.[345] Hence problems developed with regard to Spanish owners using vessels flying the flag of, or registered in, other Member States in order to circumvent their limited right of access.[345a]

[343] White, 'Fishery Rights of Non-Member States in Community Waters' (1982) EL Rev. 415.
[344] Art. 158 and Annex IX.
[345] Council Reg. 2057/82 (OJ 1982 L220/1) art. 10.
[345a] See e.g. Case 223/86 *Pesca Valentia* [1988] 1 CMLR 888.

5

Common organizations of the market: financial mechanisms

(a) European Agricultural Guidance and Guarantee Fund

It is expressly provided in art. 40(4) of the EEC Treaty that in order to enable the common organizations to attain their objectives one or more Agricultural Guidance and Guarantee Funds may be set up. It would appear that the Commission originally proposed the creation of separate funds for each product subject to a common organization of the market, with exceptional provisions for transfers from one fund to another.[1] In fact, a single European Agricultural Guidance and Guarantee Fund was established by Council Regulation 25/62 of 4 April 1962,[2] the same date as that of Council Regulation 19/62,[3] on the gradual establishment of the common organization of the markets in cereals, the first regulation dealing with common organizations of the market. This regulation provided that the Fund should form part of the Community budget and that as single market organizations were established the revenue from import levies should accrue to the Community budget and the Fund should finance export refunds and intervention purchases.

The fact that the levies accrue to the budget and the Fund finances refunds and intervention does not, however, make the agricultural policy self-financing, because there is no correlation at all between income and expenditure. If there is a high level of production of a particular agricultural product, it is quite likely that there will be a high level of intervention buying, and that is going to mean high expenditure for the Fund, whereas, at the same time, there will be a low level of imports, and, therefore, little in the way of import levies, and little income for the Fund.

Under Council Regulation 17/64[4] the Fund was split into a guarantee section which includes expenditure relating to refunds and intervention, and a guidance section which includes expenditure relating to measures undertaken in order to attain the objectives of the Common Agricultural Policy set out in Article 39; in particular, matters of structural policy. As part of the move towards the replacement of financial contributions from Member States by the Communities' own resources, Council Regulation

---

[1] Neville-Rolfe, *The Politics of Agriculture in the European Community* (Policy Studies Institute, London, 1984), p. 212.
[2] JO 1962 p. 991.   [3] JO 1962 p. 933.   [4] JO 1964 p. 586.

729/70,[5] on the financing of the Common Agricultural Policy, expressly states that both sections shall form part of the budget of the Communities. Under Article 3 of Council Decision 243/70,[6] replaced from 1 January 1986 by art. 2 of Decision 85/257,[7] the total revenue from agricultural levies is entered in the budget of the Communities.

A new feature was added by the February 1988 compromise in the European Council on the Community's future financing and new 'own resources'.[8] Under this agreement, a reference base was introduced for agricultural expenditure, fixed at 27,500 million ECU for 1988. It was further provided that the annual rate of increase in guarantee section expenditure must not exceed 80 per cent of the growth in GNP, subject to an adjustment to allow for the guarantee section's contribution towards the costs of the 'set-aside' scheme included in that same agreement [9]

However, the day-to-day administration of the Common Agricultural Policy is the responsibility of the national authorities, who both collect money on behalf of the Community, by virtue of art. 6 of Council Decision 243/70, replaced from 1 January 1986 by art. 7 of Decision 85/257, and make payments where so required under the various common organizations. Indeed, in Case 99/74, *Grands Moulins des Antilles* v. *Commission*,[10] it was held that the liability of Member States to make payments required under a common organization exists even where the Fund refuses, or is unable, to reimburse such payments. The details of the relationship between the Fund and the national authorities will be considered in the context of the administration of the Common Agricultural Policy,[11] but Community financing of the CAP manifests the principle of 'financial solidarity'.[12] Indeed, it may be observed that in its Opinion 1/84,[13] given shortly before the Fontainebleau agreement to increase the 'own resources' of the Community,[14] the Court of Auditors, which has overall responsibility for financial control in the Communities,[15] expressed the view that art. 5 of the EEC Treaty, requiring Member States to ensure fulfilment of the obligations arising out of the Treaty or resulting from actions taken by the institutions, and art. 199, requiring all items of revenue and expenditure of the Community to be shown in the budget, together imposed a legal obligation on Member States, given the exhaustion of the Community's 'own resources' in 1984, to make available the balance of the funds necessary to cover budgetary requirements in 1984. What the views of the Court of Justice and of the Court of Auditors have in common is that the

[5] JO 1970 L94/13.   [6] JO 1970 L94/19.   [7] OJ 1985 L128/15.
[8] Agence Europe Special Edition (no. 4722) 14 Feb. 1988.   [9] See *infra*, p. 135.
[10] [1975] ECR 1531.   [11] See *infra*, p. 150 ff.   [12] See *supra*, p. 41.
[13] OJ 1984 C228/5.
[14] June 1984, resulting ultimately in the enactment of Decision 85/257 (*supra*) increasing VAT 'own resources' to a flat rate of 1.4 per cent .
[15] EEC Treaty, art. 206a.

costs of the policies the Member States have agreed must ultimately be borne by those States, whether directly or indirectly. Indeed, in anticipation of the exhaustion of Community budgetary resources in 1987, Council Regulation 3183/87[16] required the Member States to make payments in accordance with the needs of the disbursing authorities when the guarantee allocation for 1987 had been used up.

(b) Common prices

The prices mentioned so far—intervention, target, and threshold prices, and also the import levies and export refunds—are all fixed in units known as 'units of account'. Indeed, the basic system of price fixing in the common organizations of the market is that there is a uniform price throughout the Community which is expressed in units of account. Whilst the need to use a unit of account which was not the currency of any one Member State may seem to be politically self-evident, it would appear that the negotiations which led to the establishment of market organizations based on a single Community price were conducted in terms of Deutschmarks,[17] and it will be seen that the Deutschmark has continued to play an important role in the calculation of agricultural prices. Under Regulation 129, of 23 October 1962,[18] the unit of account used for the Agricultural Policy was defined at a value of 0.88867088 grammes of fine gold, which happened to be the official value of the United States dollar. Art. 2 of that Regulation provided that where sums given in one currency were required to be expressed in another currency the exchange rate to be applied should be that which corresponded to the par value communicated to and recognized by the International Monetary Fund.

The basic financial mechanism, then, was that agricultural prices were fixed in uniform units of account converted into national currencies at the official parity. The problems to which this gave rise in a world of floating exchange rates will be described in the next section, since they led to the introduction of the system of monetary compensatory amounts and agricultural conversion rates.

Nevertheless, the basic principle remains that Community agricultural prices are set at a single level in units of account. Council Regulation 652/79[19] replaced the old unit of account by the European Monetary System unit of account (ECU), albeit converted into national currencies at an agricultural conversion rate rather than at its market conversion rate, and this system was consolidated in Council Regulation 1676/85,[20]

---

[16] OJ 1987 L304/1.　　　　　[17] Neville-Rolfe, *The Politics of Agriculture* p. 231.
[18] JO 1962 p. 2553.
[19] OJ 1979 L84/1.　　　　　[20] OJ 1985 L164/1.

repealing and replacing the much-amended Regulation 129/62 with effect from 1 January 1986.

The ECU is a 'basket' currency unit, defined in 1984,[21] following the inclusion of the Greek drachma, as comprising 0.719 German mark, 0.0878 pound sterling, 1.31 French francs, 140 Italian lire, 0.256 Dutch guilder, 3.71 Belgium francs, 0.14 Luxembourg francs, 0.219 Danish krone, 0.00871 Irish pounds and 1.15 Greek drachmas. Since these fixed amounts of currency do not automatically change when changes are made to the central rates, or market values fluctuate, the percentage composition of the basket in terms of these currencies is susceptible to change: the percentage share of a currency which rises in value will increase, and that of a currency which goes down in value will decrease. If the composition of the unit is formally changed, this must not have the effect of changing the overall value of the unit with regard to other currencies,[22] and the initial value of the ECU[23] was required to be the same as that of the previous European Unit of Account (EUA)[24] which had been created in 1975 for the purposes of the first Lomé Convention,[25] using the same system of a 'basket' of currencies, and had become widely used within the Community. The external value of the EUA, in turn, was derived from the value in June 1974 of the 'Special Drawing Rights' (SDR) of the International Monetary Fund,[26] based on a basket of currencies which gave a heavy weighting to the United States dollar, the original value of the SDR being, in turn, based on the gold value of the US dollar.[27] Hence, a link can be traced between the original unit of account and the modern ECU. The daily value of the ECU in terms of Member States' currencies is published in the 'C' series of the Official Journal.

There have, however, been exceptions to the principle of single prices expressed in units of account. In Case 8/78, *Milac v. HZA Freiburg*,[28] despite the reference in art. 40(3) to a common price policy, the Court was prepared to accept that different prices could be set in units of account for different Member States when, as a result of floating exchange rates, this would give rise to greater uniformity in terms of national currencies— although this could be said to add a further corrective element to the

[21] Council Reg. 2626/84 (OJ 1984 L247/1).
[22] Resolution of the European Council of 5 Dec. 1978 art. 2(3) (EC Bulletin 12/78 para 1.1.11).
[23] Defined by Council Reg. 3180/78 (OJ 1978 L379/1).
[24] Resolution of the European Council of 5 Dec. 1978 art. 2(1) (EC Bulletin 12/78 para 1.1.11).
[25] See Usher, 'Financing the Community' in *Thirty Years of Community Law* (1983) pp. 195–6.
[26] Council Decision 75/250 (OJ 1975 L104/35).
[27] International Monetary Fund Articles of Agreement art. 21 s. 2; see Mann, *Legal Aspects of Money* (Oxford 4th ed. 1982) pp. 507–8.
[28] [1978] ECR 1721.

correction already carried out by monetary compensatory amounts. On the other hand, Council Regulation 1889/87 introduced differentiation of prices expressed in ECUs as a method of trying to eliminate 'negative' m.c.a.s.[29] For different, but still pragmatic, reasons, the Court also accepted in Case 106/81 *Kind* v. *EEC*,[30] that the widely differing reference prices for sheepmeat in different regions of the Community could be accepted in the initial stages of the common organization of the market in sheepmeat, provided the aim was to achieve an eventual co-ordination of prices.

(c) *Conversion rates and monetary compensatory amounts*

Since single market organizations with single price structures were only introduced in the late 1960s (in 1967 in the case of the basic-cereals organization), the genuine single-price system only operated for about four years at most. There were incidental problems, like the fall of the French franc in 1969, which led to the restrictions on the sale of French cereals into intervention in Germany which were at issue in the *Mackprang* case,[31] but the real problems began with the collapse of the system of fixed exchange rates in 1971. The problem, then, was initially caused by the floating upwards of the German and Dutch currencies. If, for example, an intervention price had been fixed in German marks at the official parity, then, during the course of the marketing year, the value of the mark went upwards in relation to other currencies, but the number of marks a producer received per metric ton of cereals still remained the same, then there would be a very considerable inducement, for example, to French cereal growers, to sell all their cereals to the German intervention boards and, in terms of French francs, get considerably more than they would from the French intervention agencies.

The response to this was Council Regulation 974/71,[32] the full title of which makes ironic reading. It is stated to be on 'Certain measures of conjunctural policy to be taken in agriculture following the temporary widening of the margins of fluctuation of the currencies of certain Member States'. The title betrayed, however, not so much the expectation that the measures would be short-term in duration as the fact that the Regulation was enacted under art. 103 of the EEC Treaty on conjunctural policy, which allows the Council to act without consulting the European Parliament, unlike art. 43 on agricultural policy. It in fact remained in force, albeit much amended, until the end of 1985, being replaced by a consolidated and revised version enacted in Council Regulations 1677/85[33]

---

[29] OJ 1987 L182/1; see *infra*, p. 112.   [30] [1982] ECR 2885.
[31] [1975] ECR 607; see *supra*, p. 35.   [32] JO 1971 L106/1.   [33] OJ 1985 L164/6.

with effect from 1 January 1986. Council Regulation 1677/85 more honestly describes itself as being 'on monetary compensatory amounts'.

Regulation 974/71 introduced monetary compensatory amounts, in a form, in fact, appropriate for Member States whose currency had floated upwards, in that those States whose currency had fluctuated by a margin wider than the one permitted by international rules were to be authorized to charge compensatory amounts on imports, be it from Member States or third countries, and grant compensatory amounts on exports, be it to Member States or third countries. The imports and exports in question were, and still are, of products subject to the intervention procedure or of products whose price is dependent upon that of an intervention product, in circumstances where disturbances of trade would otherwise occur. Thus, the compensatory amounts compensated for the fact, in real terms, that imports had become cheaper and exports had become more expensive. The compensatory amounts were to be calculated by applying to prices the percentage difference between the official parity of Member States' currency and the arithmetic mean of the spot-market rates of this currency against the United States dollar during a particular period. So, under this system the real value of a currency was measured in terms of United States dollars. The use of the exchange rate of a currency against the dollar, doubtless intended as being synonymous with the unit of account, meant that when the dollar floated downwards in late 1971 the system of monetary compensatory amounts was able to accommodate this effective devaluation. In fact, monetary compensatory amounts were even introduced in trade with Italy, because although the lira had gone down in comparison with other European currencies in terms of the dollar its value had gone up. The Court held in Case 94/77 *Zerbone* v. *Italian Financial Administration*,[34] that the introduction of m.c.a.s in trade with Italy was valid.

Under Council Regulation 2746/72,[35] m.c.a.s were brought under direct Community control within the Common Agricultural Policy, Member States no longer being 'authorized' to charge them. A new factor was introduced, however, following the accession of the new Member States in 1973, recognizing that, for the purposes of converting prices and amounts under Common Agricultural Policy, 'conversion rates should be applied which are not based on parities but are more in line with economic realities'. Council Regulation 222/73[36] on the exchange rates to be applied in agriculture for the currencies of the new Member States, created representative rates for the conversion of the currencies of the United Kingdom and Ireland. As a matter of history, the conversion rate therein established was that £1 was equal to 2.3499 United States dollars.

---

[34] [1976] ECR 99.   [35] JO 1972 L291/148.   [36] OJ 1973 L27/4.

Following this, and for the same reason, Council Regulation 509/73[37] extended the system of monetary compensatory amounts to currencies which had effectively decreased in value as well as to those which had effectively increased in value. In the case of depreciated currencies the monetary compensatory amounts are granted on imports to make up for the fact that they have become more expensive in real terms and they are levied on exports to make up for the fact that they have become cheaper in real terms.

This regulation also introduced a new paragraph 1(a) into art. 1 of Regulation 974/71 recognizing the existence of conversion rates other than the official parity and allowing, in appropriate cases, for these conversion rates to replace the official parity for the purposes of the calculations under that regulation. The next amending Regulation 1112/73[38] introduced a new version of art. 2 of the 1971 regulation using a global formulation, 'the conversion rate used under the Common Agricultural Policy', which was apt to cover conversion both at the official parity and at representative rates where applicable. This regulation also introduced a much more important reform in the system of calculating m.c.a.s.

Following the introduction of the joint float known as the 'snake', under which the majority of Member States' currencies floated together in relation to other currencies, maintaining as between themselves a maximum variation in their spot-market rates at any given moment of 2.25 per cent, Regulation 1112/73 took account of the introduction of this system to use the snake currencies instead of the United States dollar as a reference for the calculation of monetary compensatory amounts. art. 2(1) of the 1971 regulation, as amended by this regulation, used a double method of calculating m.c.a.s. For Member States whose currencies were within the snake, the m.c.a.s were obtained by applying to the relevant prices the percentage difference between the conversion rate used under the Common Agricultural Policy and the conversion rate resulting from the central rates of those currencies. For the other Member States it was, in reality, the relationship of their currencies to the snake currencies that was important. The m.c.a.s for these Member States were obtained by applying to the relevant prices the average of the percentage differences between the relationship of their agricultural conversion rates to the parities or central rates of the snake currencies and the relationship of the spot-market rates of their currencies to the snake currencies. In other words, the currencies remaining within a band of 2.25 per cent were used as the standard for determining the real value of other Member States' currencies, and also for determining the value such currencies were deemed to have for the purposes of the Common Agricultural Policy, and

---

[37] OJ 1973 L50/1.   [38] OJ 1973 L114/4.

this system was continued even after the introduction of the European Monetary System. Monetary compensatory amounts were obtained by multiplying the relevant Community prices of individual products by the difference between these two values expressed as a percentage.

In September of that same year, Council Regulation 2543/73[39] amended the old Regulation 129[40] so as to simplify the procedure for making derogations from that regulation. Under this procedure Council Regulation 2544/73[41] was made introducing a representative rate for the conversion under the Common Agricultural Policy of the currency of one of the original Member States, the Dutch guilder. According to the recitals to that regulation, this was done so as to avoid introducing monetary compensatory amounts in the internal trade of the Benelux Customs Union. Subsequently, in October, Regulation 2985/73[42] introduced a representative rate for the Italian lira, noting in its recitals that the system of applying m.c.a.s to prices converted at official parities 'has led to different price levels in the Member States affected' and that the m.c.a.s applicable in trade with Italy could be reduced by fixing a representative conversion rate of the Italian lira at a level more closely related to the actual economic situation.

Eventually Council Regulation 475/75[43] fixed, for the first time, representative rates for the conversion of the currencies of all the Member States, creating what are popularly referred to as 'green' currencies. This process has, in fact, been repeated in each annual price-fixing round. Hence, agricultural conversion rates have become as much a matter for political decision as agricultural prices under common organizations. By 1978/9, for example, German prices in national currency were some 45 per cent higher than United Kingdom prices in national currency,[44] in terms of market exchange rates.

The introduction of the European Monetary System,[45] and the use of the ECU in agriculture by virtue of Council Regulation 652/79,[46] made no real difference, since the ECU continued to be converted at agricultural conversion rates like the old unit of account, and one of the characteristics of the European Monetary System is that, like the old 'snake', its members (except for Italy) maintain their currencies within a spread of 2.25 per cent.

The system of conversion consolidated in Council Regulation 1676/85[47] is that the agricultural conversion rate is used for conversion between the ECU and national currencies—and it clearly appears from Council

[39] OJ 1973 L263/1.   [40] JO 1962 p. 2553.   [41] OJ 1973 L263/2.
[42] OJ 1973 L303/1.   [43] OJ 1975 L52/28.
[44] See Usher,'Agricultural Markets: Their Price Systems and Financial Mechanisms' (1979) EL Rev. 147, 152.
[45] Resolution of the European Council of 5 Dec. 1978 (EC Bulletin 1978 No. 12 Point 1.1.11).
[46] OJ 1979 L84/1.   [47] OJ 1985 L164/1.

Regulation 1678/85,[48] fixing the agricultural conversion rates, that the same Member State may have different rates for different products—but for conversion between ECU and non-Member State currencies or world prices the central rate is used for Member States within the 2.25 per cent band, and for other Member States use is made of the average relationship between their spot-market rates against the currencies of those Member States within the 2.25 per cent band and their central rates. With regard to the system of m.c.a.s under Council Regulation 1677/85,[49] the basic system of calculation is as described above. Whilst the calculation of monetary compensatory amounts for currencies within the 2.25 per cent band is relatively straightforward, for the other currencies it is more complex. Taking the United Kingdom milk sector as an example, if the agricultural conversion rate is 1 ECU = £0.618655,[50] and the central rate of, for example, the Deutschmark is 1 ECU = 2.05853 DM, then the agricultural value of the pound expressed in terms of the central rate of the Deutschmark is that £0.618655 = 2.05853 DM, so that £1 = 3.327428 DM. If the spot market rate for the pound is, however, £1 = 2.9275 DM,[51] the percentage difference is 12.019133 per cent . This calculation must be repeated in terms of the other currencies falling within the narrow band of the European Monetary System, and the m.c.a. for the pound is the average of those percentage differences. Certain aspects are described in simpler terminology. In particular, the Regulation specifically defines 'positive' m.c.a.s, which constitute a charge on imports and a subsidy on exports and arise where the central or market rate is higher than the agricultural conversion rate, and 'negative' m.c.a.s, which constitute a subsidy on imports and a charge on exports, and arise where the central or market rate is lower than the agricultural conversion rate. Further, the m.c.a. is defined as filling the 'monetary gap', which is the real monetary gap between agricultural conversion rates and central or market rates, minus a small 'neutral margin', to allow for small fluctuations without changing the m.c.a.s.

This system is, however, subject to a further corrective factor introduced for a three year period by Council Regulation 855/84[52] on the calculation and 'dismantlement' of m.c.a.s, and reproduced in Regulation 1677/85.[53] This Regulation reflected a political will to narrow the differences in representative rates, and was intended to eliminate 'positive' m.c.a.s, which have a tendency to encourage over-production by allowing producers to be paid more than their competitors in other Member States.[54] This corrective factor had the effect of taking the strongest Community

[48] OJ 1985 L164/11.   [49] OJ 1985 L164/6.   [50] Example taken in Mar. 1987.
[51] Example taken in Mar. 1987.   [52] OJ 1984 L90/1.   [53] OJ 1985 L164/6.
[54] See Strauss, 'The Economic Effects of Monetary Compensatory Amounts' (1983) JCMS 261.

currencies as the basis for calculation, and had the result of reducing, therefore, positive m.c.a.s, even if it initially increased 'negative' m.c.a.s.

The 1987 target date proved optimistic, and in 1987 a graduated programme was adopted to phase out 'positive' m.c.a.s by the beginning of the 1989/90 marketing year, under Council Regulation 1889/87.[55] This provided for the corrective coefficient to be increased and in case of a realignment of currencies to be altered automatically in line with the currency the revaluation of which against the ECU was the highest. Conversely, it introduced provisions for the elimination of 'transferred negative' m.c.a.s; that is, those created by the operation of this coefficient, over a three-year period following the revaluation, and for the elimination of other 'negative' m.c.a.s created since the last realignment of parities. However, recognizing that the devaluation of the 'green rate' of a national currency to eliminate negative m.c.a.s will increase prices in national terms, hence, possibly, leading to further over-production, provision is made for the 'common' prices in ECUs to be reduced for the Member States concerned, to neutralize any increase in terms of national prices which would otherwise result from the devaluation of the 'green rate' necessary to eliminate the transferred negative m.c.a.s. It remains to be seen, however, whether such different prices will themselves require compensation in trade between Member States.

It may, however, be doubted whether m.c.a.s can be totally eliminated in a system in which agricultural prices are fixed for a whole year at a time, but there are floating exchange rates and some Member States remain outside the joint float organized under the European Monetary System.

It will be apparent from this that the original financial mechanism introduced by Regulation 974/71[56] has undergone a very considerable evolution. No longer does it compensate the difference between the official parity of a Member State's currency and the real value of that currency measured in terms of the dollar. Rather, it compensates the difference between an artificial representative rate for a Member State's currency and the real value of that currency measured in terms of those Community currencies remaining within a band of 2.25 per cent.

(d) Legal problems of monetary compensation[57]

The fundamental problem of monetary compensation relates to the legality of the system itself. It is undeniable that m.c.a.s do constitute a partitioning of the market and, indeed, the Court recognized as much in its

---

[55] OJ 1987 L182/1. [56] JO 1971 L106/1.

[57] See Gilsdorf, 'The System of Monetary Compensation from a Legal Standpoint' (1980) 5 EL Rev. 341 and 433.

earliest decisions in the matter, Case 9/73, *Schlüter* v. *Haupzollamt Lörrach*,[58] and Case 10/73, *Rewe* v. *Haupzollamt Kehl.*[59] However, the Court also recognized in those cases that the danger to the unity of the common market arose from the national monetary measures, that is, the floating of the exchange rates, for which the m.c.a.s were intended to compensate, not from the m.c.a.s themselves. The Court held that, even though m.c.a.s do constitute a partitioning of the market, diversion of trade caused solely by the monetary situation can be considered more damaging to the common interest. However, in Cases 80 and 81/77, *Ramel* v. *Receveur des Douanes*,[60] the Court went on to suggest that the failure to co-ordinate divergent monetary policies was contrary to art. 105 of the EEC Treaty, which requires such co-ordination to ensure the equilibrium of the balance of payments and to maintain confidence in the national currencies.

With regard to the legality of the agricultural conversion rates, the Court recognized in Case 138/78, *Stölting* v. *HZA Hamburg-Jonas*,[61] that the absence of representative rates could give rise to even worse discrimination, and that they did serve to remedy current monetary situations, although it may be wondered how far monetary situations can justify different exchange rates for different products in the same Member State.

Under the scheme of Regulation 974/71,[62] as re-enacted in Council Regulation 1677/85,[63] the system of m.c.a.s applies only to products covered by intervention arrangements or to products whose price depends on the price of intervention products, and m.c.a.s can only be applied where application of the monetary measures in question would lead to disturbances in trade in the relevant agricultural products. The aim of the system was stated, in Case 46/84, *Nordgetreide*[64] to be to protect the single price system, not national markets. Similarly, in Case 236/84, *Malt*,[65] the Court made clear that monetary compensatory amounts are not intended to produce a protective effect with regard to imports from third countries, but that there was no obligation to offer equal treatment to all third countries. On the other hand, where m.c.a.s are payable on import into a Member State, they are only attracted if the goods actually enter the market of the Member State of import.[66] The Court has, in fact, consistently held that the Commission enjoys a wide discretion in assessing the risk of disturbance. So, in Case 55/75, *Balkan* v. *Hauptzollamt Berlin-Packhof*,[67] it was stated that the Regulation cannot be interpreted as obliging the Commission to decide case by case or in respect of each product individually whether there is a risk of disturbance. Further, the

[58] [1973] ECR 1135.   [59] [1973] ECR 1175.   [60] [1978] ECR 927.
[61] [1979] ECR 713.   [62] JO 1971 L106/1.   [63] OJ 1985 L164/6.
[64] [1985] 3127.   [65] 24 June 1986.
[66] Case 254/85, *Irish Grain Board* (11 Nov. 1986).   [67] [1976] ECR 19.

Court held that in reviewing the legality of the exercise of such discretion it must confine itself to examining whether it contained a manifest error or constituted a misuse of power or whether the authority did not clearly exceed the bounds of its discretion. The only cases in which a manifest error has been shown concerned price dependency rather than the risk of disturbance. In Case 131/77, *Milac*,[68] a Commission Regulation was held to be invalid in so far as it applied m.c.a.s to trade in powdered whey, it being shown that there was no correlation of prices between powdered whey and skimmed-milk powder, the relevant intervention product.

The particular problem of derived products was at issue in Case 4/79, *Providence Agricole de la Champagne*,[69] and Case 145/79, *Roquette* v. *Administration des Douanes*.[70] Under the Regulations, the m.c.a. on the dependent product should be equal to the incidence on its price of the m.c.a. on the intervention product. The Court started from the premise that the aim of the system of m.c.a.s was to 'neutralize' the difference between the current exchange rate for a currency and its 'representative' or 'green' rate expressed in units of account, and went on to emphasise that m.c.a.s must be strictly neutral in character, unlike import levies which could be protective in nature. From this it concluded that m.c.a.s which obviously went beyond what was necessary to compensate the difference between prices expressed in real and representative exchange rates would no longer be helping to maintain the single price system, but would become akin to charges having equivalent effect to customs duties. Similarly, whilst recognizing that there were difficult technical and economic problems in calculating m.c.a.s on derived or dependent products, and that flat-rate m.c.a.s might not give exactly the right degree of compensation for each undertaking or producer, the Court held that, in this context, the Commission would exceed the limits of its discretion if it used a method of calculation which consistently went beyond what was necessary to take account of the incidence on the price of the dependent product of the m.c.a. on the intervention product.

In those cases, where it was admitted by the Commission that the sum of the m.c.a.s on the derived products exceeded the m.c.a. on the basic product, the Court stated as an overall limit on the Commission's discretion that, whatever the difficulties in calculating the precise m.c.a. for each derived product, this should not occur; it made clear, however, that the mathematical limit on the sum of the m.c.a.s on derived products only applied where these products could be obtained from the same manufacturing process. Hence, it distinguished the process by which maize was made into meal, flour, germs, and bran and sharps from that by which it was made into starch, gluten, and germs. On the other hand, the Court

[68] [1978] ECR 1041.   [69] [1980] ECR 2823.   [70] [1980] ECR 2917.

suggested that the mathematical limitation on the m.c.a.s on dependent products should not apply where the m.c.a. on the processed product is calculated not from that on the basic product (indeed, the Court put forward the hypothesis of a basic product not subject to m.c.a.s) but from that on a competing product.

This was the situation in the *Roquette* case with regard to potato starch. Although there was no intervention price for potatoes, and, hence, no m.c.a. on potatoes as such, it was agreed that the price of potato starch depended on that of maize starch, and the Court deduced from this that the incidence of the m.c.a. in maize on the price of potato starch must be regarded as being the same as its incidence on the price of maize starch, and, hence, that the m.c.a. on potato starch could not exceed that on maize starch. These judgments do not, however, mean that the Commission must achieve absolute mathematical equilibrium in calculating m.c.a.s on derived products. In *Providence Agricole* the error was of the order of 30 per cent, and in *Roquette* the error was about 12 per cent, but involving also a wrong basis of calculation, but in Case 39/84, *Maizena*,[71] and Case 46/84, *Nordgetreide*,[72] it was held that divergences respectively of 5.9 per cent and 4.3 per cent were not sufficient to invalidate the calculation.

A further difficulty arises largely from the fact that until the enactment of Commission Regulation 243/78,[73] currently re-enacted in Regulation 3155/85,[74] there was no mechanism for the advance fixing of monetary compensatory amounts. Hence, the Court has been faced with a large number of actions in which traders have claimed, depending on the facts of the case, that the introduction or abolition of m.c.a.s for a particular product, or the change from one system of m.c.a.s to another, or, indeed, even a change in the rates of m.c.a.s, has breached that trader's legitimate expectations.

The Court's view was clearly stated in Case 97/76, *Merkur* v. *Commission*.[75] It was there said that the aim of the system of compensatory amounts is, in particular, to obviate the difficulties which monetary instability may create for the proper functioning of the common organizations of the market, rather than to protect the individual interests of traders. The Court further said that although the possibility of protecting the legitimate interests of the trader cannot be excluded, nevertheless, the Community could only be rendered liable for the damage suffered by such traders as a result of the adoption of legitimate measures governing the system of m.c.a.s if in the absence of any overriding public interest the Commission were to abolish or modify the compensatory amounts applicable in a specific sector with immediate effect, and without warning,

[71] [1985] ECR 2115.   [72] [1985] ECR 3127.   [73] OJ 1978 L37/5.
[74] OJ 1985 L310/22.   [75] [1977] ECR 1063.

and in the absence of any appropriate transitional measures, and if such abolition or modification was not foreseeable by a prudent trader. This may be contrasted with Case 74/74, *CNTA* v. *Commission*,[76] which is, perhaps, more likely to be remembered for having established the principle that the Community can be liable even for valid legislative acts in certain circumstances rather than for the likelihood of anybody suffering from the system of m.c.a.s being able to claim to be in the same position again. The facts of the case arose in the days when m.c.a.s were calculated on the basis of the values of Member States' currencies calculated in terms of the dollar. The harm in that case was alleged to have been caused by the withdrawal by Commission Regulation of m.c.a.s applicable to colza- and rape-seeds, thus causing loss to the applicants in performing certain contracts for the sale of these seeds to purchasers in non-Member States.

With regard to the question of legitimate expectation, the Court held that the application of m.c.a.s in practice avoided the exchange risk, so that even a prudent trader might be induced to omit to cover himself against such risk. Whilst it may be that a reasonable trader could regard m.c.a.s based on the values of national currencies in terms of the dollar as covering the exchange risk, it may be doubted whether any reasonable trader could regard an m.c.a. designed to cover the difference between a politically, rather than economically, calculated representative rate and the real value of a national currency in terms of a basket of other Community currencies as being in any way necessarily related to exchange risks. In so far as the analogy may be appropriate, it was held in Case 299/84, *Neumann*,[77] that when the agricultural conversion rates themselves were changed there was no necessary implication that the Council intended to avoid a purchaser tendering before the change in 'green' rates paying more in terms of national currency than a purchaser tendering after that change.

The question of transitional measures, the absence of which gave rise to liability in the CNTA case, was first put on a general footing by Commission Regulation (EEC) 1608/74,[78] on special provisions in respect of monetary compensatory amounts. This granted a Member State discretion under certain conditions to waive m.c.a.s or a proportion thereof, where m.c.a.s were introduced or increased as a result of changes in the central rate or representative rate of the currency of that Member State or (in effect) as a result of a decision to leave the currencies kept within a band of 2.25 per cent. It was pointed out by A.-G. Mayras, in his Opinion in the *Debayser* case,[79] that the relief under this Regulation did not extend to simple changes in the rates of m.c.a.s as a result of changes in the spot-market rates for a currency. Indeed, it may well be doubted whether a trader can ever have a legitimate expectation of the maintenance

---

[76] [1975] ECR 533.
[78] OJ 1974 L170/38.

[77] [1985] ECR 3663.
[79] [1978] ECR 553, 581.

of current rates for m.c.a.s, given that they should reflect currency changes. In Case 146/77, *British Beef* v. *Intervention Board*,[80] it was specifically held that the plaintiff could not have a legitimate expectation in the maintenance in force for the whole week of a Regulation freezing m.c.a.s at the previous week's rate, when it was clear from its recitals that it had only been adopted pending a possible alteration by the Council of the representative rate for sterling. The Court held that, once it was clear that this would not be done, they could not fail to recognize that the Commission had no further grounds for not fixing new m.c.a.s on the basis of the rates of exchange recorded. In fact, the Regulation which superseded Regulation 1608/74 was itself repealed without replacement by Commission Regulation 1084/84[81] on the grounds that the system was not really workable unless a system of deposits was introduced in relation to the relevant contracts; in the recitals to that Regulation it is suggested that it should be for the parties to make suitable allowance for the introduction or increase of m.c.a.s in their contracts. The current legislation on transitional measures concerning the application of m.c.a.s contained in Commission Regulation 3156/85 relates[82] rather to the avoidance of deflection of trade.

(e) *Monetary compensation and price compensation*

It will be seen that at the external frontiers of the Community importers or exporters of agricultural products are liable to encounter two forms of compensation, which must be distinguished: price compensation covering the difference between world prices and the Community price, and monetary compensation, theoretically covering the difference between the current value of a currency and its agricultural conversion rate. There is, in fact, a danger that they may overlap. With regard to products subject to both forms of compensation, an importer who wishes to import such a product into a Member State with a revalued currency from a third State, when its world price is lower than the Commununity price, will have to pay an import levy and a monetary compensatory amount. However, the m.c.a. is, basically, calculated by applying the relevant percentage to the whole Community price, which, in reality, in this case will consist of a world price paid at current exchange rates, and a levy expressed in units of account and converted at the agricultural conversion rate into the currency of the relevant Member State. If the m.c.a. were so calculated, the result would be that the levy element in the Community price would be subject to

---

[80] [1978] ECR 1347.
[81] OJ 1984 L106/26.
[82] OJ 1985 L310/27.

procedures having the same aim twice:[83] it would be converted at the agricultural rate and then have an m.c.a. added to it to bring it in line with the agricultural rate, the result for the importer being double taxation. Conversely, export refunds in such a situation would be too large, as a result of the double conversion.

The initial solution to this problem was that the Commission calculated different m.c.a.s for trade with third countries and trade between Member States. From 1973[84] onwards a single m.c.a. has been calculated, which has been subjected to a corrective coefficient in the case of trade with third countries. The rules were consolidated into Commission Regulation (EEC) 1380/75,[85] laying down detailed rules for the application of m.c.a.s, art. 4(3)(b) of which provided that in trade with third countries the import charges and the export refunds and levies fixed in units of account should be multiplied by a coefficient to be derived from the percentage used to calculate the monetary compensatory amount. This basic principle is maintained in art. 6 of Commission Regulation 3153/85,[86] laying down detailed rules for the calculation of m.c.a.s, which in turn requires the coefficient to be applied not only to refunds and levies but also to accession compensatory amounts expressed in ECUs.

The 1975 version of this provision was considered by the Court in two cases of particular interest. In Case 79/77, *Kühlhaus Zentrum* v. *HZA Hamburg-Harburg*,[87] the plaintiff imported frozen beef from Argentina into Germany as part of a tariff quota opened under GATT agreements, giving exemption from the import levy. Nonetheless, the full rate of m.c.a. was applied. The plaintiff, however, rather than challenge the imposition of m.c.a.s as such in these circumstances, claimed that the m.c.a. should be reduced by the amount by which the levy would have been reduced by applying the corrective coefficient, if a levy had been imposed, on the basis that all monetary compensation attributable to that part of the Community price which corresponded to a notional levy should be eliminated. The Court held that the Regulation could not be so construed; it provided only for the reduction of the levy, and if there was no levy there could be no reduction. On the other hand, the Court did express strong doubts as to the appropriateness of applying m.c.a.s to tariff quotas admitted free of import levies.

Case 108/77, *Wagner* v. *HZA Hamburg-Jonas*,[88] involved the export by the plaintiff of white sugar from Germany to Bulgaria. The defendant granted m.c.a.s on this transaction, and also an export refund, which it subjected to the corrective coefficient derived from the m.c.a., which had

---

[83] See the Opinion of Warner A.-G. in Case 108/77, *Wagner* v. *HZA Hamburg-Jonas* [1978] ECR 1187, 1200.

[84] Commission Reg. 1463/73 (OJ 1973 L146/1).   [85] OJ 1975 L139/37.

[86] OJ 1985 L310/4.   [87] [1978] ECR 611.   [88] [1978] ECR 1187.

the effect of reducing the refund. Thus stated, the facts would appear to fall squarely within the scope of Regulation 1380/75. However, the export refunds in this case were granted under the system of partial invitations to tender for export refunds under Commission Regulation 2101/75,[89] whereby the tenders were expressed in national currency, and were converted into units of account for the purposes of comparison and to check that they fell within the maximum refund. The assumption underlying the legislation appears to be that refunds fixed under the tendering system were, in reality, fixed in units of account,[90] and this was the view taken by A.-G. Warner in his Opinion.[91] The plaintiff, however, argued that the export refunds really were fixed in national currency, and so did not fall within the scope of art. 4(3)(b), which referred only to sums fixed in units of account. This was the line taken by the Court, which held that 'the refunds in question were fixed in national currency, and . . . their conversion into units of account constituted only an internal operation within the Commission in order to make tenders comparable'. Hence, the coefficient could not be applied to the refund.

It may be wondered whether the plaintiff was thinking in terms of 'green' marks or real ones when he put in his tender. The situation is not made any simpler by the fact that of the nine export licences at issue in this case only one had been tendered for in marks by the plaintiff; the other eight were issued by the French intervention agency as a result of tenders in French francs (the current and agricultural values of which happened to be the same at the time) by a French company, and had been subsequently transferred to the plaintiff.

The reaction of the Commission was to enact Regulation 1392/78,[92] applying the coefficient to refunds and levies the amount of which had been set in a national currency in the statement of award following an invitation to tender. An unsuccessful attempt to challenge this legislative reversal was made by the same plaintiff in Case 162/78, *Wagner* v. *Commission*,[93] and the provision has been continued in art. 7(1)(c) of Commission Regulation 3153/85.[94]

Where accession compensatory amounts are involved as well as levies or refunds, art. 6(4) of Regulation 3153/85 provides a step-by-step method of calculation: first, the accession compensatory amount is added to or subtracted from the levy or refund, as the case may be; then such part of the resulting sum as is expressed in ECUs must be multiplied by the monetary coefficient, and, finally, that amount is converted into national currency and the monetary compensatory amount is added to it or subtracted from it as appropriate.

[89] OJ 1975 L214/5.
[90] See (1978) 3 EL Rev. 383 (n. 4).
[91] [1978] ECR 1187, 1205.
[92] OJ 1978 L167/53.   [93] [1979] ECR 3467.
[94] OJ 1985 L310/4.

Even where a product is not subject to monetary compensation within the Community the differences between agricultural conversion rates may have to be corrected in external trade. This is illustrated in the rice sector by Commission Regulation 3294/86, fixing the conversion rate to be applied for levies and refunds in that sector.[95] It was there recited that the conversion of levies and refunds at the agricultural conversion rate had given rise to deflection of trade with third countries, and the solution adopted was to provide that the agricultural conversion rate should be multiplied by a monetary coefficient based on the 'real monetary gap' defined in Council Regulation 1677/85,[96] on monetary compensatory amounts. Under this legislation, therefore, monetary compensation was used only in the context of the price compensation at the external frontiers of the Community.

(f) Accession compensation

Accession compensatory amounts, despite their terminological similarity to monetary compensatory amounts, fulfil an entirely different function. They have been used in successive Acts of Accession as the basic transitional mechanism to cover differences between agricultural price levels in new Member States and agricultural price levels in the other Member States, until these prices are co-ordinated. They are comparable with the import levies and export refunds established under most common organizations of the market, replacing such levies and refunds in trade between the new Member States and the rest of the Community, and being added to or subtracted from such levies and refunds in trade with non-Member States.

The analogy with import levies and export refunds was recognized by the European Court in Case 6/78, *Union Française de Céréales* v. *HZA Hamburg-Jonas*.[97] In that case, the French applicants had exported a cargo of wheat from Germany intending it to be unloaded in the United Kingdom. However, the ship sank in the North Sea, and the German customs authorities refused to pay the accession compensatory amounts which would otherwise have been due on such a transaction, on the basis that the exporters had not fulfilled the requirement expressed in art. 5(2) of Commission Regulation 269/73[98] laying down detailed rules for the application of the system of accession compensatory amounts, that, in the circumstances, the compensatory amount should be paid only upon proof that 'import formalities have been completed and duties and taxes of equivalent effect payable in the Member State of destination have been

[95] OJ 1986 L304/25.   [96] OJ 1985 L164/6.
[97] [1978] ECR 1675.   [98] OJ 1973 L30/77.

collected'. Since the wheat had never arrived in the United Kingdom, such proof could not, of course, be produced. Nonetheless, it was suggested on behalf of the exporters that it would be possible to apply the legislation in the related field of export refunds by analogy. Under art. 6(1) of Commission Regulation 192/75,[99] laying down detailed rules for the application of export refunds in respect of agricultural products, payment of the refund was conditional not only on the product having left the geographical territory of the Community but also on its having been imported into a third country 'save where it has perished in transit as a result of *force majeure*'.

The exporters appealed to the Finanzgericht of Hamburg against the German customs authorities' refusal to pay the accession compensatory amounts, and the Finanzgericht referred the case to the European Court, asking specifically whether art. 6(1) of Regulation 192/75 on export refunds could be applied by analogy to the payment of accession compensatory amounts, so as to exonerate the exporter from the need to prove that the goods had arrived in a third country when they had perished in transit as a result of *force majeure*.

In answering this question, the Court examined the system of accession compensatory amounts established under art. 55 of the 1972 Act of Accession, and held that they were intended to replace the export refunds which had been payable in trade with the new Member States when they were still third countries; that is, to enable Community producers to sell in markets in which the level of prices was lower, and, in particular, that they were intended to encourage Community preference in trade between the original Member States and the new Member States. It was found that the insurance contracted on behalf of the purchaser would only cover the value of the goods in the country of destination, and that to require the exporter to bear the difference or insure it himself would place him in an unfavourable position in comparison with exporters in third countries and conflict with the principle of Community preference. The Court concluded that in not allowing for *force majeure*, Regulation 269/73 contained an omission which, given the similarity between accession compensatory amounts and export refunds, could be remedied by applying art. 6(1) of Regulation 192/75 by analogy, and that the principle of Community preference required that the exporter should receive 'accession' compensatory amounts at the rate at which he would have received them if the goods had reached their destination and the import formalities had been completed.

A general limit on accession compensatory amounts is that, as under art. 55(6) of the 1972 Act of Accession, art. 61(5) of the Greek Act of

---

[99] OJ 1975 L25/1.

Accession, and arts. 72(5) and 240(5) of the Spanish and Portuguese Act of Accession, they may not exceed the total amount levied by the relevant Member State on imports from third countries, and in Case 169/73, *Compagnie Continentale France* v. *Council*,[100] it was held that a Council resolution published several months before accession indicating what the compensatory amounts would be in trade with the United Kingdom had to be read subject to this overall limitation, so that traders who knew the market could not simply rely on the resolution.

On the other hand, although the case was not directly concerned with accession compensation, a rather different view was taken of the level of knowledge of traders in Greece following Accession in Case 160/84, *Oryzomyli Kavallas*,[101] where the facts that a Greek language text of the relevant Community legislation was not available, that local civil servants had not received instructions in the matter, and that the head of service was absent at the relevant time were found to constitute 'special circumstances' triggering the operation of art. 13 of Council Regulation 1430/79,[102] allowing the remission of import and export duties in situations arizing from special circumstances in which no negligence or deception may be attributed to the person concerned; with regard to the latter requirement, it was held that small undertakings far from Athens could not, in those circumstances, be expected to know the European Community rules for themselves.

[100] [1975] ECR 117.   [101] 15 May 1986.   [102] OJ 1979 L175/1.

6

Common organizations of the market: legal consequences

(a) Powers of national authorities

(i) Introduction

The situations where common organizations themselves confer powers on national authorities or require action on the part of national authorities will be considered in the context of the administration of the Common Agricultural Policy.[1] Greater legal problems have, however, been raised in determining the extent to which national authorities retain the power to act in their own right in relation to products governed by common organizations. Here, two different approaches may be detected in the case-law of the European Court. On one view, the existence of a common organization precludes unilateral national legislation within its scope; on the other view, unilateral national legislation may be permitted provided it is not incompatible with the rules of the common organization. The development of these views may be illustrated in relation to certain specific aspects of common organizations.

(ii) Problems created by the rules of the common organization itself

It is, unfortunately, not unknown for the provisions of a common organization to create a new problem which they fail to resolve. This came clearly to light in Case 159/73, *Hannoversche Zucker* v. *HZA Hannover*,[2] in relation to the common organization of the market in sugar. This provided for a system of annual-production quotas, and laid down the consequences of over-production, but failed to make provision for determining the marketing year to which an excess should be attributed when discovered on a stock-taking which might occur at intervals of several years. The problem being created by the Community rules themselves, the European Court held that the rules of the common organization must be regarded as forming a complete system, in the sense that it did not leave the Member States the power to fill such a lacuna by resorting to their national law. The Court, therefore sought a Community solution in the

---

[1] See *infra*, p. 158.   [2] [1974] ECR 121.

light of the aims and objectives of the common organization, and concluded that an excess must be treated as arising during the marketing year in which it was ascertained—which happened to be the solution that the Commission had in the meantime adopted by way of Regulation.

This refusal to allow national solutions to such problems was repeated in the context of the system operated in the beef market, which required security to be lodged to guarantee the performance of contracts for the private storage of certain products subject to Community aids. In Case 117/83, *Koenecke*,[3] a trader in Germany had obtained the release of such a security by fraud, and the goods had been removed from storage. The German authorities sought to recover the security from the trader, but faced the difficulty that the Community legislation failed to provide for such recovery, and, therefore, wished to invoke the relevant German legislation. Again, the European Court held that the storage system for beef must be regarded as a complete system, so that it did not allow Member States to resort to their national law to fill the lacuna unless they were so authorized under the Community legislation—although the national authorities had both the right and the duty to apply the rules of their national criminal law with regard to the fraud itself. However, it was held in Case 124/83, *Corman*,[4] that where a security was wrongly released, allowing a tenderer to acquire goods at a reduced price, he could be required as a matter of Community law to pay the difference between the reduced price and the normal intervention price.

(iii) Price systems of common organizations

The question of the legal effects of the price systems of common organizations with regard to the powers of national authorities first arose in Case 31/74, *Galli*.[5] Galli was charged with breaches of Italian prices legislation in relation to the sale of cereals subject to the common organization of the market in flour cereals and in relation to the sale of flour derived from oil seeds subject to the common organization of the market in oils and fats. The Court was, in effect, asked to what extent the Community price system established within the context of the common organization of the market may exclude a national price control system. Its view was expressed in rather wide-ranging terms: 'It must be concluded that in sectors covered by a common organisation of the market . . . Member States can no longer interfere through national provisions taken unilaterally in the machinery of price formation as established under the common organisation'. Even more strongly it was stated that 'the only way compatible with Community law of enabling Member States to attain, in a

---

[3] [1984] ECR 3291.   [4] [1985] ECR 3777.   [5] [1975] ECR 47.

sector covered by a common organization of the market, the objectives sought by the national legislation and intended to combat a rise in prices, is for those States to take, at the Community level, the necessary action for the purpose of prompting the competent Community authority to institute or authorize measures which are consistent with the requirements of the single market' set up by the Regulations in question. However, in the next paragraph the Court also stated that the price system established by the Regulations in question was applicable solely at the production and wholesale stage, with the result that those provisions left Member States free to take the appropriate measures relating to price formation at the retail and consumption stages, provided they did not jeopardize the aims or functioning of the common organization of the market in question.

However, shortly afterwards the Court was again faced with the effects of price systems, this time under the common organization of the market in sugar, in Case 65/75, *Tasca*,[6] and Cases 88 to 90/75, *SADAM*[7] In its judgments the Court expressly repeated certain of the passages form its Galli judgment quoted above, but then went on to say that a distinction between maximum consumer prices and maximum prices applicable at previous marketing stages was difficult, and concluded that the unilateral fixing by a Member State of maximum prices for the sale of sugar, whatever the marketing stage in question, was incompatible with Regulation 1009/67,[8] introducing the common organization of the market in sugar, once it jeopardized the objectives and the functioning of this organization and, in particular, its system of prices. The Court then went on to consider how such incompatibility could arise. It held, having looked at the structure of the sugar market and the sugar price system in the common organization, that a Member State would jeopardize the objectives and functioning of the sugar markets if it regulated prices in such a way as, directly or indirectly, to make it difficult for the sugar manufacturers to obtain an ex-factory price at least equal to the intervention price. The Court added that such an indirect obstruction would exist when a Member State, without regulating the prices at the production stage, fixed maximum selling prices for the wholesale and retail stages at such a low level that the grower found it practically impossible to sell at the intervention price. It was finally concluded that it was for the national court to decide, having regard to these considerations, whether the maximum prices which it was called upon to consider produced such effects as to make them incompatible with the Community provisions on sugar.

Nevertheless, the Court returned to the distinction it had made in Galli in two cases decided in 1979. In Case 10/79, *Toffoli*,[9] which involved local legislation by the Region of Venice fixing a regional price for milk at the

[6] [1976] ECR 291.   [7] [1976] ECR 323.
[8] JO 1967 no. 308 p. 1.   [9] [1979] ECR 3301.

production level, it was repeated that Member States can no longer interfere through national provisions taken unilaterally in the machinery of price formation established under a common organization, but in the judgment delivered the same day on references from the Belgian Cour de Cassation in Cases 16–20/79, *Danis and Others*,[10] the Court again added the rider that Member States still have the power to take unilateral measures relating to price formation at the retail and consumption stages, provided that they do not jeopardize the aims or functioning of the common organization of the market in question.

In the result, despite the difficulties of distinguishing the economic effects of price controls at different levels in the chain of distribution, it would appear that in areas subject to common organizations based on production prices Member States have no power to enact legislation relating to prices at the production level, and such legislation is presumed incompatible with the Community rules, whereas the compatibility of national legislation governing prices at other marketing stages with the Community rules must be considered in the light of the circumstances of each case.

(iv) **Other aspects of common organizations**

This latter approach is one which was followed with regard to other aspects of common organizations. Here, it was not said that national legislation was excluded, but rather, as the Court put in in Case 111/76, *Officier van Justitie* v. *Van den Hazel*,[11] that it was the duty of Member States, once a common organization of the market had been established, to refrain from taking any measures which might derogate from or harm that organization. This approach was illustrated in Case 50/76, *Amsterdam Bulb* v. *Produktschap voor Siergewassen*.[12] This was concerned with Dutch legislation firstly providing for a minimum export price for bulbs smaller than those for which Commission Regulation 369/75[13] laid down a minimum price, and secondly providing a minimum price for bulbs of a type not covered by the Regulation. The Court held, again, that the compatibility of these provisions with the Community Regulations must be examined, having regard not only to the express provisions of the regulations but also their aims and objects. With regard to the first problem, that of the small bulbs, the Court found that under the Community scheme bulbs smaller than those specified in Council Regulation 315/68[14] could not, in fact, be exported, and that the minimum price for those falling within that Regulation but not mentioned in Regulation 369/75 should be the lowest

---

[10] [1979] ECR 3327.　　　　　[11] [1977] ECR 401.
[12] [1977] ECR 137.　　　　　[13] OJ 1975 L41/1.
[14] JO 1968 L71/1.

fixed in that Regulation. With regard to the second problem, that of the types of bulbs not covered by the Community Regulations on prices, though falling within the scope of the common organization as a whole, the Court found there was no express prohibition on the fixing of national minimum prices for exports, and inferred from the minimum system applied by the Commission that such prices could continue to be fixed until replaced at the Community level. There is, however, no discussion in the judgment of the question whether the imposition of minimum export prices under national law constituted a measure equivalent to a quantitative restriction on exports prohibited under art. 34 of the EEC Treaty.

The situation can also arise where the practical problems involved in applying the rules of a common organization may lead the Court to infer that certain national legislation is compatible with that organization. In three sets of French wine cases heard in 1975[15] the question was asked, in effect, whether the Community rules in the wine sector enabled Member States to apply a presumption in law of over-alcoholization based on the proportion of alcohol to 'reduced extract' which, in turn, was obtained by 'the hundred degree method'.[16] The Commission Regulation determining Community methods for the analysis of wines provided, in fact, for measuring the dry extract by 'the densimetric method'. However, the Court found that under the Regulations on the common organization of the market in wine the Member States were required to take effective measures of control. It also found that the use of the densimetric method laid down by the Community regulations was not an aim in itself, and that in the absence of Community measures of control it would be contrary to the aims of the Community rules to require that this method be used at the cost of invalidating the only method of control then acknowledged to be appropriate for the detection of over-alcoholization. So it was stated that, until more appropriate methods had been worked out, Community rules in the wine sector did not prohibit Member States from using the hundred-degree method to measure the dry extract of wine in order to apply a presumption in law of over-alcoholization based on the proportion of alcohol to dry extract.

Compatibility was tested not only against the express provision of a Regulation establishing a common organization, but also against its

---

[15] Cases 89/74 and 19/75, *Procureur Général (Bordeaux)* v. *Arnaud and Others* [1975] ECR 1023. Cases 10–14/75, *Procureur de la République (Aix-en-Provence)* v. *Lahaille and Others* [1975] ECR 1053. Case 64/75, *Procureur Général (Lyon)* v. *Mommessin and Others* [1975] ECR 1599.

[16] The '100-degree' method consists in weighing what is left after evaporating the volatile substances in the wine at 100°C. The 'densimetric' method consists in calculating the dry extract indirectly from the specific gravity of the wine from which the alcohol has been removed and which has been brought up to the initial volume by adding water. See [1975] ECR 1023 at p. 1026.

underlying principles, as in Case 83/78, *Pigs Marketing Board* v. *Redmond*,[17] in relation to Regulation No. 2759/75[18] on the common organization of the market in pigmeat. This case was a reference from a Northern Irish Resident Magistrate in the context of a prosecution brought by the Northern Irish Pigs Marketing Board; under the relevant Northern Irish legislation, only producers who were registered with the Board could sell bacon pigs and only to or through the agency of the Board. In laying down the test for determining whether such a scheme was compatible with the common organization, the Court looked to what might be described as the underlying concept, stating that the common organization of the market in pigmeat was based on the concept of an open market to which every producer had free access, and the functioning of which was regulated solely by the instruments provided for by that organization. It concluded that 'any provisions or national practices which might alter the pattern of imports or exports or influence the formation of market prices by preventing producers from buying and selling freely within the State in which they are established, or in any other Member State, in conditions laid down by Community rules, and from taking advantage directly of intervention measures or any other measures for regulating the market laid down by the common organization are incompatible with the principles of such organization of the market'. In any event, measures of the type there at issue were specifically found to contravene the Treaty provisions prohibiting measures having equivalent effect to quantitative restrictions on imports and exports.

However, the idea of looking at the underlying concepts of a common organization rather than its express provisions was taken a step further in another judgment involving the common organization of the market in pigmeat in Case 107/78, *Pigs and Bacon Commission* v. *McCarren*.[19] This involved a marketing system in the Irish Republic under which the Pigs and Bacon Commission was empowered to impose a levy on the production of all pig carcasses intended for the manufacture of bacon, whilst paying a bonus to those exporting bacon through its agency. Regulation No.2759/75[20] and the provisions on the free movement of goods held to be an integral part of it do not appear expressly to prohibit the payment of bonuses. Nonetheless, the Court found that 'according to the idea on which the regulation dealing with the common organization of the market in pigmeat is based, the products referred to therein are in fact required to move freely within the Community at the price level resulting from the operation of the machinery for the common organization of the market, and neither Member States nor agencies on which they have conferred powers are entitled to create advantages for the marketing of national products as

[17] [1978] ECR 2347.   [18] OJ 1975 L282/1.
[19] [1979] ECR 2161.   [20] OJ 1975 L282/1.

against those of other Member States by means of financial machinery such
as the grant of bonuses'. However, earlier in the judgment it was said that
the marketing system established by the Regulation precluded 'any
intervention by Member States in the market otherwise than as expressly
laid down by the Regulation itself'. Taken literally, this would appear to
exclude unilateral national competence in any market governed by a
common organization, which would represent a considerable change in
attitude, and would be difficult to reconcile with the contemporaneous
cases allowing national prices legislation at the retail level so long as it did
not interfere with the functioning of a common organization.

(v) Development of exclusivity

The principle of exclusivity enounced in McCarren appears, nevertheless,
to indicate the approach followed by the Court in its more recent case-law.
Case 222/82, *Apple and Pear Development Council*,[21] involved, inter alia,
the quality standards laid down by the United Kingdom Apple and Pear
Development Council. The Court there stated that the common organization of the market in fruit and vegetables laid down an *exhaustive* system
of quality standards for the relevant products, so that Member States and
bodies such as the Development Council were prevented from imposing
unilateral provisions concerning the quality of the fruit marketed by
growers—although the Development Council might make simple recom-
mendations. This view that the Community rules in the fruit sector on
quality standards are exhaustive was repeated in Case 218/85, *Le
Campion*,[22] where it was held that a Member State could not make the
rules of a national producers' organization compulsory with regard to
weight, presentation etc. Furthermore, in Case 16/83, *Prantl*,[23] involving the
common organization of the market in wine, it stated categorically that
where a common organization of the market constitutes a complete system
Member States no longer have any competence in the matter, unless a
provision of Community law provides otherwise; the dispute in that case
involved German rules concerning bottle shapes, and it was, in fact, found
that a provision in the Regulation establishing the common organization
did authorize Member States to regulate bottle shapes—although it was
then found that the German rules at issue constituted measures equivalent
to quantitative reduction on imports prohibited under art. 30 of the EEC
Treaty. Finally, in a case involving quality standards for poultrymeat,[24] the
Court applied the exclusivity theory as developed in the context of fisheries
to a land-based common organization. The Regulation establishing the

---

[21] [1983] ECR 4083.   [22] 25 Nov. 1986.
[23] [1984] ECR 1299.
[24] Cases 47 and 48/83, *Pluimveeslachterij Midden-Nederland* [1984] ECR 1721.

common organization provided for the Council to lay down the relevant quality standards, but it had totally failed to do so. After referring to its decision in Case 804/79, *Commission* v. *UK*,[25] in relation to fisheries policy, the Court held that the Member States, faced with such a failure to act, had no competence of their own, but could nonetheless act on behalf of the Community in taking interim measures on a provisional basis—although it added that their interim measures should themselves be compatible with the principles of the common organization.

Given this clear move towards the exclusivity of Community competence in areas covered by common organizations of agricultural markets, it is at first sight, surprising that in Case 237/82, *Jongeneel Kaas*,[26] decided in the same period, concerning the common organization of the market in milk, it was held that in the absence of any specific rules in the Regulation establishing the common organization Member States had power to lay down quality standards for cheese, provided they were compatible with the other provisions of the common organization. However, it may be argued that the Regulation was construed as authorizing Member States to take such measures, again, therefore, making it a matter of exclusive Community competence, or that there was not a complete common organization of the type described in *Prantl* with regard to quality standards for cheese.

It may, therefore, be suggested that the modern principle is that the existence of a common organization precludes unilateral national legislation on the matters which it covers, unless it can be shown to be incomplete, in the sense of not covering or not purporting to cover the matter at issue. National legislation may only be enacted where required or permitted by the rules of the common organization. This was illustrated in Case 207/84, *De Boer*,[27] where it was held that Council Regulation 1353/83,[28] on herring quotas, did empower Member States to lay down how the quota should be used, so that the Netherlands could determine how boats participating in the quota should be equipped, but that Council Regulation 3796/81,[29] on the common organization of the market in fish products, left Member States with no competence to determine how fish caught under the quota should be processed and marketed, so that the Netherlands could not require the fish caught to be sold in a particular form. As summarized in Case 48/85, *Commission* v. *Germany*,[30] Member States are only competent in matters not governed by a common organization, or where they are authorized to act by the Community. On the other hand, as was pointed out in Case 118/86, *Nertsvoederfabriek*,[31] the existence of a common organization does not exempt producers from national legislation pursuing objectives different from those of the common organization.

---

[25] [1981] ECR 1045; see *supra*, p. 24.
[26] [1984] ECR 483.   [27] 3 Oct. 1985.   [28] OJ 1983 L139/54.
[29] OJ 1981 L379/1.   [30] 18 Sept. 1986.   [31] 6 October 1987.

(b) Role of national organizations of the market

Whilst common organizations may expressly provide for a particular function to be performed by national organizations, in particular producer organizations,[32] it was clearly stated by the European Court in Case 83/78, *Pigs Marketing Board* v. *Redmond*,[33] that the institution of a common organization replaces any pre-existing national organization of the market, in the sense that the national organization ceases to have any special legal position, even if, as in that case, the overall time limit for the replacement of national organizations by common organizations under the 1972 Act of Accession had not yet expired. On the other hand, Community law itself may, as with the United Kingdom Milk Marketing Boards,[34] permit the continuance of national organizations within the limits of a common organization.

[32] See *infra*, p. 159.   [33] [1978] ECR 2347.   [34] See *supra*, p. 81.

7

Structural and guidance measures

(a) General structural policy

The references in art. 39 of the EEC Treaty on the one hand to increasing agricultural productivity and on the other to the need to take account of the structural and natural disparities between the various agricultural regions themselves indicate that the Common Agricultural Policy must do more than simply offer a system of price support, a view further evidenced by the reference in art. 40(3) to an agricultural guidance fund, as well as to an agricultural guarantee fund. Indeed, the problems caused by large numbers of small farms were well recognized even when Community agricultural legislation was first discussed, and the Commission did propose the establishment of a separate European Fund for Structural Improvement.[1] However, the Council decided to add structural measures to the guidance section of the General Agricultural Guidance and Guarantee Fund (EAGGF) when that was split into two sections in Council Regulation 17/64.[2] It may be said that the guidance section received relatively little of the Community funds spent on agriculture, the fundamental legal obligation under the common organizations being to finance the guarantee measures provided under those organizations. However, Council Regulation 870/85,[3] on the financial framework of the guidance section of the EAGGF, has established the principle that there should be a five-year financial framework for the guidance section, and attributed 5250 million ECUs to that section for the period 1985–89, with the proviso that this sum could be increased.

Although Regulation 17/64 created the guidance section, and laid down a procedure under which particular projects could be submitted for aid, it was not immediately followed by any measures of structural policy. Then, in 1968, the Commission put forward its 'Memorandum on the Reform of Agriculture in the EEC', commonly called the 'Mansholt Plan' after the name of the Commissioner responsible for agriculture. Its basic aim was to lead to the creation of larger farms, so that high guaranteed prices could be reduced, on the basis that a larger, more efficient unit could provide an adequate income at lower prices. This proposal also indicated that it would

---

[1] See Hill, *The Common Agricultural Policy: Past, Present and Future* (Methuen, London, 1984) pp. 26–27.

[2] JO 1964 p. 117. [3] OJ 1985 L95/1.

involve some five million people leaving farming, and that some five million hectares should be taken out of production. This proved politically unacceptable as such, but did lead to the enactment in 1972 of a trio of Directives which remained in force as the backbone of Community structural policy until 1985.

Council Directive 72/159,[4] on the modernization of farms, was basically intended to help farmers with low incomes, a criterion adopted also in the new legislation. It was largely implemented in the United Kingdom through the Farm and Horticulture Development Schemes. Council Directive 72/160,[5] on measures to encourage the cessation of farming and the reallocation of utilized agricultural areas, enabled payments to be made to farmers between fifty-five and sixty-five who left farming, it being required either that their land should be leased or sold to farmers falling within the first Directive or that it should be withdrawn from agricultural use. This was implemented in the United Kingdom under the Farm Amalgamation Scheme. The Council returned to this pattern in Reg. 1096/88 establishing a general Community scheme to encourage the cessation of farming over the age of fifty-five, intended to ensure that the land either was taken out of production or at least that it was not used to increase production of surplus products.[6] The third of this series was Directive 72/161,[7] on the provision of socio-economic guidance for, and the acquisition of occupational skills by, persons engaged in agriculture, the improvement of agricultural skills remaining an objective of the new legislation.

These Directives were amended in 1981 to enable a greater share of EAGGF funding to be made available in the Mediterranean area and the West of Ireland, and their validity was successively extended until they were replaced with effect from 30 September 1985 by Council Regulation 797/85,[8] on improving the efficiency of agricultural structures. This Regulation replaced not only the three 1972 Directives but also the aid provisions of Council Directive 75/268,[9] on mountain and hill farming and farming in less-favoured areas, although, even as originally drafted, these had been treated as 'common measures' under Directive 72/159.

Although, according to its recitals, Council Regulation 797/85 was made under the agricultural provisions of the EEC Treaty, it may be said that in some respects it appears to be as much related to rural social policy as to agricultural policy in the strict sense. Essentially, it is concerned with aids subject to a financial contribution from the guidance section of the EAGGF, but it does also deal with certain national aids. However, the purpose of these structural aids was dramatically altered by Council

[4] JO 1972 L96/1.   [5] JO 1972 L96/9.
[6] OJ 1988 L110/1.   [7] JO 1972 L96/15.
[8] OJ 1985 L93/1.   [9] OJ 1975 L128/1.

Regulation 1760/87,[10] introducing a scheme for conversion and 'extensification' of production into the scope of the legislation. Conversion simply involves the conversion of products to non-surplus products (as defined by the Council), but extensification is defined as a reduction in output of the product concerned by at least 20 per cent without other production capacity being increased. Initially, this system applied only to cereals (where the area devoted to production must be reduced by 20 per cent), beef and veal (where the number of livestock units must be reduced by at least 20 per cent), and wine (where the yield per hectare must be reduced by at least 20 per cent). The dairy sector is not included in 'extensification', but an independent compensation scheme had already been introduced in that market,[11] and although dairy products are eligible for the conversion aid under this Regulation provision is made for the deduction from that aid of any premiums paid under Council Regulation 775/87[12] withdrawing a proportion of the milk reference quantities. Social considerations are, however, taken into account in art. 1a(3), which enables the Commission to authorize Member States not to apply these arrangements in regions or areas in which production should not, because of natural conditions or the danger of depopulation, be reduced. This concept of extensification was adapted to produce a 'set-aside' scheme under the European Council's February 1988 compromise on the Community's future financing and new 'own resources'.[13] Under this scheme, a producer must set aside at least 20 per cent of his arable land for at least five years, and if he sets aside at least 30 per cent he will be exempted the co-responsibility levy on 20 tonnes of cereals.[14] Such a producer would be entitled to a premium of between 100 ECU per hectare and 600 ECU per hectare, the Community contribution to this premium varying between 50 per cent at the bottom of the scale and 15 per cent at the top. A particular novelty of the scheme, however, is that 50 per cent of the Community contribution is to be found from the guarantee section of the Agricultural Guidance and Guarantee Fund,[15] leaving only 50 per cent to be found by the guidance section.

The more traditional structural provisions of Council Regulation 797/85 (that is, those which are capable of leading to an increase in production) enable investment aid to be granted to beneficiaries who practize farming as their main occupation, who have adequate occupational skill, who submit a plan for materially improving their holding, and who undertake to keep simplified accounts, subject to the fundamental criterion that the labour income per man-work unit is less than a level not exceeding the average gross wage of non-agricultural workers in the relevant region. The

---

[10] OJ 1987 L167/1.   [11] See *supra*, p. 74.   [12] OJ 1987 L78/5.
[13] Implemented by Council Reg. 1094/88 (OJ 1988 L106/28).
[14] See *supra*, p. 56.   [15] See *supra*, p. 104.

plan may relate not only to, for example, reduction of costs, but also to the protection and improvement of the environment. On the other hand, it must not take milk production over the quota limits,[16] and limits are imposed on pig production. The aid may take the form of capital grants, interest-rate subsidies, or deferred repayments, but it may not cover the purchase of land, or of pigs, poultry, and calves for slaughter, the latter being very short-term investments. There are overall financial limits on the aid,[17] and it must not exceed 35 per cent of the investment, in the case of fixed assets, or 20 per cent in other types of investment. However, for less-favoured areas as defined in Directive 75/268, that is, hill farmers, the limits are raised to 45 per cent and 30 per cent respectively. The investment may relate to a merger plan, in which case the investment limits are multiplied by the number of participants, subject to an overall ceiling. Aids may also be granted for afforestation, and woodland improvements, in holdings falling within the criteria set out above.

Special aids may be provided for 'young' farmers under forty, including a premium on first installation, interest-rate subsidies, and an additional investment aid. Financial encouragement may also be given to various associations and groups, such as groups for the joint use of equipment, or the operation of a group holding, or associations operating farm-relief services and farm management services. Special aid may be paid for the improvement of agricultural skills, independently of measures submitted to the European Social Fund.

For farmers in 'less-favoured areas' as defined under Directive 75/268, an annual compensatory allowance, originally provided under that Directive itself, may be paid to assist farming activities. The beneficiary must undertake to pursue his farming activity for at least five years from the first payment and must have at least three hectares of land (a requirement reduced to two hectares for some areas). Member States may also, in such areas, provide aid for investment in tourist- or craft-industry projects on the agricultural holding (which suggests a broad view of agriculture).

With regard to these permitted investment aids, the guidance section of the EAGGF may pay 25 per cent of their cost, but this limit is raised to 50 per cent for the special aids for young farmers. The overall limit is raised to 50 per cent for certain aids in certain areas, but these do not include any in the United Kingdom, although they do include some areas of Ireland. The cost over the first five years to the EAGGF was calculated in the Regulation at the surprisingly precise figure of 1988 million ECU.

The Regulation imposes restrictions on other national aids to holdings which do not qualify under its criteria, requiring them, in general, to be

---

[16] See *supra*, p. 74.
[17] 60,000 ECU per man-work unit, or 120,000 ECU per holding.

less than the aids specifically authorized, although, subject to the express application of the general Treaty rules on state aids, there is no limit on aids for land purchase or special national schemes in 'environmentally sensitive areas'. The environmental aspects of the Regulation were, in fact, considerably strengthened by Council Regulation 1760/87,[18] in so far as it introduced a new art. 19 and new arts. 19a–c allowing for the development of specific aid schemes for areas which are 'particularly sensitive' from the point of view of protection of the environment or preservation of the landscape and the countryside, these areas being determined by the Member States. The aid takes the form of an annual premium per hectare paid to farmers in such areas who undertake, under a specific programme for that area, to introduce or maintain, for at least five years, farming practices compatible with the requirements of the protection of the environment and of natural resources or with the requirements of the maintenance of the landscape and of the countryside. This conversion of Community agricultural policy to encourage the protection of the environment was expressly stated to be 'to contribute to the adaptation and the guidance of agricultural production according to market needs',[19] and Regulation 1760/87 was enacted solely on the basis of art. 43 of the EEC Treaty on agricultural policy, and not under arts. 100 and 235 which were the usual provisions cited to justify environmental legislation before the entry into force of the specific provisions introduced by the Single European Act.[20]

It might finally be observed that in what appears to be a reversion to the aims of Directive 72/160,[21] the European Council, in the context of the February 1988 agreement on the Community's future financing and new 'own resources',[22] agreed to introduce optional Community arrangements for promoting the cessation of farming by encouraging early retirement.[22a]

(b) Specific structural measures

(i) Hill farming

One of the more obvious legislative consequences of United Kingdom accession to the Communities was the enactment of Council Directive 75/268[23] on mountain and hill farming and farming in less-favoured areas. The benefits now accorded such areas under the general structural policy

---

[18] OJ 1987 L167/1.   [19] Art.19 of Reg. 1760/87 (OJ 1987 L167/1).
[20] See Usher, 'The Scope of Community Competence: Its Recognition and Enforcement' (1985) 24 JCMS 121.
[21] JO 1972 L96/9.   [22] Agence Europe Special Edition (no. 4722) 14 Feb. 1988.
[22a] Implemented in Reg. 1096/88, see p. 134 above.   [23] OJ 1975 L128/1.

have been explained in the preceding paragraphs.[24] Of particular interest is the definition of mountain areas as being areas where either, because of altitude, difficult weather conditions substantially shorten the growing season, or, at lower altitudes, the slopes are too steep for the use of machinery, or require the use of very expensive special equipment. Such areas are, in fact, listed in further Council Directives, the amended United Kingdom list being contained in Council Directive 84/169.[25] This defines the relevant areas by reference in England and Scotland to named parishes falling wholly or partly within such areas (with the additional refinement of certain land falling outside parishes, and isolated farms in some instances), in Wales to 'communities' and in Northern Ireland to 'district electoral divisions'. These units are listed under county names, the names in the English and Welsh list being those which resulted from local government reorganization in the 1970s, the names of the Scottish list, however, being those which preceded the introduction of 'regions' under such reorganization.

In effect, the 'less-favoured areas' would appear to include most of Scotland, apart from the east coast, most of Wales, most of Northern Ireland, the parts of England bordering Scotland and Wales, and much of the north-east, north-west and south-west of England, in so far as a generalization may be made.

(ii) Fisheries

The fisheries sector provides an example of a developed system of structural legislation. Community measures to improve and adopt structures in the fisheries and aquaculture sector are currently derived from Council Regulation 4028/86,[26] which is expressed to apply for ten years from 1 January 1987, and replaced Council Regulation 2908/83,[27] which expired at the end of 1986.

The essential aim of this legislation is the development of multiannual guidance programmes to establish a viable fleet and to adjust fishing capacities to demand. Against this background, structural support may be provided under nine different headings. Assistance may be given for the purchase or construction of new vessels, which must be more than nine metres in length, or twelve metres if they are capable of being used for trawling, and this aid may be increased where the beneficiary is aged under forty, owns at least 40 per cent of the vessel concerned, and undertakes to remain skipper of that vessel for at least five years, with priority being given to an owner-skipper whose current ship is more than fifteen years old. Help may also be given with modernization, defined as work not

---

[24] See *supra*, p. 136.
[25] OJ 1984 L82/67.
[26] OJ 1986 L376/7.   [27] OJ 1983 L290/1.

exceeding 50 per cent of the value of a new vessel. Detailed rules on modernization were adopted in Commission Regulation 894/87.[28]

With regard to aquaculture, and 'structural works in coastal waters', assistance may be given, under art. 11(3), where that activity is purely commercial, it is carried out by persons possessing sufficient occupational competence, and it gives satisfactory assurance of yielding a profit. There is a link with the rationalization of sea fishing in that the aid may be increased where the project involves the redeployment of sea fishermen and provides for the scrapping of operational fishing vessels.

A further positive aspect lies in the encouragement of exploratory fishing, with regard to which detailed rules were laid down by Commission Regulation 1871/87.[29] Under art. 15 of the basic Regulation 4028/86 an incentive premium of up to 20 per cent of the costs of the voyage may be paid, provided, inter alia, the vessel is more than eighteen metres long, it is involved in more than sixty days' fishing per year, and provision is made for scientific observation. Encouragement may also be given to joint ventures in the form of a co-operation premium under arts. 18 to 21, where joint exploitation is developed with persons in third countries with which the Community maintains relations in fisheries matters.

On the negative side, provision is made for the adjustment of capacities in the form of a laying-up premium or a final-cessation premium. Under art. 23, the laying-up premium covers boats over eighteen metres in length which fished for at least 120 days in the year preceding the claim, and which are laid up for between 45 and 150 days per year, whereas under art. 24 the final cessation premium is paid when a vessel is permanently withdrawn from fishing by scrapping, transfer to a third country, or assignment to non-fishing purposes, provided it was more than twelve metres in length and had fished for at least 100 days in the year preceding the claim. An example of what might, perhaps, be termed the new budgetary realism may, however, be found in art. 26, under which the Community contribution to these premiums depends on the availability of budget appropriations, and may not in any event exceed 50 per cent.

Assistance may also be given to the development of facilities at fishing ports, but this is linked to a programme under Council Regulation 355/77,[30] on processing and marketing, and should be prepared by a producers' organization recognized under Council Regulation 3796/81,[31] on the marketing of fish products. Marketing is more obviously involved in so far as the Regulation enables support to be given to the search for new markets for fish products, although under art. 30(2)(b), to be eligible for support, a scheme must not be oriented towards any particular commercial brands, and must not make reference to a particular country or production

[28] OJ 1987 L88/1.   [29] OJ 1987 L180/1.
[30] OJ 1977 L51/1. See *infra*, p. 140.   [31] OJ 1981 L379/1.

region. Finally, the Commission may be empowered, under art. 32, to implement other specific measures. Like the general structural Regulation 797/85,[32] the fisheries structural Regulation was costed from the outset, and under art. 40 it was estimated to involve an expenditure of 800 million ECU during the period 1987 to 1991.

(iii) Processing and marketing

Council Regulation 355/77,[33] on common measures to improve the conditions under which agricultural products are processed and marketed, was extended in its operation to 30 April 1995 by Council Regulation 1932/84.[34] It is intended to provide support for measures which guarantee producers an adequate and lasting share in the resulting economic benefits, and, in particular, will aid the development of new outlets where they ease the burden on intervention mechanisms. In principle, there is a 25 per cent contribution from the guidance section of the EAGGF and the beneficiary must find 50 per cent of the cost. In order to qualify for support, a project must, under art. 10 of the Regulation, form part of a programme, offer adequate guarantees that it will be profitable, and contribute to the lasting economic effect of the structural improvement aimed at by the programme. However, by an amendment introduced by Council Regulation 1760/87,[35] the first and third of these three conditions need not be met where the project is for the marketing or processing of 'organically grown products' (an expression which is not defined), and is a pilot or experimental project. The explanation given in the recitals to Regulation 1760/87 was that this was to aid the achievement of the objectives of Regulation 355/77 'in respect of the adjustment and reorientation of agriculture made necessary by the economic consequences of the common agricultural policy'; presumably, this indicates that there was felt to be a demand for such products, and that the techniques used would be less likely to lead to surplus production.

There are also more specific marketing measures. In particular, Council Regulation 1079/77,[36] introducing the milk co-responsibility levy, also provided for Community support for promotional and publicity measures to encourage the human consumption of milk. The implementation of such measures has continued on a regular basis, being governed for the 1987/8 marketing year by Commission Regulation 568/87.[37] Under this scheme, measures such as seminars, courses, and conferences designed to provide personnel engaged in marketing milk and milk products with information and training may qualify for a Community contribution of up to 90 per cent of the expenditure, and the purchase of refrigerators and refrigerated

[32] OJ 1985 L93/1. [33] OJ 1977 L51/1. [34] OJ 1984 L180/1.
[35] OJ 1987 L167/1. [36] OJ 1987 L131/6. [37] 1987 L57/22.

dispensers may qualify for support of 50 per cent. It is also made clear that promotion should not be brand-orientated, and that Community milk products should be promoted without reference to their country or region of manufacture, unless that arises from the traditional name of the product.

(iv) **Producer organizations**

Mention has already been made of the role to be played by producer organizations in the support mechanisms of certain common organizations of the market, such as those concerned with the marketing of fishery products under Council Regulation 3796/81,[38] or with the marketing of fruit and vegetables, where, following the amendments introduced by Council Regulations 3284 and 3285/83,[39] certain marketing rules can even be extended to non-members. Their role will also be considered in the context of the administration of the Common Agricultural Policy.[40]

However, the encouragement of producer organizations may also be regarded as aiding the improvement of agricultural structures, and it is this that lies behind Council Regulation 1360/78,[41] on producer groups and associations of producer groups. This was, essentially, intended to promote the development of such groups and associations in areas where they were weak or non-existent. It was originally drafted to cover only Italy, Belgium, and parts of the South of France, but following successive Accessions, it has been extended to Greece, Portugal, and Spain.[42] Even in these countries, however, it only applies to producers of products defined in art. 3, and under art. 5 the 'producers' concerned are any persons working in an agricultural holding situated within Community territory who produce the products of the soil and livestock products listed in art. 3 or, while being primary producers, produce the processed products listed in art. 3. To qualify for support, groups of such producers must contribute to the objectives of art. 39; notably, by laying down common rules for production and common rules for placing goods on the market, and the aid may be granted for the first five years following recognition of the group at a rate of up to 5 per cent of the value of the products coming from the members for the first year, and up to 5 per cent, 4 per cent, 3 per cent and 2 per cent in the subsequent years, provided this does not exceed the actual cost of setting up and running the group.

Under art. 13, the EAGGF may pay up to 25 per cent of this aid, but this may be increased to 50 per cent where 2/3 of the members of the group or association are recognized as 'encountering special difficulties in adapting

[38] OJ 1981 L379/1.   [39] OJ 1983 L325/1.   [40] See *infra*, p. 159.
[41] OJ 1978 L166/1.
[42] See Council Reg. 2224/86 (OJ 1986 L194/4).

to the conditions and economic implications of the Common Agricultural Policy'.

By virtue of Council Regulation 1760/87,[43] the operation of this common measure was extended to the end of 1991.

(c) *Integrated development projects*

The rural-policy aspects of the Regulation on structural efficiency illustrate that agricultural policy cannot always be regarded as totally separate from other aspects of regional and social policy. Hence, there is an obvious utility, at least in the poorer areas of the Community, in bringing together the various sources of Community finance to promote common activity. However, the first group of measures to refer expressly to integrated programmes, which included Council Regulation 1939/81,[44] on an integrated development programme for the Western Isles (Outer Hebrides), eventually involved only the financial participation of the guidance section of the EAGGF. It was intended to aid agriculture, fisheries, tourist amenities, crafts, industrial, and 'other complementary activities essential to the improvement of the socio-economic situation', and enabled the guidance section of the EAGGF to finance up to 40 per cent of the costs of projects for the improvement of agricultural structures, the planting of windbreaks, the improvement of marketing and processing of agricultural products, the improvement of agricultural infrastructure, the provision of shore facilities for inshore fisheries, and the development of aquaculture. This aid was to be paid over a period of five years from the notification of a programme by the United Kingdom for the relevant area, with a total financial contribution of thirteen million ECU. On the other hand, it may be observed that Council Regulation 1402/86,[45] introducing common action for the encouragement of agriculture in the Scottish islands off the north and west coasts with the exception of the Western Isles, was simply made under art. 18 of the general structural Regulation 797/85.[46]

The pilot actions for integrated mediterranean programmes, on the other hand, initiated by Council Decisions 84/70 to 84/82,[47] whilst clearly only pilot actions, did enable the Commission to use EAGGF, Social Fund, Regional Development Fund, or fisheries restructuring appropriations, or a special budgetary line within the limits of available budgetary resources. These pilot schemes were subject to specific decisions of the Commission on individual projects, these decisions themselves fixing the Community's contribution to their financing. They eventually led to the adoption of Council Regulation 2088/85 concerning integrated mediterranean

---

[43] OJ 1987 L167/1.   [44] OJ 1981 L197/6.   [45] OJ 1986 L128/9.
[46] OJ 1985 L93/1.   [47] OJ 1984 L44.

programmes.[48] This enables support to be given for multiannual operations covering not only agriculture, food, and 'agri-food industries' (sic), but also for energy projects, crafts, and industry, including building and public works, and services, including tourism. The funds used may be those of the Regional Development Fund, the Social Fund, or the guidance section of the EAGGF, as well as specific additional appropriations, and the operations may also involve loans from the European Investment Bank or under the New Community Instrument.[49] Under art. 13, the Community may meet up to 70 per cent of the cost of such operations.

In turn, these mediterranean programmes may be regarded as the precursors of the general provisions on economic and social cohesion introduced as arts. 130a–e of the EEC Treaty by the Single European Act. In particular, art. 130d requires amendments to be made to the structure and operational rules of the existing structural Funds to increase their efficiency and to co-ordinate their activities between themselves and with the operations of the existing financial instruments.

[48] OJ 1985 L197/1.

[49] Created under art. 235 of the EEC Treaty by Council Decision 78/870 (OJ 1978 L298/9), in the absence of express borrowing powers under the Treaty, to enable the Commission to contract loans on behalf of the Community so as to finance investment projects contributing to greater convergence and integration of the economic policies of the Member States. The current framework is contained in Council Decision 83/200 (OJ 1983 L112/26).

8

Administration of the Common Agricultural Policy

(a) The basic pattern

Although art. 43 of the EEC Treaty conferred specific powers on the Commission to make general proposals for the implementation of the Common Agricultural Policy duringtheearly stages of the original transitional period, power to issue agricultural legislation is conferred only on the Council of Ministers. The exercize of this power is subject to consultation with the European Parliament, and in Case 138/79, *Roquette* v. *Council and Commission*,[1] it was held to be a breach of that requirement not to wait to receive the Parliament's opinion after a proposal had been sent to that body, even if the Council was not ultimately obliged to follow the Parliament's opinion. However, in the absence of any emergency procedure in the agricultural provisions of the Treaty, it was held to be legitimate, when the system of monetary compensatory amounts was introduced to combat the problems caused by floating exchange rates in 1971, for the Council to legislate under art. 103 of the Treaty,[2] which enables it to decide upon measures of conjunctural policy appropriate to the situation without consulting the Parliament. This no doubt explains why Council Regulation 974/71,[3] introducing monetary compensatory amounts, referred in its title to 'measures of conjunctural policy to be taken in agriculture'. When, however, it was amended by Council Regulation 2746/72,[4] which had itself been enacted under the art. 43 procedure, its recitals were actually altered so as to include a reference to art. 43 as an enabling provision. To the extent that the Council may, in the context of common organizations, confer upon itself power to adopt implementing legislation without consulting thc European Parliament, which tends to be the case with regard to general rules on levies, refunds, and minimum prices, it was held in Case 46/86, *Romkes*,[5] that the Council must observe the essential elements of the basic Regulation upon which the Parliament was consulted.

It was noted at the beginning of this book that art. 43 provided for qualified majority voting as from 1 January 1966, and can, therefore, be linked to the French failure to attend Council meetings in the second half

---

[1] [1980] ECR 3333.
[2] Case 5/73, *Balkan* v. *HZA Berlin-Packhof*, [1973] ECR 1091.
[3] JO 1971 L106/1.   [4] JO 1972 L291/148.   [5] 16 June 1987.

of 1965, leading to the 'Luxembourg accords' of January 1966, in which France recorded its view that 'where very important interests are at stake the discussion must be continued until unanimous agreement is reached'. Whilst this view was, in effect, treated as a constitutional convention during the 1970s, although it had no force in law, in 1982 agricultural price legislation was adopted by the Council on a qualified majority vote, despite the fact that the United Kingdom invoked the Luxembourg Accords.[6] Although subsequently qualified majorities have not always been sought or obtained where they could have been used (in 1985 for example)[7] they have become more widely used in practice, and it would appear that the contentious 1987 legislation[8] was adopted by qualified majorities which differed on different points. Indeed, in the area of health protection, the United Kingdom brought Case 68/86, *UK* v. *Council*,[9] seeking the annulment of Council Directive 85/649,[10] prohibiting the use in livestock farming of certain substances having a hormonal action, claiming that it should have been adopted under the general harmonization procedure of art. 100, which required unanimity, rather than by a qualified majority under art. 43. However, July 1987 saw the entry into force of art. 100a introduced into the EEC Treaty by art. 18 of the Single European Act, allowing the Council to adopt measures for the approximation of laws by a qualified majority, and in co-operation with the European Parliament, for the purpose of establishing the internal market by 31 December 1992.

A further aspect of the Community legislative process which is particularly illustrated in the context of agriculture is its sectoral nature: Community agriculture legislation is normally adopted by a Council composed of Ministers of Agriculture, whose meetings are prepared not by the usual Committee of Permanent Representatives expressly recognized in art. 4 of the Merger Treaty, but by a 'Special Committee for Agriculture' composed of senior national civil servants responsible for agricultural matters.[11]

Under the Regulations establishing common organizations of agricultural markets enacted pursuant to art. 43, the Council does generally retain a limited number of powers for itself, notably the power to fix the basic target and intervention prices for each marketing year. Unfortunately, it is notorious that these price decisions are not always taken in time, so that

---

[6] For a critical account, see Hill, *The Common Agricultural Policy: Past, Present and Future* (Methuen, London, 1984) pp. 134–136.

[7] Giving rise to the adoption by theCommission of the 'precautionary measures' described below.

[8] Which, in particular introduced a 'buying-in' price for cereals: see *supra*, p. 54.

[9] 23 Feb. 1988; see *supra*. p. 26.

[10] OJ 1985 L382/228.

[11] For the history of this Committee, see Neville-Rolfe, *The Politics of Agriculture in the European Community* (Policy Studies Institute, London, 1984) p. 208.

previous marketing years were often deemed to continue for a while longer. In 1985 it was proposed by the Commission, for the first time, that cereal prices expressed in European currency units should actually be reduced. The Council was unable to reach agreement on the matter by the appropriate date, but, whilst it may be possible to 'stop the clock' when prices are likely to rise or stay the same, and pay the previous year's prices on a temporary basis, much greater difficulty arises if the aim is to reduce the guaranteed prices. If the previous year's prices were to be paid in such a case, producers would be paid an excessive price, part of which would have to be recovered once the new lower prices were agreed. The matter came to a head in June 1985 since, under the version of art. 3 of Regulation 2727/75[12] then in force, the intervention prices valid on 1 June in Greece, Italy, and certain regions of France had to be adjusted in the light of the intervention prices fixed for August, which was then the first month of the new marketing year. In the light of the Council's failure to act on its proposals, the Commission, on 20 June 1985 adopted Decision 85/309[13] on 'precautionary measures' with regard to the buying in of cereals in Greece, Italy and those regions of France, requiring the Member States to reduce certain of the previous year's prices by 1.8 per cent. This was replaced by Commission Regulation 2124/85,[14] adopted on 26 July 1985 (i.e. just before the start of the marketing year), applying general 'precautionary measures' (in other words, fixing lower prices) in the cereals sector other than durum wheat. In October 1985, the Commission exercised its express power under art. 13 of Regulation 2727/75 to fix import levies on cereals, adopting in Regulation 2956/85[15] levies calculated from the basic prices it had itself enacted. The outline history may be completed by stating that no Council legislation was adopted in the matter until Council Regulation 1584/86 of 23 May 1986,[16] fixing the cereal prices for the 1986/7 marketing year, which expressly continued some of the prices fixed by the Commission.

In adopting its 'precautionary measures' the Commission declared, in the recitals both to the Decision and to the subsequent Regulation, that it was acting under arts. 5 and 155 of the EEC Treaty. Art. 5 requires the Member States to take all appropriate measures to ensure fulfilment of the obligation resulting from the action taken by the institutions of the Community, to facilitate the achievement of the Community's tasks, and to abstain from any measure which could jeopardize the attainment of the objectives of the Treaty, whereas art. 155 empowers the Commission, inter alia, to ensure that the provisions of the Treaty and the measures taken by the institutions pursuant thereto are applied. Presumably therefore the

---

[12] OJ 1975 L281/1.
[13] OJ 1985 L163/52.
[14] OJ 1985 L198/31.
[15] OJ 1985 L285/8.
[16] OJ 1986 L139/41.

rationale of the Commission's action was that the failure of Member States in Council to fix the cereal prices in due time constituted a breach of their duties under art. 5, and that the Commission's duty under art. 155 was to ensure the application of the common organization of the market in cereals. What is, however, particularly remarkable is that no direct challenge to the Commission's legislation was mounted either by the Council as such or by any of the Member States, though it remains to be seen whether the validity of that legislation will be attacked by individual traders or producers through the national courts.

It would seem that the Commission is willing to follow its own precedent, since in 1987, when it seemed that agreement in the Council was unlikely, the Commission again adopted a series of Regulations[17] on precautionary measures, expressed to be without prejudice to the ultimate decisions to be taken by the Council. In this case, however, the Council did reach agreement in July 1987.

(b) *Management committee system*

The power to enact most implementing legislation in relation to common organizations is, however, expressly delegated by the Council to the Commission, as authorized under art. 155 of the Treaty. Hence, the vast majority of the thousands of EEC agricultural Regulations have been issued by the Commission. In practice, the Council has delegated not only powers of simple administration, but also powers requiring the exercise of discretion. In this latter case, however, it has usually required the Commission to consult a committee representing national interests, known as a 'Management Committee', established for each common organization.

The model for these committees is contained in arts. 25–7 of Council Regulation 2727/75,[18] on the common organization of the market in cereals. It consists of representatives of the Member States (normally civil servants responsible for the particular market), with a representative of the Commission as chairman. The national representatives have votes weighted accordance with the qualified majority procedure laid down in art. 148(2) of the EEC Treaty, so that the number of votes and the majority required has been automatically altered every time art. 148(2) has been amended in successive Acts of Accession. Where the Commission is required to act under this procedure, it must submit a draft of the measures to be adopted to the Committee, which must deliver its opinion within the time-limit set by the Chairman. A qualified majority as defined in art. 148(2) is required

[17] Commission Regs. Nos. 1213/87 (OJ 1987 L115/33), 1503/87 (OJ 1987 L141/13), and 1826/87 (OJ 1987 L173/7).
[18] OJ 1975 L281/1.

by the Committee to give either a favourable opinion or an unfavourable opinion. To take as an example the information published in Table 13 to the twentieth General Report of the EC (1986), the twenty-six agricultural management and regulatory committees gave in that year a total of 2,179 favourable opinions (897 of them in the cereals market) and no unfavourable opinions at all, a situation which would appear to be not untypical. If, however, the Committee does issue an opinion which is unfavourable, the Commission is not prevented from putting its measures into operation; it must refer the matter to the Council itself, but it has a discretion whether or not to defer the application of its measures. The Council, in turn, may take a different decision by a qualified majority within a month, but, if it fails to do so, the Commission's measures remain in force. It would appear, in fact, that by 1986 the Council had only once reversed a Commission measure since the system began in 1962.

The legality of the management committee system was challenged in Case 75/70, *Einfuhr- und Vorratsstelle Getreide* v. *Köster*,[19] on the basis that it interposed between the Council and the Commission a body which was not provided for by the Treaty. The Court, however, held that it formed part of the detailed rules to which the Council could legitimately subject a delegation of power to the Commission, on the basis that it was really a method of permanent consultation between the Council and the Commission, the Committee had no power to take a decision in place of the Council or the Commission, and it had the beneficial effect of enabling the Council to delegate to the Commission an implementing power of appreciable scope. In the result, similar, if not identical, committees have been established in relation to other areas of Community legislation.

However, this led to the development of procedures which differ marginally one from the other, and the establishment of hundreds of different committees. In the light of this, art. 10 of the Single European Act amended art. 145 of the EEC Treaty so as to require the Council to lay down a framework of rules and principles governing such procedures, which, in turn, led to the enactment of Council Decision 87/373,[20] of 13 July 1987, laying down procedures for the exercise of implementing powers conferred on the Commission. This recognizes three basic procedures: the first merely requires the Commission to obtain the opinion of the relevant committee, the second effectively reproduces the 'management-committee' system outlined above, and the third, in principle, requires the Commission to obtain the consent of the relevant committee before it can act. Variants on these procedures are, nevertheless, recognized, and art. 4 of the Decision expressly provides that procedures in acts which predate its

[19] [1970] ECR 1161.
[20] OJ 1987 L197/33.

entry into force may be retained when such acts are amended or extended. It would, therefore, seem likely that the existing pattern of agricultural committees will continue.

What the Commission may not do, however, is to sub-delegate powers which it should exercise through the management committee system so as in effect to circumvent that procedure. This appears from Case 23/75, *Rey Soda* v. *Cassa Conguaglio Zucchero*,[21] where the Court was concerned, in fact, with a sub-delegation of powers by the Commission to the Italian government. The provision in question was art. 6 of Regulation 834/74.[22] This provided that 'Italy shall take national measures to prevent disturbances on the market resulting from the increase on 1 July 1974 in the price of sugar expressed in Italian lire. These provisions shall consist in particular of a payment to beet growers of the increased value of stocks'. The action with which the Court was concerned was a reference from an Italian court before which the plaintiff was seeking to recover the amounts which he had had to pay to the Italian sugar authority under the Italian legislation made subsequent to this provision.

It was held that the Commission should have defined in its regulation what was meant by 'stock' and by 'increased value', but, most importantly, the Court stated that by not specifying the bases of the calculation of the tax in the provision in question, and leaving Italy to choose them, the Commission discharged itself of its own responsibility to adopt the basic rules and to submit them by way of the Management Committee procedure to the approval if need be of the Council; therefore the art. was invalid. On the other hand, many examples can, of course, be found of Community agricultural legislation which directly confers discretionary powers on the Member States, particularly in the context of sugar and milk quotas. Indeed, in Cases 103–109/78, *Société des Usines de Beauport* v. *Council*,[23] it was held that Council Regulation 298/78,[24] amending the basic Regulation on the allocation and alteration of the basic quotas for sugar, was not of 'direct and individual concern' to the applicants in terms of art. 173 of the EEC Treaty[25] precisely because that Regulation allowed France a discretion whether or not to reduce the basic quotas fixed for sugar producers in its overseas departments, and also as to whether the basic quotas of all or only of certain undertakings were to be reduced.

---

[21] [1975] ECR 1279.
[22] OJ 1974 L99/15.
[23] [1979] ECR 17.
[24] OJ 1978 L45/1.
[25] See Usher, 'European Court Practice' (1983) paras. 1.25–1.32.

(c) *Control functions of the Agricultural Guidance and Guarantee Fund and the Commission*

(i) Introduction

As will have been observed, the Commission has frequently used its general power to take enforcement proceedings against Member States under art. 169 of the EEC Treaty with regard to breaches of agricultural legislation, and to the extent that the relevant substantive rules apply to agriculture, the Commission may also use its normal methods of enforcing the competition rules under arts. 85 and 86 of the Treaty and the state-aids rules under arts. 92–4 of the Treaty.

A distinctive feature of the agricultural sector, however, is the degree of financial control which may be exercised by the Commission through the EAGGF, and which arises from the fact that Member States are responsible, under art. 6 of Council Decision 243/70,[26] on the system of own resources (replaced from 1 January 1986 by art. 7 of Council Decision 85/257),[27] for the collection of agricultural levies, and from the fact that the various common organizations make them responsible for the payment of intervention purchases, refunds, aids, etc. The legal possibilities of this situation were clearly revealed in a group of three cases brought by the Netherlands,[28] Germany,[29] and France[30] against the Commission for the annulment of Commission Decisions relating to the discharge of accounts with regard to EAGGF guarantee section expenditure in 1971 and 1972.

(ii) Legal basis of EAGGF liability

The legal basis under which the EAGGF should become liable for agricultural expenditure was at issue in both the Dutch and German cases. Council Regulation 729/70,[31] on the financing of the Common Agricultural Policy, states in its art. 1(2) that the guarantee section shall finance 'refunds on exports to third countries' and 'intervention intended to stabilize the agricultural markets'. Art.2(1) provides more specifically for the financing of refunds on exports to third countries 'granted in accordance with the Community rules within the framework of the common organization of agricultural markets', and art. 3(1) provides, more specifically, for the financing of intervention intended to stabilize the agricultural markets 'undertaken according to Community rules within the framework of the common organisation of agricultural markets'. The

[26] JO 1970 L94/19.   [27] OJ 1985 L128/15.   [28] Case 11/76 [1979] ECR 245.
[29] Case 18/76 [1979] ECR 343.
[30] Cases 15 and 16/76 [1979] ECR 321.   [31] JO 1970 L94/13.

provision invoked by the Dutch and German governments, however, was art. 8(2), the first subparagraph of which is to the effect that 'in the absence of total recovery, the financial consequences of irregularities or negligence shall be borne by the Community, with the exception of the consequences of irregularities or negligence attributable to administrative authorities or other bodies of the Member States'. The two governments argued that this provision must be taken to mean that the Community must bear the financial consequences of an incorrect interpretation of a provision of Community law by a national authority, where the interpretation was adopted in good faith and was not the 'fault', in the sense of a wrongful action, of that national authority.

After looking at the different-language versions of art. 8, the Court reached a conclusion which gives rise to concern with regard to the drafting and translation of Community legislation; it found that art. 8 'contains too many contradictory and ambiguous elements to provide an answer to the questions at issue'. Looking at the whole of art. 8 in its context, however, the Court found that it was concerned with the prevention of fraud and irregularities, and with the recovery of sums wrongly paid. Without going so far as to say, with the Commission (and A.-G. Capotorti), that art. 8(2) only refers to irregularities or negligence on the part of individuals, the Court found there to be a general principle common to the Community legal system and to 'most' of the national legal systems that it was not possible to recover from the recipients sums paid in error by the national authorities on the basis of an incorrect interpretation of Community law adopted by them in good faith, and from this it concluded that art. 8(2) did not apply to such a situation, it being concerned with situations where recovery was legally possible.

On the basis that art. 8(2) could not apply, the Court held that the situation should be considered in the light of arts. 2 and 3 of the Regulation, requiring the Community to finance refunds granted and intervention undertaken 'in accordance with the Community rules'. From this, given that the sums at issue were not only refunds or intervention payments, the broader principle was deduced that the Commission could charge to the EAGGF 'only sums paid in accordance with the rules laid down in the various sectors of agricultural production while leaving the Member States to bear the burden of any other sum paid', in particular, any amounts which the national authorities wrongly believed themselves authorized to pay in the context of the common organization of the market. This strict, indeed absolute, rule was justified on the grounds that a Member State should not be able to favour its own traders by a wide interpretation of a provision of Community law, and certainly should not be able to do so with Community finance.

Although a detailed analysis of the items of expenditure at issue in the cases would be out of place, given their highly specific nature, a general consideration of them may furnish useful examples of the way in which the rule was applied by the Court: indeed, only one item was held to be liable to be financed by the EAGGF.

(iii) **Expenditure for which the EAGGF is not liable**

The first item in the Dutch case concerned the release of securities lodged to ensure the export within thirty days of 'sale' of intervention butter sold at reduced prices under Commission Regulation 1308/68.[32] The Dutch government had allowed the securities to be released where the butter was exported thirty days after removal from storage, whereas the Commission took the view that it should have been exported within thirty days of the contract of sale. The Court held quite simply that 'sale' meant sale, and not removal, and, hence, that the EAGGF was not liable to meet the cost of repayment of the securities. The same point also arose in the German case and was answered in the same way. The second item in the Dutch case involved payments of export refunds for lactalbumin, a product in the milk sector, under legislation which the Court had held in Case 150/73, *Hollandse Melksuikerfabriek* v. *Hoofdproduktschap voor Akkerbouw-produkten*,[33] only to apply to ovalbumin, a product in the egg sector. Although it was accepted that there might be doubts as to the exact scope of that legislation, it was found that its incorrect application was not the result of the Commission's conduct. Hence, the refunds could not be charged to the EAGGF.

The first item in the French cases involved the payments of aid to skimmed-milk powder exported from France to Italy and intended for use as animal feed, where the aids had been paid without the control copies of the Community transit document having been produced, as required under the relevant legislation. It would appear that this lapse had later been rectified, but the Court held that aid paid in disregard of a condition that certain formalities relating to proof are complied with at the time of payment is not paid in accordance with Community law and, therefore, cannot be charged to the EAGGF. The second aspect of the French cases involved the payment of aids for the distillation of wines. The French government had taken the view that the aids payable to this end under Council Regulation 766/72[34] were inadequate, and supplemented them with national aids. The Commission then initiated the procedure under EEC art. 169 against France in relation to the breach of a Treaty obligation involved in the payment of national aids, but did not pursue the matter when the aids ceased to be paid. However, when it came to the discharge

---

[32] JO 1968 L214/10.   [33] [1973] ECR 1633.   [34] JO 1972 L91/1.

of the EAGGF accounts, the Commission refused to accept liability for the amounts of aid payable under Community law, on the grounds that the national measures had had the effect of distorting the distillation operation by extending it. Before the Court, the French government claimed that the EAGGF should meet the proportion of the aid granted which corresponded to the rates fixed by Community rules, but it was held that it was impossible to ascertain to what extent the total effect of the combined national and Community aid was due to one or other component part, and, in particular, that it was impossible to establish with certainty what quantities of wine would have been distilled in France if the national measure had not been adopted. With regard to the discontinuance of the proceedings under EEC art. 169, the Court pointed out that such discontinuance does not constitute recognition that the contested conduct is lawful. So, by adding a national element to a Community aid, France found itself having to finance the whole amount.

On the other hand, if a Member State does not add its own national aid, but pays a Community aid to recipients falling outside its scope, the Member State will not necessarily lose the whole aid. In Case 49/83, *Luxembourg* v. *Commission*,[35] it was held that where the Member State had acted in good faith it may still obtain reimbursement to the extent that it can prove that the aid was properly paid—but the burden is on the Member State.

(iv) Expenditure for which the EAGGF is liable

The only item in the trio of cases for which the EAGGF was held to be liable to pay involved German expenditure on aid for the purchase of butter by persons in receipt of social assistance. Council Regulation 414/70[36] enabled the Commission to decide that Member States could grant aid to enable, inter alia, persons in receipt of social assistance to purchase butter at reduced prices. Its validity was initially limited to 1970, but it was later extended to the end of 1971. Commission Decision 70/228,[37] made under the Regulation, enabled Member States to implement the aid by a scheme of individualized vouchers, allowing 0.5 kg. per month to be bought at a reduced price. In order to save administrative costs, the German authorities issued vouchers early in 1970 valid for each month of the whole year, and did the same in 1971. However, the Commission Decision was repealed with effect from 1 May 1971; nonetheless, the German authorities continued to allow the vouchers to be used until the end of the year, on the grounds that by distributing the vouchers it had created a legal position for their holders which it could not

---

[35] [1984] ECR 2931.   [36] JO 1970 L52/2.   [37] JO 1970 L77/15.

terminate prematurely. The Commission refused to meet the cost of the aid after 30 April 1971, but the Court held that, since the Commission decision remained in force without any amendment for an indeterminate period after the period of validity of the enabling regulation had been extended to the end of 1971, it could not be said that the German government had exceeded what it was lawfully entitled to do to implement the Commission's decision within its territory by maintaining the system it had initially adopted without making provision for the possibility of terminating the operation in the course of the year. In this the Court differed from A.-G. Capotorti, who had suggested that no Member State was entitled to grant to the recipients, at the expense of the Community, rights more extensive than those conferred by the Commission decision. It is, perhaps, the case that this could not at first sight be construed as an example of expenditure in accordance with the letter of Community law, but the Court found that the relevant legislation allowed the Member States 'great freedom' to choose the methods and administrative procedures for its implementation, and that what the German government had done did not exceed the limits of that freedom. In other words, it was a reasonable exercise of its discretion, at the time the discretion was exercised.

In the result, a very simple and virtually absolute rule can be stated with regard to the recovery of Member States' expenditure under the Common Agricultural Policy from the EAGGF: a Member State may recover only sums spent in accordance with Community rules as ultimately interpreted by the European Court of Justice, whatever interpretation that State may itself have put on those rules. The only exceptions are that where the Community rules grant the Member States a discretion expenditure falling within a reasonable exercise of that discretion may be recoverable, and that where the incorrect application of Community law is attributable to a Community institution the Community should bear the financial consequences.

(d) *Introduction of EC Agricultural Law into the United Kingdom*

As is well known, the general provisions of the European Communities Act are drafted on the basis of a distinction between the rules of Community law which do not require national enactment in order to be law in a Member State, converted into what are termed 'enforceable Community rights' and obligations, etc., under s. 2(1), and rules of Community law which do require national implementation, with regard to which s. 2(2) enables Orders in Council to be made and enables designated Ministers or departments to make regulations.

At the outset, it may be observed that there is not always a clear-cut distinction between provisions of Community law which require domestic implementation in the United Kingdom and those which do not. By definition, an EEC Regulation is directly applicable throughout the Community and its terms therefore do not need national re-enactment; indeed, the European Court has held that they must not receive national re-enactment since the Community law origin of the legislation might thereby be disguised, and those affected might not realise that Community law remedies were available in relation to the legislation.[38] Nevertheless, there are many EEC Regulations which, as the European Court has recognized,[39] expressly or implicitly require domestic ancillary or implementing legislation. However, in implementing under s. 2(2) what is already law under s. 2(1), it is clear that the role of the statutory instruments is to provide machinery to aid the application of the Community law, and not to alter or add to the directly applicable provision.

On the other hand, although Directives are defined under art. 189 of the EEC Treaty as binding only on the Member States to which they are addressed, leaving to the Member States the choice of form and methods to achieve the required result, it is now clear that certain provisions of EC Directives may confer on individuals rights enforceable by them before national courts once the time-limit for the implementation of the Directive has expired,[40] thus, falling within s. 2(1) of the European Communities Act. Nevertheless, as a matter of Community law the Member States remain under a Treaty obligation expressly to implement such provisions.[41]

Even where a relevant Community obligation does exist, the powers under s. 2(2) and (4) of the European Communities Act do not preclude the use of parallel powers in other legislation or the implementation of Community obligations by separate Act of Parliament, as, for example, the Importation of Milk Act 1983, which was enacted as a result of the judgment of the European Court in Case 124/81, *Commission* v. *United Kingdom*.[42]

Although directly applicable Community legislation may, as a matter of Community law, render automatically inapplicable any conflicting provisions of national law,[43] there may still be a Community obligation formally to repeal those provisions,[44] since their apparent maintenance in force may give rise to a state of uncertainty as to the possibility of relying on

[38] Case 34/73, *Variola* v. *Italian Finance Administration* [1973] ECR 981.
[39] e.g. Case 31/78, *Bussone* v. *Italian Ministry for Agriculture* [1978] ECR 2429.
[40] Case 148/78 *Ratti* [1979] ECR 1629.
[41] Case 102/79, *Commission* v. *Belgium* [1980] ECR 1473.
[42] [1983] ECR 203.
[43] Case 106/77, *Italian Finance Administration* v. *Simmenthal* [1978] ECR 629.
[44] Case 167/73, *Commission* v. *France* [1974] ECR 359.

Community Law. Hence, the European Communities Act itself expressly repealed certain redundant agricultural legislation.

Section 2(2) refers also to the implementation of rights enjoyed by the United Kingdom by virtue of the Community Treaties. It may be wondered whether the word 'rights' in s. 2(2) is intended in a broader sense than in s. 2(1), where 'rights' are apparently to be distinguished from 'powers', since it would appear to be far more usual for Community instruments to grant powers or permissions to Member States than expressly to confer rights upon them. In particular, it may be doubted whether s. 2(2) could be used to implement a bare permission of the type found in art. 3(1) of EC Council Regulation 855/84,[45] on the calculation and dismantlement of monetary compensatory amounts, declaring that 'any special aid granted to German agricultural producers under the conditions referred to below shall be deemed to be compatible with the common market'. Similarly, the view appears to have been taken that art. 4(1) of EC Council Regulation 857/84[46] on the milk quota system, providing that Member States 'may grant to producers undertaking to discontinue milk production definitively compensation paid in one or more annual payments', amounted in reality to a declaration that such compensation would not constitute unlawful state aid rather than a clearly defined right for the Member States.[47] This scheme was ultimately implemented by a separate statute, the Milk (Cessation of Production) Act 1985.

In any event, wide as the apparent scope of s. 2(2) may be, it is subject to express limitations in Schedule 2 which may make it necessary to resort to primary legislation or parallel powers. Section 2(2), as there restricted, does not include power to make any provision imposing or increasing taxation, or to issue retrospective legislation, for example. The inability to issue retrospective legislation under s. 2(2) is reflected in other enabling provisions of the Act, and the fact that under s. 6(7) agricultural produce could only be taken out of the scope of s. 1 of the Agriculture Act 1957 prospectively led to a retrospective change in the period of application of United Kingdom guaranteed prices for pigmeat being effected in the directly applicable EC Commission Regulation 1822/75.[48]

It may, finally, be observed that the last paragraph of s. 2(2) specifies that, unless the implementation of Community legislation is itself to be by Order in Council, the minister or department wishing to make regulations must be designated for that purpose by an Order in Council. Such designation orders may be broad in scope, and, in the case of agriculture, the European Communities (Designation) Order 1972[49] quite simply

---

[45] OJ 1984 L90/1.   [46] OJ 1984 L90/13.
[47] The aid was originally paid on a non-statutory basis in the United Kingdom.
[48] OJ 1975 L185/10.   [49] S I 1972 No. 1811.

designates the Secretary of State and the Minister of Agriculture, Food, and Fisheries with regard to the implementation of the Common Agricultural Policy. Regulations concerning the Common Agricultural Policy in Scotland are, therefore, made by the Secretary of State.

As well as providing the general mechanism by which Community Law becomes available in the United Kingdom, the European Communities Act did itself implement certain substantive provisions of European Community Law, or lay down specific mechanisms by which they may be implemented.

Formal repeals and amendments of United Kingdom legislation were effected or enabled to be effected by s. 4 and Schedules 3 and 4. Part II of Schedule 3 repealed certain legislation relating to sugar, and Part III repealed legislation relating to seeds. Schedule 4, on the other hand, introduced amendments to United Kingdom legislation. On the related matter of food legislation, s. 4(1) of the Food and Drugs Act 1955, enabling regulations concerning the composition of food to be made by statutory instrument subject to the negative resolution procedure, was amended to allow such regulations to be made if 'called for by any Community obligation' and a new s. 123a was added enabling the ministers to make such provision by regulation as they considered necessary or expedient to ensure that any 'directly applicable' Community provision relating to food was administered, executed, and enforced under that Act; in particular, enabling sampling, analysing, testing or examining to be carried out. This indicates a preference for the use, or extended use, of specific powers rather than the general implementing power under s. 2(2) of the European Communities Act wherever possible, and specifically envisaged ancillary legislation where the substantive rules were laid down by directly applicable Community legislation. Similarly, whilst produce subject to Community grading rules (defined as 'directly applicable' Community provisions establishing standards of quality for fresh horticultural produce) was specifically excluded from regulations made under s. 11(1) of the Agriculture and Horticulture Act 1964, ministers were empowered to provide for the application of the enforcement provisions of the Act as if such produce were regulated produce. The Plant Varieties and Seeds Act 1964 was amended to broaden the power to issue seeds regulations governing the marketing or the importation or exportation of seeds, seed potatoes, and any other vegetable-propagating material or silvicultural-planting material. The Agriculture Act 1970 was amended to enable regulations to be made to control in the public interest the composition or content of fertilizers and of material intended for the feeding of animals, and to apply other provisions of the Act with a view to implementing or supplementing any Community instrument relating to fertilizers or to material intended for the feeding of animals. With regard to animal and plant health, the Diseases of Animals Act 1950 was amended to enable orders to be made excluding prescribed animals imported from other Member States from the requirement of slaughter on landing, and for regulating the exportation from Great Britain to other Member States of animals, or poultry, or carcasses thereof; the Plant Health Act 1967 was amended to enable orders to be made for the control of pests if 'called for by any Community obligation'.

However, the major provision of the European Communities Act with regard to the implementation of the Common Agricultural Policy is s. 6, which created the Intervention Board for Agricultural Produce, the role of which will be considered in the next section.

(e) National agencies and producer organizations

In anticipation of the need to provide for the administration at the national level of the Common Agricultural Policy, s. 6 of the European Communities Act 1972 provided for the establishment of the Intervention Board for Agricultural Produce, and provision for its constitution and membership was made before Accession under the Intervention Board for Agricultural Produce Order 1972.[50] In general, it is charged with such functions as the ministers may from time to time determine in connection with the carrying out of the obligations of the United Kingdom under the Common Agricultural Policy, and s. 6(4) specifically requires levies on the export of agricultural goods to be paid to, and recoverable by, the Board. On the other hand, s. 6(5) requires levies on agricultural imports, which are, in practice, far more important, to be levied, collected, and paid as if they were Community customs duties, even if as a matter of law, they are not,[51] and their collection is, therefore, entrusted to the Commissioners of Customs and Excise. Nevertheless, under the Customs and Excise (Positive Monetary Compensatory Amounts) Regulations 1980,[52] the Commissioners are required to pay to the Board a sum equivalent to the amounts paid to them as positive, monetary compensatory amounts (when the value of the pound is higher than its agricultural exchange rate) on imports of agricultural goods from other Member States.

As has already been noted, s. 6, further, enabled regulations to provide for the charging of fees in connection with the discharge of any functions of the Board, and also enabled regulations to be issued modifying or adding to the constitution or powers of any other statutory body concerned with agriculture or agricultural produce either to enable them to act for the Board or to require them to discontinue activities prejudicial to the proper

[50] S I 1972 No. 1578.   [51] See *supra*, p. 63.   [52] S I 1980 No. 927.

discharge of the Board's functions, and the 1972 Order specifically enabled the Board, with the approval of the ministers, to arrange for the performance of any of its functions by another such statutory body.

A delegation of powers was, in fact, effected before Accession under the Intervention Functions (Delegation) Regulations 1972[53] to the Home-Grown Cereals Authority and to the Meat and Livestock Commission. It was there provided that the Home-Grown Cereals Authority should have power to carry out in the United Kingdom such of the Board's functions with respect to wheat, barley, oats, rye, maize, and oil-seed rape as the Board might with the approval of the ministers and the agreement of the Authority delegate to the Authority in writing. This is of some legal interest in so far as, under Community law, oil-seed rape falls within the common organization of the market in oils and fats rather than under the common organization of the market in cereals.

With regard to the Meat and Livestock Commission, it was, similarly, provided that the Commission should have power to carry out in Great Britain such of the Board's functions with respect to livestock and livestock products as the Board might, with the approval of the ministers and the agreement of the Commission, delegate to the Commission in writing.

Intervention functions have also been delegated to the Milk Marketing Boards under the Intervention Functions (Delegation) (Milk) Regulations 1982,[54] under which the Boards have power in the area in which each operates to act for the Intervention Board by carrying out in that area such of the functions of the Intervention Board with respect to milk as the Intervention Board may, with the approval of the Ministers and the agreement of the milk marketing boards, delegate in writing to them. More specifically, in the context of the guarantee threshold for milk and the quotas imposed thereunder, the Dairy Produce Quotas Regulations 1986[55] provide that the Intervention Board and any milk marketing board may enter into an agreement providing for the discharge by the milk marketing board, on behalf of the Intervention Board, of any functions of the Intervention Board under the regulations or the Community legislation specified in the agreement, on such terms as may be specified in the agreement.

Moving from the Milk Marketing Boards to producer organizations as such, their encouragement is often regarded as, essentially, a structural or guidance measure,[56] but it has usually been achieved by authorising such organizations to effect certain guarantee measures, such as operating a withdrawal system, withdrawing goods from the market when prices fall below a certain level. This appears to have been first introduced in relation to the markets in fruit and vegetables in Council Regulation 159/66,[57]

---

[53] S I 1982 No. 1679. [54] S I 1982 No. 1502. [55] S I 1986 No. 470, Reg. 26.
[56] See *supra*, p. 133–7. [57] JO 1966 p. 3286.

repeated in Council Regulation 1035/72,[58] and strengthened by Council Regulation 3284/83[59] enabling fruit-and-vegetable-producers' organizations to extend their marketing rules to non-members in certain circumstances. Similar provision may, for example, be found in the common organization of the market in fish products under Council Regulation 3796/81,[60] under which non-members may be required to abide by certain of the rules of producer organizations.

In the case of the common organization of the market in milk, however, the basic legislation was amended in effect to accommodate the United Kingdom Milk Marketing Boards, as has been noted in the context of that common organization. Council Regulation 1421/78[61] amended Regulation 804/68[62] on the common organization of the market in milk, so as to allow certain rights to be granted to organizations representing 80 per cent in number and 50 per cent of production of milk producers in the relevant area; these special rights were the exclusive right to buy (coupled with an obligation to buy milk satisfying certain minimum requirements) and the right to equalize prices paid to producers, provided this did not jeopardise the basic price and intervention arrangements. Council Regulation 1422/78[63] arranged for a poll to be held in relation to the Milk Marketing Board for England and Wales, the Scottish Milk Marketing Board, the Aberdeen and District Milk Marketing Board, the North of Scotland Milk Marketing Board and the Milk Marketing Board for Northern Ireland, but also provided that the exclusive rights were not to apply to milk withheld for export or to milk withheld for conversion into butter or skimmed-milk powder for sale into intervention,, that is, the fundamental individual rights to sell into another Member State and to sell into intervention were preserved. Following the poll (and provision was made for fresh polls to be held), Council Regulation 1565/79[64] confirmed the grant of the special rights, but provided expressly that producers should be enabled to determine the milk price resulting from the intervention prices for skimmed-milk powder and butter. However, it may be observed that, by virtue of United Kingdom secondary legislation,[65] intervention functions with regard to milk are effected by the selfsame Milk Marketing Boards.

(f) Legal consequences of national administration of the CAP

Although agricultural levies form part of the Communities' 'own resources' under Council Decision 243/70[66] (replaced from 1 January 1986 by Council

[58] JO 1972 L118/1.   [59] OJ 1983 L325/1.   [60] See *supra*, p. 92.
[61] OJ 1978 L171/12.   [62] JO 1968 L148/13.   [63] OJ 1978 L171/14.
[64] OJ 1979 L188/29.   [65] See *supra*, p. 159.   [66] JO 1970 L94//19.

Decision 85/257),[67] their collection is expressly stated to be the responsibility of the Member States. Hence, in Cases 178–180/73, *Belgium and Luxembourg* v. *Mertens and others*,[68] which were references made in criminal proceedings relating to fraud in the context of the export and import of agricultural products, the European Court held that it was for the Member States to take the necessary criminal or civil proceedings to enforce or recover agricultural levies. This view was taken further in a ruling given on a reference in criminal proceedings before an Italian magistrate, the pretore of Cento, in 1977,[69] where the Court held that the Community institutions are not empowered, in the present state of the law, to take proceedings before national courts for the purpose of claiming payment of Community revenue constituting own resources. On the other hand, the implementing legislation, currently re-enacted in art. 18 of Council Regulation (EEC) no. 2891/77,[70] provides that the Commission may be 'associated' at its request with measures of control carried out by Member States, but it was pointed out by the Court in Case 267/78, *Commission* v. *Italy*,[71] that this does not enable the Commission to carry out measures of control itself, and that it does not, for example, alter national rules as to the secrecy of criminal investigations and of documents related thereto.

Conversely, there is a series of judgments holding that an individual trader who wishes to recover agricultural levies which he thinks the national authorities have wrongly charged him must bring his action against the national authorities rather than the Community, even though the levies may constitute the Community's own resources. This was first clearly stated in Case 96/71, *Haegeman* v. *Commission*,[72] where an importer brought an action against the Commission for recovery of charges levied by the Belgian authorities under Commission legislation on imports of Greek wine. It was held that since the collection of 'own resources' was, basically, the responsibility of the national authorities, disputes concerning the levying of such charges should be resolved by the national authorities, or before the national courts, subject to the possibility of referring any question as to the interpretation of Community law to the European Court. It might merely be noted that in subsequent cases it has not always proved easy to distinguish between actions for the recovery of agricultural levies and actions for damages for harm caused by the wrongful acts of the Community institutions.

Just as traders seeking to recover agricultural levies must, in principle, act against the national authority which collected them, so, also, a trader seeking payment of sums due under Community agricultural legislation must act against the national authority entrusted with making such a

---

[67] OJ 1985 L128/15. [68] [1974] ECR 33. [69] Case 110/76, [1977] ECR 851.
[70] OJ 1977 L336/1. [71] [1980] ECR 31. [72] [1972] ECR 1005.

payment. The clearest example of this is perhaps, Case 99/74, *Grands Moulins des Antilles* v. *Commission*,[73] where the applicants were claiming export refunds and carry-over payments due under the relevant Community legislation in relation to cereals respectively exported from or stocked in French overseas departments. It was held that the action should be brought against the national authorities, even though their refusal to pay arose because the EAGGF, in turn, refused to finance such payments in relation to overseas *départements*, since by art. 227(2) of the Treaty the benefits of the Fund did not automatically extend to overseas *départements*. Similarly, it was held in Cases 89 and 91/86, *Société l'Etoile Commerciale*,[74] that the payment and recovery of Community aids was a matter of the national authorities, despite the refusal of the Agricultural Guidance and Guarantee Fund to make the relevant payment.

Legislative reinforcement of the view that payments are the responsibility of the national authorities was given in the context of the exhaustion of Community budgetary resources in 1987, when Council Regulation 3183/87[75] required Member States to make payments in accordance with the needs of the disbursing authorities when the guarantee allocation for 1987 had been used up. On the other hand, where the Community legislation fails to provide for the payment claimed, and this is alleged to be a wrongful act, an action may be brought directly against the responsible Community institution, as was confirmed in 1979 in Case 238/78, *Ireks Arkady* v. *Council and Commission*,[76] one of a group of cases in which damages were for the first time awarded to applicants harmed by Community legislation which seriously breached a superior rule of law for the protection of the individual.

Particular problems may arise in considering whether a trader has suffered harm as a result of the action of the Community authorities or as a result of the action of the national authorities implementing the Community legislation. In Case 133/79, *Sucrimex* v. *Commission*,[77] it was held that where the application of the relevant Community rules was a matter for the national authorities it was their actions which should be treated as harming the applicants, even though they had acted on the basis of a (non-binding) telex from the Commission. A similar approach was taken in Case 12/79, *Wagner* v. *Commission*,[78] where the dispute related to the refusal by the German authorities to allow the applicant to cancel a sugar export licence on 1 July 1976. The German authorities thought they were acting on the basis of a Commission Regulation which purported to come into force on 1 July 1976. It transpired, however, that, because of a strike, the copy of the Official Journal containing the Regulation was only published the next day, and it, therefore, could only enter into force on that day. The view of

[73] [1975] ECR 1531.   [74] 7 July 1987.   [75] OJ 1987 L304/1.
[76] [1979] ECR 2985.   [77] [1980] ECR 1299.   [78] [1979] ECR 3657.

the Court was that it was the German authorities which had, thus, acted unlawfully in the absence of binding Community legislation, and the legality of their conduct should be challenged before the national courts.

However, in Case 175/84, *Krohn* v. *Commission*,[79] where telexes sent by the Commission to the German authorities were interpreted, in the context of the legislation in question,[80] as instruction to the German authorities, it was held that the alleged unlawful conduct was to be attributed to the Commission itself, and an action for damages could, therefore, be brought against the Commission.

(g) *Enforcement by and against national authorities*[81]

It is in the context of the Common Agricultural Policy that most of the basic principles have been laid down concerning the enforcement of Community law by and against national authorities.

With regard to the enforcement of Community law *by* national authorities, the basic principle is that, in the absence of specific Community rules,[82] the national authorities must enforce Community law by national methods, but that, in so far as the national authorities have wrongly paid out Community moneys, they enjoy no discretion as to whether they should attempt to recover such moneys;[83] on the other hand, it would appear to be permissible for the national courts to protect a bona fide payee who did not give wrong information, where such a payee would be protected in relation to an incorrect payment under national law.[84] The fundamental rule, however, is that the power to recover sums due to the Community under national law must not be more restricted than the powers granted to the same authority in relation to sums due under national law.[85] Finally, whilst Member States may not fill a lacuna created by Community legislation, as where a Regulation failed to provide for the recovery of a deposit where its release was obtained by fraud,[86] they remain under a duty to take any available national criminal proceedings with regard to such conduct.[87]

---

[79] [1986] ECR 753.

[80] Art. 7(1) of Commission Reg. 2029/82 (OJ 1982 L218/8).

[81] For a fuller account of the author's views, see paras. 3.71–3.76 of 'Law of the European Communities' ed. Vaughan (Butterworths, London, 1986), also printed in vol. 51 of Halsbury's *Laws of England*. See also, Oliver 'Enforcing Community Rights in the English Courts' (1987) MLR 881.

[82] Community rules do exist, for example, in relation to certain aspects of customs legislation.

[83] Cases 205 to 215/82, *Deutsche Milchkontor* v. *Germany* [1983] ECR 2633.

[84] Case 265/78, *Ferwerda* v. *Produktschap voor Vee-en-Vlies* [1980] ECR 617.

[85] Cases 66, 127 and 128/79, *Italian Finance Administration* v. *Salumi* [1980] ECR 1237.

[86] Case 117/83 *Koenecke* [1984] ECR 3291; see *supra*, pp. 124–5.   [87] Ibid.

Where an individual or trader wishes to enforce Community law *against* national authorities before national courts, the basic principle remains that, in the absence of any relevant Community rules, normal national remedies should be used provided that they do not make it practically impossible to exercise enforceable Community rights,[88] and that these national rules are non-discriminatory[89] and subject to the overriding obligation on national courts to protect directly effective rights under Community law.[90] Hence, the relevant national limitation periods apply[91] if they comply with these conditions. However, whilst in a claim for restitution of sums paid to the national authorities the national courts may take account of the fact that those charges were actually passed on to the plaintiff's customers so as to prevent the unjust enrichment of the plaintiff, if national law so provides,[92] they cannot impose an excessive burden of proof that such charges were not passed on to the customers, even if such a burden would be imposed in relation to an analogous claim arising under national law alone.[93] On the other hand, if it is possible to recover an over-payment on grounds of equity in relation to a national tax, it should also be possible to recover an over-payment made under Community law.[94]

With regard to the enforcement of Community agricultural legislation against the public authorities in the United Kingdom, the aspect of judicial review most frequently involved is the action for a declaration. Actions for a declaration have been used in two separate ways: either to challenge the validity of United Kingdom acts in the light of Community law, or to challenge the validity of Community acts. In the first category was *Meijer* v. *Department of Trade*,[95] where a declaration was sought that the United Kingdom was no longer authorized to control the importation of potatoes from other Member States. The second category includes the English isoglucose cases[96] where declarations were sought to the effect that a series of EC Council Regulations were void and of no effect and that the United Kingdom government was not entitled to implement those Regulations. Hence, the action for a declaration provides a very attractive method of avoiding the restrictions on actions for the annulment of regulations brought by private individuals under art. 173 of the EEC Treaty.

---

[88] Case 33/76, *Rewe* v. *Landwirtschaftskammer Saarland* [1976] ECR 1989; Case 45/76, *Comet* v. *Produktschap voor Siergewassen* [1976] ECR 2043; Case 826/79, *Mireco* v. *Italian Finance Administration* [1980] ECR 2559; Case 130/79, *Express Dairy Foods* v. *Intervention Board* [1980] ECR 1887; Case 199/82, *San Giorgio* v. *Italian Finance Administration* [1983] ECR 3595.

[89] *Express Dairy Foods*, supra, n. 85.

[90] Case 61/79, *Denkavit Italiana* [1980] ECR 1205.   [91] *Rewe, Comet, supra*, n. 85.

[92] *Express Dairy Foods*, supra, n. 85; *Denkavit Italiana*, supra n. 87.

[93] *San Giorgio, supra* n. 85.   [94] Case 113/81, *Reichelt* [1982] ECR 1957.

[95] Case 118/78, [1979] ECR 1387.

[96] Cases 103 and 145/77, *Royal Scholten Henig* v. *Intervention Board, Tunnel Refineries* v. *Intervention Board* [1978] ECR 2037.

Whilst the application for judicial review may, in general, involve a consideration of the law rather than of the facts, it was held in *R.* v. *MAFF ex p. Irish Dairy Board*,[97] where the applications sought both declarations and mandamus with regard to the designation of exclusive ports of entry for UHT milk, that the court was entitled to consider whether, and to what extent, the detailed measures of control were capable of constituting an impermissible restriction on intra-Community trade under art. 30 of the EEC Treaty,[98] on the basis that where, in a matter of public law, the application for judicial review was the only available form of proceeding, the United Kingdom should not be left in a situation where those persons with rights under European Community law should be denied the means of enforcing them.

That a breach of Community law giving rise to rights enforceable by individuals before national courts may constitute the tort of breach of statutory duty under English law was indicated by the House of Lords in *Garden Cottage Foods* v. *Milk Marketing Board*,[99] which involved an alleged abuse by the MMB of its dominant position in the milk market, with regard to its policy on the sale of bulk butter. After referring to the judgment of the European Court in *BRT* v. *SABAM*,[100] holding that 'as the prohibitions in arts. 85(1) and 86 tend by their very nature to produce direct effects in relations between individuals, these articles create direct rights in respect of the individuals concerned which the national courts must safeguard', Lord Diplock concluded that a breach of art. 86 may be categorized in English law as 'a breach of a statutory duty that is imposed not only for the purpose of promoting the general economic prosperity of the Common Market but also for the benefit of private individuals to whom loss or damage is caused by a breach of that duty'. The majority of the House of Lords concurred in this view, although Lord Wilberforce, in his dissent, regretted that the House should take a position on the point in interlocutory proceedings. These proceedings concerned the activities of the Milk Marketing Board (MMB) as an 'undertaking' in the context of the EEC competition rules,[101] rather than as a statutory organization. However, a similar view has been taken in proceedings where the pricing system adopted by the MMB was alleged to breach the EEC regulations governing the common organization of the market in milk and milk products.[102] It was held that, although the price system may be a matter of public law, EEC regulations which had direct effect created direct rights in private law which national courts must protect, so that a common-law

[97] [1984] 2 CMLR 502, per Forbes J.
[98] A form of words borrowed from Case 132/80, *United Foods* v. *Belgium* [1981] ECR 995.
[99] [1984] AC 130.   [100] [1974] ECR 51.
[101] i.e. arts. 85 and 86 of the EEC Treaty.
[102] *Irish Dairy Board* v. *MMB* [1984] 1 CMLR 519 and 584.

claim for damages should not be struck out. The same approach was also followed at first instance in *Bourguoin* v. *MAFF*,[103] where damages were claimed in respect of the revocation by the Ministry of Agriculture of a general licence to import turkeys from France, later held by the European Court to constitute a breach of art. 30 of the EEC Treaty.[104] Notice was taken of the case-law of the European Court holding that art. 30 produces direct effects and creates individual rights which national courts must protect,[105] and it was held that no differentiation could be made between the direct effects of art. 30 and the direct effects of art. 86, which had been at issue in the *Garden Cottage Foods* case, so that the statement of claim did disclose a cause of action for breach of the statutory duty imposed by art. 30. It was further held in this case, however, that for a minister (or other official) to do something which he had no power to do under Community law, where he knew that he had no power so to act and that his act would injure the plaintiff (in this case French turkey producers and traders), could also give rise to a cause of action for 'misfeasance in public office'.

The Court of Appeal was in agreement with regard to the question of misfeasance in public office, but the majority invoked the case-law of the European Court on the liability of the Community institutions to pay damages for harm caused by legislative acts as a justification for limiting the circumstances under which liability may occur when Community law is breached by a United Kingdom minister. Their view appeared to be that, where the minister acted in good faith, judicial review was the appropriate remedy, and that this mere breach of art. 30 did not give rise to an action for breach of statutory duty, unless an abuse of power was involved. Whatever the merits of this view,[106] the matter did not get to the House of Lords, since the case was settled on the basis that the French turkey producers would be paid the sum of £3.5 million.[107] The case does, however, illustrate the extent to which EC agricultural law may influence even basic principles of tortious liability in English law.

---

[103] [1985] 3 All ER 585.
[104] Case 40/82, *Commission* v. *UK* [1982] ECR 2793.
[105] Case 74/76, *Ianelli and Volpi* v. *Meroni* [1977] ECR 557.
[106] See Temple Lang, *The Duties of National Courts under the Constitutional Law of the European Community* (Exeter, 1987) pp. 9–15.
[107] Hansard 23 July 1986 vol. 102 no. 156 col. 116.

Index